Investment Strategy and State and Local Economic Policy

INVESTMENT STRATEGY AND STATE AND LOCAL ECONOMIC POLICY

VICTOR A. CANTO,
ARTHUR B. LAFFER,
AND
ROBERT I. WEBB

QUORUM BOOKS
Westport, Connecticut • London

Library of Congress Cataloging-in-Publication Data

Canto, Victor A.
    Investment strategy and state and local economic policy / Victor
  A. Canto, Arthur B. Laffer, and Robert I. Webb.
        p. cm.
    Includes bibliographical references and index.
    ISBN 0-89930-405-2
    1. Finance, Public—United States—States. 2. Fiscal policy—
  United States—States. 3. Investments—United States—States.
  4. Competition—United States—States. 5. Taxation—United States—
  States. I. Laffer, Arthur B. II. Webb, Robert Ivory.
  III. Title.
  HJ275.C28   1992
  338.973—dc20   91-48060

British Library Cataloguing in Publication Data is available.

Library of Congress Catalog Card Number: 91-48060
ISBN: 0-89930-405-2

First published in 1992

Quorum Books, 88 Post Road West, Westport, CT 06881
An imprint of Greenwood Publishing Group, Inc.

Printed in the United States of America

The paper used in this book complies with the
Permanent Paper Standard issued by the National
Information Standards Organization (Z39.48-1984).

10 9 8 7 6 5 4 3 2 1

Contents

Illustrations

DIAGRAM

FIGURES

TABLES

Preface

It is difficult to believe now with the collapse of communism that there ever was a time in the United States when the commonsensical idea that individuals respond to economic incentives was controversial. Yet not so long ago in the world center of capitalism, the United States, the conventional wisdom was that the disincentive effects of federal government fiscal policy on economic activity could be largely ignored. Essentially, it was believed that the basic philosophy of neoclassical economics somehow did not apply to the area of public finance. While it was understandable when politicians voiced these beliefs out of political expediency, it was disconcerting when professionally trained economists did so. Not surprisingly, in this Alice in Wonderland world, sound principles were turned on their heads, and bizarre notions often took hold. Fortunately, those days are past, and reason has prevailed.

In recent years, the fiscal policy of the U.S. government has drawn the attention of academicians, pundits, and policymakers alike. At the same time, the fiscal policies of the several states have been largely ignored. This is unfortunate because the aggregate impact of the fiscal policies of the individual states is often substantial. This book seeks to redress that deficiency.

This book owes its origin to the grass roots tax revolt that swept California in the late 1970s. The public's frustration with high and rising state and local (particularly property) taxes found expression in the passage in 1978 of Proposition 13—an initiative to limit state and local spending and taxation. The success of Proposition 13 sparked similar initiatives elsewhere, including Massachusetts's Proposition 2½. Some observers contend that the tax revolt at the state and local levels helped frame the debate of the 1980 presidential campaign over federal tax policy. In any event, the subsequent election of Ronald Reagan as president ultimately led to sweeping cuts in federal income tax rates in 1981 and again in 1986, which often increased the pressure to change state taxes. The debate accompanying the 1981 and 1986 federal tax rate cuts increased interest in the effects of state and local fiscal policies on state and local economic growth.

The authors of this volume were early and active participants in the public policy debate on tax policy. At the federal level, they conducted some of the early empirical academic research on the revenue effects of the Kennedy tax rate cuts, which provided intellectual support for the Reagan tax rate cuts. At the state level, they were also involved in a consulting study for the Commonwealth of Massachusetts during Governor Edward King's administration to determine the impact of state fiscal policy on state economic growth. The research conducted in that study formed the basis for an article later published in the *Southern Economic Journal* that explained persistent differences in real per capita factor income across states in terms of differences in state fiscal policies. More important, the simple neoclassical model developed in that article provided the conceptual analysis for natural extensions of the impact of state fiscal policy on other variables.

The approach taken in this book emphasizes both empiricism and classical economic theory. Three ideas permeate the book. One is that individuals respond to economic incentives, in particular, to perceived changes in *after-tax* income or returns. The second is that in an integrated economy with a high degree of factor mobility it is changes in *relative* state tax burdens (i.e., relative prices) that matter. And the third is that individual states are *competitors* in terms of their economic policies. The emphasis throughout the book is on the economic consequences of alternative public policy actions. In addition, the implications for investment strategy are assessed.

Unlike the 1980s, when economic growth was fueled by federal fiscal policy, the 1990s promise to be quite different. The current federal budget situation and the dismantling of the Soviet empire point to an era of tax rate increases and reduced spending. If the United States is to grow, this "fiscal drag" will have to be offset by state and local actions.

In the coming decade, every state in the United States will be striving for its share of economic growth—some with enviable success; others with disappointing results. As states seek to attract and hold industries and workers within their borders, the winners and the losers will be separated by their ability to "read" the competitive environment and then influence events in such a way as to enhance their own state's appeal.

The forces at play in this environment touch on all the elements of competition. Climate, waterways and seaports, the location of airport facilities, and the price of energy all have differential effects on economic development among states. But as suggested by research reported in this book, fiscal policy is the most important factor common to all states, strongly influencing competitiveness and hence relative economic growth rates. Within fiscal policy, the change in a state's tax burden relative to the nation is most important. The importance of the responsiveness of a state's relative growth rate to changes in tax rates goes well beyond the changes in each state's relative position.

In Chapter 1, Victor Canto and Robert Webb develop a theoretical framework based on an integrated national economy with a combination of mobile and immobile factors. An analysis of the responsiveness of the economies of individual states to changes in their relative tax rates provides insight into the importance of fiscal policy to the health of a national economy. In essence, each state is being treated as a country with an open economy. Just as states compete with each other for the location of factories, offices, and jobs within the U.S. economy, the United States must compete with countries around the world for the location of economic activity. Moreover, since monetary policy is the same for all the states, the effect of fiscal policy is isolated. The model is then used to derive implications relating state and local fiscal policy and a state's economic performance. The empirical results are uniform across states.

In an open economy such as ours, where factors are free to move across state political boundaries, state governments are essentially competitors with respect to their economic policies. The idea that state and local governments compete with one another in the conduct of their economic policies was first recognized by Charles Tiebout. This competition results, in large part, from the ability of mobile factors of production to "vote with their feet" by relocating to political jurisdictions pursuing more favorable economic policies. Indeed, the observed persistent differential in factor incomes across states in the United States may be largely explained by differences in state economic policies. States are analogous to monopolists with respect to their taxing power over fixed or relatively fixed factors of production. It is only the output of these factors of production that a state is able to influence through changes in its tax policies. The mobile factor of production is able to escape all but the lowest state tax rate in an integrated economy without internal barriers to factor migration. The evidence suggests that, more often than not, increases in the relative tax burden will then result in a lower level of economic activity. This, in turn, will reduce the tax base and possibly affect the overall fiscal health of the state (i.e., state general fund ending balance).

In Chapter 2, Victor Canto explores and develops some of the practical applications of the model. In Chapter 3, Victor Canto and John Silvia apply the framework developed to analyze the effect of state and local fiscal policies on business starts and failures.

The empirical evidence reported shows a clear connection between changes in a state's relative tax burden and business starts and failures in the state. The evidence indicates that increases in the relative tax burden are associated with a decline in business starts.

For investors and corporate planners, knowledge of a company's exposure to a state where taxes are either rising or falling relative to the nation can be an important input in investment or location decisions. Companies with production facilities concentrated in a state where relative tax rates are declining, for example, can, in general, expect to reap higher after-tax rates of return than those companies in states with rising tax burdens.

The extent of the duration and magnitude of such gains or losses is tied inextricably to the mobility of each company's competitors, workers, and the sensitivity of its customers to the price of its goods. Part II of the book extends the development of the model to its investment implications. In Chapter 4, Arthur Laffer and Christopher Hammond apply the basic framework to the California real estate market.

Laffer and Hammond examine the economic sequence of events. The starting point is the effect of California's taxes on the state's business climate (i.e., unemployment, personal income, etc.). The next link examined is the relation between the business climate and population growth. The final link is how population growth affects home prices. Based on historical relations and recent political changes in California (i.e., a significant tax burden increase), Laffer and Hammond conclude that is hard to visualize a continuation of California's frenetic prosperity and population growth and thereby a continuation of California's real estate appreciation.

Traditionally, real estate is considered the quintessential fixed factor since immobile factors of production are unable to escape state and local taxation. It follows that the burden of taxation will ultimately fall on real estate and will be reflected, among other things, in residential real estate prices.

In Chapter 5, Victor Canto examines the relation between single family home prices in different states and the states' relative tax burden. The empirical evidence is quite robust. Increases in a state's relative tax burden are associated with a below-average performance in the state's single family home market relative to the national average.

The empirical evidence reported identifies a negative relation between relative tax burden and the level of economic activity, the percent change in single family home prices, and business starts. A positive relation is seen between increases in the relative tax burden and a state's unemployment rate and business failures relative to the national average. In short, the change in tax burden may affect the overall business climate and fiscal conditions. In that case, a link between the tax burden and a state's general obligation (GO) bond rating may be established. In Chapter 6, Victor Canto, Christopher Charles, and Arthur Laffer examine the relation between state fiscal policy and GO rating changes.

The experience during the 1985-91 period shows that of the 46 credit rating changes 19 of the 26 credit rating upgrades occurred in states lowering their relative tax burden, and 12 of the 20 downgrades occurred in states raising their tax burden. Changes in state GO bond ratings occur infrequently and thus are likely to represent significant changes in perceived economic and financial conditions. The distribution of the changes clearly indicates that state competitiveness is related to their timing and direction.

This chapter develops a method of constructing probability estimates of a rating upgrade or a rating downgrade for each of the states. Since the data used in the estimation of these probabilities are readily available at the beginning of each fiscal year, the estimated probabilities may be legitimately used in constructing a portfolio strategy. The probabilities are then used to construct a buy and a sell portfolio. If the economic environment is related to the relative yields of state general obligation bonds, the portfolio strategy can yield significant results even if rating changes do not occur. The buy portfolio may include GO bonds for all states that simultaneously rank in the top half of the range of estimated probabilities of upgrades as well as in the bottom half of the range of estimated probabilities of downgrades. A more stringent cutoff, such as a ranking in the respective top or bottom 30 percent of states, may also be employed. The sell portfolio would consist of the mirror image of the buy portfolio.

Applying the portfolio strategy to the available data sets yields interesting results. In three of the four years, the buy portfolio yield declined relative to the average yield, whereas that of the sell portfolio increased in every year. The buy portfolio outperformed the sell portfolio in three of the four years. When more stringent requirements are applied, the buy portfolio outperformed the sell portfolio in each of the four years. Given the estimated sample size, the results are only suggestive. Nevertheless, they are quite encouraging, for they suggest that a differential of up to 25 basis points may be realized using the strategy.

Owing to the connection between state and local tax policy and economic performance, the values of assets located in states that alter their tax policies will fluctuate in predictable directions. Assets will tend to become more valuable in states that are cutting tax rates, whereas tax rate increases will tend to depress asset values.

The investment implications for stock selection are straightforward: Buy the stocks of companies located in states that are lowering tax rates and sell the stocks of companies in states that are raising tax rates. As simple as this strategy is, it is difficult to apply in practice because most major corporations operate in many states and, perhaps, in several countries. Thus, the impact of a particular state's tax changes on the values of the stocks of multistate corporations may be relatively minor.

An investment strategy based on changes in the state competitive environment may be even more rewarding if it is applied to small companies. The operations of small companies are more likely to be concentrated in one or a few states, and small companies typically are less able to pass tax rate changes forward to consumers or backward to suppliers. Thus, changes in states' relative tax burdens may have more pronounced effects on the after-tax returns and stock market performances of small corporations. The negative relation between relative tax burden and economic growth combined with knowledge of enacted and proposed tax legislation can be used to forecast the states most likely to gain or lose competitiveness. Changes in state and local taxes can be used to develop a portfolio strategy. This strategy requires the identification of changes in state tax policies and identification of producers who are unable to pass state and local taxes forward or backward. Under ideal circumstances, the strategy would be applied to companies having all their production facilities located in one state. Few companies with publicly traded securities satisfy this requirement. As an alternative, the strategy can be applied to the stocks of small-capitalization companies. Small-cap corporations are more likely to have their operations concentrated in one or a few states. It also is likely that small companies are less able to pass tax rate changes forward or backward. Thus, state taxes may be relatively more important for small-cap stocks than for large-cap stocks.

The changes in tax burden have been used to forecast the relative perfor-mance of the various state stock portfolios. The stocks examined are those of companies in the lowest market value quintile of the New York and American stock exchanges. The corporate headquarters for each of these small-cap companies was determined. Small-cap companies headquartered in the states with declining relative tax burdens are in the "buy" portfolio, and companies based in states with rising relative tax burdens are in the "sell" portfolio.

The efficacy of the change in relative tax burden as a possible screen in selecting stocks is reported in the study. This screen identifies companies that would have an above-average appreciation in stock performance. How-ever, if, on average, stock prices decline, this strategy would not ensure positive stock returns; it would only provide above-market-average returns. The differential performance is examined in Chapter 7 by Canto, Laffer, and Webb. As discussed in Chapter 7, the relative performance of the stocks is consistent with our framework.

Part III of the book focuses on the political economy aspects of the state competitive environment. Mobile factors will move into states that are lowering tax rates and emigrate from states that are raising tax rates. Changes in relative population may, in turn, result in a reapportionment of congressional seats.

If migration costs are nontrivial, there will be a gradual adjustment of the population, arbitraging the differences in after-tax income across localities. In Chapter 8, Canto and Webb examine the relation between reapportion-ment and state and local fiscal policy. Empirically, we have chosen changes in state relative tax burden at a particular point in time as well as lagged changes in state relative tax burden and state population growth as our characterization of the tax structure that may induce migrations across states. The variables as well as lagged values of population growth characterize adjustment costs.

The results reported in Chapter 8 suggest that state fiscal policy during the 1970-87 period is useful in forecasting state population growth. This result is consistent with the costly/partial adjustment hypothesis. Decadal changes in state relative tax burden, contemporaneous plus lagged, do have a significant and negative impact on state population growth.

The negative relation between changes in relative tax burden and economic growth combined with knowledge of enacted and proposed tax legislation can be used to forecast the states most likely to gain or lose congressional seats. To estimate the changes, we have used the following procedure: The changes in tax burden and previous population growth are used to calculate a projected population growth in each state. The projected increase plus the original state population are then divided by the U.S. population, thereby obtaining the state pro rata share of the congressional delegation. The fraction multiplied by the number of congressional seats, 435, and rounded to the nearest integer gives the projected congressional delegation by state.

California has been at the forefront of the tax revolt. The remaining three chapters examine the origins of the tax revolt. Chapter 9 reproduces Charles Kadlec and Arthur Laffer's analysis of the economic effects of Proposition 13. The forecast was quite bullish at the time and, in retrospect, not too far off the mark. California's fiscal issues were reversed a decade later as discussed by Arthur Laffer in his analysis of Proposition 111 (see Chapter 10). This time the forecast for the outlook for California's economy is not as optimistic.

Chapter 11, the final chapter, contains Victor Canto and Arthur Laffer's development of a tax system geared to raising the current level of revenues yet minimizing the disincentive effects of distorting state taxes. Thus, on a static revenue basis the switch to the proposed tax system would be revenue neutral, yet additional benefits would be derived by the ensuing improved competitive environment that the proposed tax reform would bring about.

Acknowledgments

During the last few years, we have been fortunate to participate in joint research with several of our colleagues. While this cooperation has greatly enhanced our productivity, it has also made it difficult to claim sole property rights to the projects and ideas that have emanated from the original research. This book is an example of a project whose origins can be traced to our interaction with several of our colleagues. Although we are claiming the property rights to this project, we wish to acknowledge several of our colleagues whose comments and suggestions have greatly enhanced the quality of this book. This list is headed by Tim W. Ferguson. Other people who have directly or indirectly contributed to the manuscript are Dorothy A. Cooper, Christopher S. Hammond, and Edward Mooney. We also would like to thank summer interns Daniel B. Johnston, James J. Lerner, Alan MacEachern, and Russell Silberstein, who proved to be capable research assistants.

Part I

Economic Activity and State Economic Policy

1

The Effect of State Fiscal Policy on State Relative Economic Performance

Victor A. Canto and Robert I. Webb

INTRODUCTION

The relative performance of different state economies has been a matter of much interest to both policymakers and the public in general. In a neoclassical world where factors are free to move across political boundaries, one would not expect to observe the existence of persistent product price or factor income differentials. Such differentials would disappear through either the trading of goods or factor migration. Yet in seeming violation of neoclassical economic theory, apparent persistent differences in factor incomes have been repeatedly observed among states or regions in the United States.[1] The intent of this chapter is to develop and empirically examine a neoclassical model that explicitly incorporates both state and federal fiscal policies in order to explain persistent differences in the levels of market income of the states' economies.[2]

In the section that follows, a simple neoclassical model of an integrated economy is developed. Within this framework, we show that trade in market goods and migration of the mobile factor may result in factor price equalization across states on a before-tax basis. Our model differs from others (Borts 1960; McLure 1970) in that the assumption of factor price equalization does not necessarily imply equality in per capita market income across states. This result may be traced to our assumption that each factor has the choice of working in either the market or the household sector. Consequently, although *full* incomes may be equated, *market* incomes need not be. In our model, divergences in *market* incomes across states are attributable, in part, to the impact of state government fiscal policies on the supply of services of the immobile factor of production across states.

In the comparison of the model's statics, it is shown that if prices are equalized across states, a change in relative prices will tend to have the same proportionate effect in all states. Thus, part of the change in economic activity attributable to the relative price change will generate a component common to all states, and to a large extent, this component will be exogenous to individual state governments. However, to the extent that state and local governments can influence the full income and the net-of-tax factor reward of the fixed factor, the utilization rate—and thus the total services supplied by the fixed factor—can be influenced by state spending and tax policies. As a result, output per unit of factor of production may differ across states.

Finally, data on federal and (continental 48) state spending, transfer payments, and taxes covering the period 1957-77 are employed to examine the influence of relative spending or tax rate policies on individual state economic performance as measured by personal income. The empirical results reported later in this chapter can be used to make inferences about a number of important issues. With a few exceptions, the empirical results suggest that state and local taxes have a negative and significant effect on the level of state income. However, the magnitude of estimated coefficients does not necessarily support the hypothesis that a reduction in a state's tax burden will elicit an increase in the state's tax revenues.

THE MODEL

The basic model is characterized by the following equations:

$$H_{Mi} = H_M[\Omega_{Mi}/N_{Mi}), R_M(1-t_{Mi})] \quad \text{(mobile factor demand for time) (1)}$$

$$H_{Ii} = H_I[\Omega_{Ii}/N_{Ii}), R_I(1-t_{Ii})] \quad \text{(immobile factor demand for time) (2)}$$

$$Y_i = F(N_{Mi}S_{Mi}, N_{Ii}S_{Ii}) \quad \text{(aggregate production function) (3)}$$

$$\Omega_{Mi} = (N_{Mi}R_{Mi} + \alpha [\gamma_f G_f + \Psi_f TR_f] + a_i[\gamma_{Si}G_{Si} + \Psi_{Si}TR_{Si} - T_{Si}]) \quad \text{(mobile factor full income) (4)}$$

$$\Omega_{Ii} = (N_{Ii}R_{Ii} + (1-\alpha)[\gamma_f(-1)G_f + (\Psi_f-1)TR_f] + (1-a_i)[(\gamma_{Si}-1)G_{Si} + (\Psi'_{Si}-1)TR_{Si}]) \quad \text{(immobile factor full income) (5)}$$

Where:

Y_i = the ith state production of market goods

N_{Mi} = the number of units of the mobile factor within the ith state

N_{Ii} = the number of units of the immobile factor within the ith state

S_{Mi} = the ith state utilization rate of the mobile factor

S_{Ii} = the ith state utilization rate of the immobile factor

H_{Mi} = the amount of time spent on household production by the mobile factors in the ith state

H_{Ii} = the amount of time spent on household production by the immobile factors in the ith state

R_M = the before-tax return to the mobile factor

R_I = the before-tax return to the immobile factors

t_{Mi} = the tax rate faced by the mobile factor in the ith state

t_{Ii} = the tax rate faced by the immobile factor in the ith state

α = the share of federal government services accruing to the mobile factors

G_f = federal government purchases of goods and services

γ_f = market value of the services provided by federal government purchases

TR_f = federal transfer payments

Ψ_f = the value of transfer payments

T_f = federal tax revenues

a_i = the share of state and local services accruing to mobile factors located within the state

Ψ_S = the value of services provided by the state and local government

G_S = state and local government purchases of goods and services

TR_{Si} = state and local transfer payments in the ith state

Ψ_{Si} = the value of state and local transfer payments in the ith state

T_{Si} = state and local tax revenues in the ith state

In order to abstract from issues of capital accumulation or population growth, the total supply of each factor of production is assumed to be exogenously determined. The absence of capital accumulation suggests that factors of production may be viewed as different types of labor.

The services of the factors of production can be employed either in the production of market goods or in the production of a household commodity. The decision to work to produce market goods and/or the household commodity [Equations (1) and (2)] is based in part on the opportunity cost of the factor's services.[3] In this chapter we adopt as the operational measure of the opportunities the full-income concept developed by Becker (1965).[4] In addition to the value of the total endowment of services, factors of production will also include in their full-income measure the actions of the federal government.[5]

For the purposes of this chapter, we assume that each state produces a single market good using similar technology. The market good production process [Equation (3)] is assumed to be linear, homogeneous, and twice differentiable with two indispensable inputs.

In order to capture as wide a spectrum of factor mobility as possible, factors of production are divided into those that are mobile (factor M) and those that are not (factor I)[6]. With respect to the mobile factor, it is assumed that all forms of barriers, both natural and man-made, among the different states are absent. The mobile factor, therefore, is presumed to incur no cost when moving across state boundaries. Neither factor faces any moving costs within a state. The immobile factor, on the other hand, faces a prohibitive cost if it were to move across state boundaries. Immobile factors of production must therefore be employed within the state where they are located.

For convenience of exposition, it is assumed that neither the mobile nor the fixed factor can move across national boundaries (i.e., both factors are immobile across countries). In addition, federal taxes and government services are assumed to be distributed between the two factors according to their proportion in the economy. In any state, the full-income measure of the mobile factor can be expressed as equations (4) and (5).[7]

In the absence of natural barriers to trade (e.g., transportation costs), arbitrage will ensure that the price of market goods will be the same in every state. Furthermore, through migration, the mobile factor equalizes its income across states.[8] The assumption of a common technology across states, combined with the assumption that both the price of market goods and mobile factor income are equated respectively across states, ensures that factor returns of the immobile factor will be equalized across states on a before-tax basis as well.[9] However, the after-tax factor return and/or income of the immobile factor need not be equalized across states. Therefore, within this scenario, state and local fiscal policy can influence the income and after-tax return of the immobile factor across states. Thus, insofar as state and local fiscal policies influence the amount of work of the fixed factor, the relative economic performance of the state will also be affected.

STATE EQUILIBRIUM: COMPARATIVE STATICS

The equalization of factor prices combined with the assumption of a similar linear homogeneous technology implies that the proportion of factor services used in the production of market goods in any state will be the same as that of the rest of the economy. That is,

$$(N_{Mi}S_{Mi}/N_{Ii}S_{Ii}) = (N_{Mj}S_{Mj}/N_{Ij}S_{Ij})V_{ij} \ldots \qquad (6)$$

Thus, the ratio of output produced in a state to that of the U.S. economy will be equal to the ratio of the immobile factor services supplied in the state relative to that of total services supplied by the factor in the U.S. economy that is:

$$Y_i = (N_{Ii}S_{Ii}/N_{IUS}S_{IUS})Y_{US} \qquad (7)$$

Substituting equations (1), (2), (3), (4), (5), and (6) into equation (7) and differentiating totally yields

$$
\begin{aligned}
E(Yi) = {} & \phi\eta_{I\Omega}(\gamma - 1)d(G_{Si}/N_{Ii} - G_S/N_{IUS}) \\
& + (\Psi - 1)d(TR_{Si}/N_{Ii} - TR_{Si}/N_{IUS}) - \phi\eta_{BR}[dt_{Ii}/(1 - t_I) \\
& - dt_{IUS}/(1 - t_{IUS})] + E(Y_{US})
\end{aligned} \qquad (8)
$$

where E is the change in the log operator, and G_S and TR_S denote the sum of all state purchases of goods and services, and transfer payments, respectively. N_{IUS} denotes the U.S. endowment of the immobile factor.[10]

A simple interpretation can be provided in equation (8). Within an integrated economy framework, two separate types of equilibria are of interest. The first is state-specific equilibrium, that is, the equation of the demand and supply of goods and services and for factors of production within a given state. This may be achieved through a redistribution of goods and/or the mobile factor of production among states. The second is overall equilibrium, that is, the equation of total demand and supply of goods and factors of production within the United States.

The important point is simply that if prices are equalized across states, a change in relative prices will tend to have the same proportionate effect in all states. Thus, part of the change in economic activity attributable to the relative price change will generate a component common to all states [i.e., the $E(Y_{US})$ term in equation (8)] and to a large extent, this component will be exogenous to individual state governments. However, to the extent that state and local governments can influence the full income and the net-of-tax factor reward of the fixed factor, the utilization rate—and thus the total services supplied by the fixed factor—can be influenced by state spending and tax policies. As a result, output per unit factor of production may differ across states.

The change in state economic activity attributable to the state's economic policies will differ from that of the "average" performance in the other states to the extent that the state's spending and tax rate policies differ from those of the average of the other states. The terms in equation (8) summarize the basic hypotheses of the model. First, if factor prices are equalized across states on a before-tax basis, then the coefficient for the percent change in the U.S. real income will be unity. Second, the effect of government purchases and transfer payments on state personal income depends crucially on the private sector's valuation of these services. Third, increases in a state's relative tax burden will reduce that state's personal income level.

The simplicity of the model developed in this chapter can be largely attributed to a couple of sets of assumptions—the first one being the assumption that the value of government services is the same across state and federal governments. This assumption allows us to aggregate the government spending variables into the two spending variables (government purchases and transfer payments). We would like to point out, however, that these potential aggregation problems are not unique to our work here.

The second set of assumptions that play a key role are those leading to the factor price equalization result. Notice that the equalization of factor prices across states could have been achieved in a variety of ways, such as the number of traded goods equaling the number of factors of production. This suggests that factor price equalization, and not migration, is more critical in our model.

Alam (1981) has extended the framework developed in this chapter to analyze the effects of fiscal policy on the trade balance. In his analysis, he investigates the effects of relaxing the factor price equalization assumption and finds that as this assumption is relaxed, the basic equation used in the empirical analysis [equation (8)] does not change qualitatively. However, the coefficient of the percent change in equation (8) will no longer equal unity. Thus, whether the coefficient for the percent change in national personal income is unity or not may be interpreted as an indirect test of the validity of the factor price equalization assumption.

The factor price equalization result on a before-tax basis suggests that the incidence of the state and local fiscal policy will fall on the factors of production that cannot move across state boundaries. Therefore, our analysis implies that when state and local fiscal policies result in a state experiencing above-average performance, the state's fixed factors will earn local rents.

EMPIRICAL EVIDENCE: THE STATE'S PERFORMANCE

A stochastic version of equation (8) was estimated for each state, with per capita personal income—deflated by the consumer price index (CPI)—used to measure state economic activity. Personal income was used owing to constraints on the availability of data on other measures of state economic activity. One of the explanatory variables in our model is state real expenditures (i.e., deflated by the CPI). For purposes of estimation, this variable was subdivided into state government purchases and state transfer payments. A third explanatory variable used in our analysis is the differential tax burden among the various states.[11]

Single equations were first estimated for each state. Unfortunately, the single equation estimates are predicated on the assumption that each state's explanatory variables are predetermined. This may be a reasonable assumption for the U.S. growth rate variable if the state is small relative to the union. It may also be a reasonable assumption for the local government purchases of goods and services variable. However, it is clearly not a reasonable assumption for the state transfer payments and tax rate variables. This becomes apparent when one considers that the automatic stabilizer feature of modern fiscal policy ensures that part of the spending variable is related to the level of economic activity.[12] Thus, by construction, the transfer payment and tax rate variables used in this study will be endogenously determined, and as a result, the ordinary least squares estimates may suffer from simultaneous equation bias. In order to allow for this, equation (8) was reestimated using two-stage least squares.

The instrumental variables technique is likely to produce better estimates only if the instruments are reasonably highly correlated with the explanatory variables that they replace and largely uncorrelated with the error term. Since the errors are unobservable, the determination of the appropriateness of an instrumental variable can only be made on a priori grounds. The two-stage results are consistent with those of the single equation estimates. This can be interpreted in one of two ways. Either the single equation estimates are consistent, or both approaches have the same degree of inconsistency. Furthermore, the structure of the theoretical model advanced above might lead one to expect correlation of the disturbances across equations. Zellner (1962) has suggested the use of seemingly unrelated regression analysis to obtain more efficient estimates in such cases. We estimated a variant of equation (8) using the seemingly unrelated regression technique to measure state economic performance relative to its region and economic performance relative to the national economy. As it turns out, the seemingly unrelated results are consistent with the single and simultaneous equation estimates. Thus, in what follows, only the single equation estimates will be discussed.[13] Finally, although controversial, tests of econometric exogeneity are possible (Zellner 1984). However, owing to the sample size limitations imposed by the availability of the state and local data variable, we did not perform Granger-Sims "causality" or econometric exogeneity tests.

Table 1.1 reports the single equation estimates for each of the states. The empirical results reported in Table 1.1 are consistent with the implications of the model developed in this chapter. The significance level of the intercept term of each of the estimated equations can be used to draw inferences about two competing views regarding the relationship between factor rewards across states. One view argues that trade in goods and factor migration will equalize the before-tax factor return in all states and at all times (for simplicity in what follows, we will refer to this view as the *factor price equalization hypothesis*), thus holding state fiscal policy constant; all states will tend to grow at the same rate, in which case, if the model is properly specified, the intercept term will be insignificant.

Table 1.1
State Performance Relative to the National Economy Single Equation Estimates

Δ in Y	Constant	Δ in Y	Δ[(G_i/POP_i)-(G_US/POP_US)]	Δ[(TR_i/POP_i)-(TR_US/POP_US)]	Δ(t_i - t_US)	R²	F	DW	ρ	SE
Alabama	.00825 (0.00557)	.969* (0.169)	.000174 (0.000324)	.000623 (0.000896)	-4.39* (1.77)	.699	8.70 (4,15)	1.86	--	.0147
Arizona	.00787 (0.00708)	.649* (0.193)	-.0000389 (0.000295)	-.00101 (0.00156)	-4.32 (1.05)	.716	8.83 (4,14)	--	-0.272	.0176
Arkansas	.00475 (0.00939)	1.08* (0.270)	.000492 (0.000299)	.000578 (0.00166)	-6.13* (1.71)	.672	7.16 (4,14)	--	-0.086	.0226
California	.00405 (0.00366)	.638* (0.138)	.000110 (0.000197)	.0000298 (0.000344)	1.37 (0.908)	.699	8.11 (4,14)	--	-0.506	.0122
Colorado	.0148 (0.00919)	.567* (0.238)	-.0000772 (0.000362)	.00205 (0.00145)	-2.34* (1.22)	.441	2.76 (4,14)	--	.124	.0191
Connecticut	-0.0120* (0.00626)	1.11* (0.221)	.0000557 (0.000140)	-.00140 (0.00179)	-0.463 (1.02)	.692	8.42 (4,15)	1.73	--	.0175
Delaware	.0186 (0.0122)	-.222 (0.452)	.000280 (0.000260)	-.00212 (0.00292)	-3.45* (1.72)	.475	3.16 (4,14)	--	-0.569	.0377
Florida	-0.00400 (0.00922)	1.14* (0.255)	-.000353 (0.000376)	.0000284 (0.00238)	2.95 (2.22)	.703	8.91 (4,15)	1.88	--	.0203
Georgia	.00240 (0.00380)	1.22* (0.114)	.000341 (0.000266)	.000760 (0.000760)	-4.79* (1.19)	.895	29.96 (4,14)	--	-0.582	.0116
Idaho	.0123 (0.0118)	1.44* (0.368)	.000844 (0.000483)	.00733 (0.00204)	-4.79 (0.949)	.757	10.87 (4,14)	--	-0.336	.0310
Illinois	.00144 (0.00466)	.816* (0.156)	-.000239 (0.000220)	.000412 (0.000556)	-1.31* (0.680)	.807	14.60 (4,14)	--	-0.170	.0119
Indiana	-0.00341 (0.00426)	1.45* (0.139)	.000466 (0.000277)	.00459* (0.00108)	-1.76 (0.602)	.915	37.50 (4,14)	--	-0.525	.0116

State						R^2?	F (df)			
Iowa	-0.00315 (0.000974)	1.03* (0.383)	-0.000114 (0.000469)	.00139 (0.00128)	-6.72* (2.11)	.798	13.86 (4,14)	--	-0.178	.0256
Kansas	-0.00331 (0.000639)	1.22* (0.233)	-0.0000888 (0.000359)	.00141 (0.000910)	-2.40* (1.13)	.785	12.75 (4,14)	--	-0.376	.0192
Kentucky	.00971* (0.00404)	.979* (0.127)	.000169 (0.000163)	-0.000990 (0.000821)	.546 (0.698)	.816	16.6 (4,15)	1.90	--	.0117
Louisiana	.00208 (0.00817)	.915* (0.199)	.000466* (0.000245)	-0.00105 (0.00142)	-1.62 (1.08)	.644	6.79 (4,15)	1.73	--	.0181
Maine	-0.00414 (0.00527)	1.11* (0.184)	.000337 (0.000252)	.00288* (0.00142)	-2.54* (0.974)	.801	14.11 (4,14)	--	-0.931	.0207
Maryland	.00706 (0.00619)	.775* (0.193)	-0.000137 (0.000237)	0.0000169 (0.00150)	-1.02* (0.581)	.611	5.89 (4,15)	2.26	--	.0165
Massachusetts	.00477 (0.00604)	.891* (0.184)	.00121 (0.000281)	-0.000507* (0.000193)	-1.98 (1.30)	.717	8.88 (4,14)	--	.234	.0135
Michigan	-0.0174* (0.00652)	1.71* (0.208)	-0.000408 (0.000480)	-0.000113 (0.00103)	-2.22* (1.13)	.860	22.99 (4,15)	1.75	--	.0182
Minnesota	-0.00659 (0.00698)	1.39* (0.232)	-0.000384 (0.000411)	.00574 (0.00110)	-3.22* (1.21)	.741	10.0 (4,14)	--	-0.375	.0205
Mississippi	.0120 (0.00905)	1.11* (0.253)	.000437 (0.000362)	.000515 (0.00135)	-1.61 (1.54)	.632	6.00 (4,14)	--	-0.282	.0204
Missouri	-0.00432 (0.00806)	.878* (0.236)	.000769 (0.000666)	-0.00309* (0.00179)	-4.64* (1.90)	.604	5.74 (4,15)	1.81	--	.0212
Montana	-0.00850 (0.00565)	.841* (0.203)	-0.0000653 (0.000198)	-0.00311* (0.00159)	-5.42* (0.762)	.884	26.59 (4,14)	--	-0.738	.0223
Nebraska	-0.00654 (0.00552)	1.25* (0.178)	.000166 (0.000300)	-0.000566 (0.00129)	-4.41* (0.758)	.893	29.08 (4,14)	--	-0.585	.0170
Nevada	.00116 (0.0170)	.548 (0.337)	-0.00138 (0.000282)	-0.00126 (0.00182)	-4.32* (1.30)	.500	3.48 (4,14)	--	-0.372	.0315

Table 1.1 (continued)

Δ in Y	Constant	Δ in Y	Δ[(G_i/POP_i)-(G_US/POP_US)]	Δ[(TR_i/POP_i)-(TR_US/POP_US)]	Δ(t_i-t_US)	R^2	F	DW	ρ	SE
New Hampshire	.00362 (0.00664)	.853* (0.208)	-0.00140 (0.000441)	-0.000316 (0.00149)	-5.16* (1.39)	.822	17.34 (4,15)	2.18	--	.0176
New Jersey	.00134 (0.00423)	.768* (0.130)	.00363* (0.000213)	.000644 (0.000740)	-1.73* (0.730)	.761	11.92 (4,15)	1.80	--	.0109
New Mexico	.0110 (0.00745)	.569* (0.227)	.000543* (0.000246)	-0.000545 (0.00137)	-2.38* (1.22)	.635	6.09 (4,14)	--	-0.494	.0217
New York	-0.00419 (0.00442)	.976* (0.164)	.0000794 (0.000129)	.000534 (0.000442)	-2.59* (1.09)	.765	11.43 (4,14)	--	-0.274	.0131
North Carolina	.0114* (0.00462)	.874* (0.164)	-0.000167 (0.000365)	-0.0000160 (0.00127)	-4.37* (2.07)	.805	15.47 (4,15)	1.65	--	.0128
North Dakota	.00920 (0.0119)	.290 (0.414)	.000166 (0.000451)	-0.000790 (0.00239)	-8.77* (0.799)	.944	59.17 (4,14)	--	-0.68	.0404
Ohio	-0.0139* (0.00391)	1.37* (0.130)	.000411* (0.000233)	.000544 (0.000815)	-4.18* (1.53)	.908	37.40 (4,15)	1.97	--	.0144
Oklahoma	.000914 (0.00658)	.920* (0.192)	.000233 (0.000224)	-0.000828 (0.000710)	-1.75 (1.23)	.572	4.68 (4,14)	--	-0.361	.0163
Oregon	.000944 (0.00703)	.843* (0.256)	.000356* (0.000208)	-0.000229 (0.00108)	-1.78 (1.14)	.642	6.29 (4,14)	--	-0.458	.0165
Pennsylvania	-0.00570 (0.00426)	1.09* (0.124)	.0000156 (0.000247)	.000543 (0.000696)	-1.17 (0.748)	.864	23.90 (4,15)	2.01	--	.0097
Rhode Island	.00820 (0.00612)	.875* (0.205)	.000223 (0.000240)	-0.00249 (0.00180)	-3.11* (1.69)	.728	9.38 (4,14)	--	-0.559	.0204

State						R^2	F			
South Carolina	.00914 (0.00763)	1.01* (0.263)	.000436 (0.000393)	-0.00147 (0.00158)	-3.04 (1.99)	.635	6.07 (4,14)	--	-0.197	.0199
South Dakota	.00309 (0.0115)	.577 (0.400)	.00103* (0.000564)	.000256 (0.00266)	-7.74* (0.644)	.929	49.12 (4,15)	2.06	--	.0321
Tennessee	.00467 (0.00456)	1.11* (0.137)	-0.000139 (0.000229)	.00201 (0.00121)	-4.54* (1.04)	.860	22.97 (4,15)	2.02	--	.0116
Texas	.0110* (0.00491)	.625* (0.136)	.000451 (0.000352)	-0.00126 (0.000996)	-3.90* (0.786)	.832	17.30 (4,14)	--	.277	.0103
Utah	.00584 (0.00590)	.629* (0.181)	.000260 (0.000328)	-0.00134 (0.00239)	-0.907 (1.33)	.523	3.84 (4,14)	--	-0.335	.0153
Vermont	.00397 (0.0100)	.913* (0.328)	.000372 (0.000224)	.00151 (0.00176)	-4.54* (0.749)	.823	17.50 (4,15)	2.19	--	.0281
Virginia	.00628 (0.00644)	1.10* (0.224)	.0000290 (0.000341)	.000877 (0.00168)	-1.94 (1.07)	.674	7.73 (4,15)	1.91	--	.0155
Washington	-0.00203 (0.00597)	1.10* (0.195)	-0.000359 (0.000230)	.00147 (0.00115)	-4.33* (1.61)	.731	10.18 (4,15)	2.11	--	.0175
West Virginia	.0134 (0.00873)	.614* (0.269)	-0.000253 (0.000310)	.000733 (0.00144)	-3.77* (1.45)	.459	3.18 (4,15)	1.88	--	.0249
Wisconsin	-0.00401 (0.00461)	1.19* (0.114)	-0.000249 (0.000210)	.0000744 (0.000604)	-0.907 (0.641)	.838	19.43 (4,15)	1.88	--	.0126
Wyoming	.0269* (0.0156)	.354 (0.521)	.000271 (0.000202)	.00232 (0.00271)	-4.61* (1.38)	.458	3.16 (4,15)	1.85	--	.0446

Note: Standard errors in parentheses. Significant at the 5% level

The other view, which we shall call the *adjustment costs hypothesis*, argues that although trade in goods and factor migration mitigate regional differences in income, differences in factor returns and income will remain for long periods of time owing to some market imperfections, such as movement costs. This view suggests that if all else is constant over time, low-income states will catch up with the national average. In order to do so, these states will experience above-average growth rates. Furthermore, if the model is properly specified, the catching-up effect will be picked up by the constant term. Thus, according to the adjustment costs hypothesis, after accounting for the potential effects of fiscal policy, states with income below the national average should have a positive and significant intercept term, whereas states with income above the national average should have a negative intercept.

In the majority of estimated equations, the intercept term was not found to be statistically significantly different from zero. There are, however, seven states for which the intercept was significantly different from zero. Interestingly, the states with negative intercepts (i.e., a below-average growth rate after controlling for state fiscal policy)—Connecticut, Michigan, and Ohio—are located in the Snowbelt or older industrial area of the country, whereas the states with a positive intercept (i.e., above-average growth rate after controlling for the effects of fiscal policy)—Kentucky, North Carolina, Texas, and Wyoming—are primarily southern states. These results lend support to the adjustment costs hypothesis.

An alternative explanation of the significant coefficients may be due to changes in the composition of output of the various states and the existence of industry-specific factors of production.[14] It is worthwhile to point out that two of the states with negative intercepts—Michigan and Ohio—have basic industries (automobile and steel, respectively) that have been declining during recent years. Similarly, two of the states with high positive intercepts—Wyoming and Texas—have fossil fuel deposits that have significantly increased in value during the last few years. However, these states appear to be the exception rather than the rule. Thus, the results overwhelmingly favor the hypothesis of factor price equalization over the adjustment costs hypothesis.

Upon inspection of Table 1.1, it is apparent that the estimated coefficient for the percent changes in the U.S. real per capita income is not statistically significant in only 5 states—Delaware, Nevada, North Dakota, South Dakota, and Wyoming; the U.S. coefficient is positive and significant in the remaining 43 states. Three states—Indiana, Michigan, and Ohio—have a coefficient more than two standard errors above unity. And two states—California and Texas—have a coefficient more than two standard errors below unity. Notice that in the case of Michigan, Ohio, and Texas the coefficient of the intercept is also statistically significant and that the states with above-unity coefficients tend to have a negative intercept. In the remaining 38 states, the coefficient is within two standard errors of unity. Thus, for these states we cannot reject the unit coefficient predicted by the factor price equalization hypothesis.

The pattern of estimated coefficients for the intercept term and the percent change in U.S. real personal income $[E(Y_{US})]$ provides additional support for the factor price equalization hypothesis. This is important for several reasons. First, it suggests that the degree of mobility for the most mobile factors of production in a state plays an important role in the incidence of state and local fiscal policy. To the extent that there is perfect mobility for one of the factors of production, the short- and long-run incidence of state and local fiscal policy will be the same. Alternatively stated, state fiscal policy will have a contemporaneous effect on state real personal income. In contrast, the view that movement costs lead to imperfect factor mobility implicitly assumes a partial adjustment of income over time. Lagged values of fiscal policy will have a significant effect on current levels of expenditures and taxes. To summarize, the estimated coefficients for the intercept and $E(Y_{US})$ terms favor the factor price equalization hypothesis.

Another feature in the empirical results reported in Table 1.1 is the insignificance of the states' relative spending and transfer payment variables. Only in six states—Louisiana, New Jersey, New Mexico, Ohio, Oregon, and South Dakota—was the spending variable positive and significant. In no state was the variable both negative and significant. The transfer payment variable was negative and significant in three states—Massachusetts, Missouri, and Montana—and positive and significant in only one state—Maine. The insignificance of the estimated coefficients does not support the view that increases in relative spending lead to increases in the state output.

The regression coefficient of the change in relative government expenditures represents the effect that would result from a one-unit increase in such expenditures if the other right-hand-side variables in the regression, including the relative tax rates, were held constant. The insignificance of the coefficient implies either that the public views increases in expenditures as being perfect substitutes for private goods (i.e., $\gamma = 1$) or that the demand for time is unresponsive to changes in income.

If the demand for household time is responsive to income at the margin, the empirical estimates suggest that on the margin the value of the government services equals their cost (i.e., $\gamma = 1$) and, as a result, would have no impact. The fact that government expenditures do not appear to have an impact on economic activity does not imply that government expenditures are necessarily wasteful. On the contrary, these results are consistent with "optimal" behavior on the part of the government. Abstracting from the substitution effects that nonneutral taxation may generate, a government policy that maximizes the economy's total wealth (exclusive of government services) is one that makes the value of government services equal to their costs (i.e., $\gamma = 1$). Thus, if anything, the evidence suggests that state governments have pursued an optimal spending policy, as defined above. A note of caution is in order, however, since, as we mentioned, this optimum neglects the substitution effects generated by tax rates that may reduce the level of income. Once the distortionary effects of *nonneutral* tax rates on the economy are taken into account, it becomes apparent that an optimal government spending policy requires that the value of the services provided be sufficiently large to cover the factor costs of the services provided as well as the costs generated by the nonneutral tax rate (i.e., $\gamma > 1$). In this case, the reduced form coefficient for the public spending variable will be unambiguously negative. Interpreted in this light, the empirical results suggest that in the case of Louisiana, New Jersey, New Mexico, Ohio, Oregon, and South Dakota—and possibly for most of the other states—state expenditures are beyond their optimal level. A similar argument applies to the expenditures on social progams in Indiana and Maine.

The results reported in the previous paragraphs strongly suggest the possibility of homogeneity of coefficients across states, in which case the data could be pooled into a single time series–cross section regression and the effects of the different variables on personal income reported in a more compact manner. However, this hypothesis is rejected by the data. Therefore, a separate equation for each of the states must be estimated.[15]

The homogeneity of the intercept, the percent change in U.S. per capita income, and state and local expenditure across equations imply that the rejection of the homogeneity of coefficients across equations is due to the variability of the coefficient of the relative tax burden. This differential response of state personal income changes to changes in the relative tax burden is not totally unexpected since states, in general, use a different mix or structure of various taxes (i.e., property, sales, income, corporate, etc.). In addition, the level of taxation is likely to differ across states, and since the different taxes have different degrees of incidence on the various factors of production, they will have different distortionary effects on the work-leisure choice. As a result, one would not expect to find the coefficient for the tax variable to be equal across states, although the model suggests the tax coefficient to be both negative and significant.

The results reported in Table 1.1 indicate that the coefficient of the relative tax burden is positive and insignificant in only 1 state—California; negative and insignificant in 9 states—Connecticut, Florida, Kentucky, Oklahoma, Oregon, Pennsylvania, South Carolina, Utah, and Wisconsin; and negative and significant in the remaining 38 states.

It should be noted that the data employed for the tax rate variable are highly aggregated and represent *effective average* (i.e., the states' tax burden) tax rates and, as such, do not account for progressivity in the tax system.[16] Clearly, the use of effective average tax rates as a proxy for state marginal tax rates will result in less precise estimates. Further, given the level of aggregation, one cannot tell which types of taxes are important but merely that a disincentive effect appears to exist.

A natural question that arises in the empirical estimation of equation (8) concerns possible multicollinearity among the state explanatory variables. The state government budget constraint can be viewed as the sum of purchases and transfer payments—or equivalently, taxes, borrowing, and revenue sharing. To the extent that borrowing and revenue sharing differ from zero, this would tend to reduce the correlation between spending and the effective tax rates. In addition, it must be noted that the explanatory variables are expressed as changes in the deviation from the mean, which also tends to reduce any correlation between spending and tax revenues.[17]

The results suggest that increases in local taxes have a contemporaneous effect on state incomes. Before discussing the magnitude of the coefficient, a word of caution is in order: For reasons previously explained, the coefficient differs substantially across states. Upon inspection of Table 1.1, it is apparent that the range of significant coefficients varies from low values in the neighborhood of 1 to high values in the neighborhood of 8, with values between 3 and 4 being the most frequent, although the coefficients suggest that the effects of state and local taxes on states may be quite sizable indeed. However, in no states are the coefficients sufficiently large that a reduction in state tax rates would generate an increase in tax revenues (Kadlec and Laffer 1979).[18]

Our results differ from those of other studies in this area, such as Genetski and Chin (1978) and Kadlec and Laffer (1979). Our analysis, which encompasses the time period of the Genetski and Chin study, suggests that the pooling of the data across states (and thus cross-sectional analysis) is inappropriate since one may not reject the hypothesis of homogeneity of coefficients.

CONCLUSIONS

Data on percent changes in state real personal income, real per capita state spending, and the state tax burden were examined to ascertain the effect of state fiscal policies on relative economic performances. A stochastic version of equation (8) that included a constant term was estimated. The empirical results indicate that the model is quite robust and the results are fairly consistent across the techniques employed. In particular, the constant term was rarely significant. Furthermore, in the majority of states, one could not reject the hypothesis that the coefficient for the percent change in U.S. real per capita personal income was different from unity. These results are contrary to the implications of theories that explain income differentials as temporary phenomena that are eliminated over time as factor prices are equilibrated across regions (Borts 1960;

Newman 1980). The results reported in this chapter favor the hypothesis that through trade in goods and factor migration, *before-tax* factor incomes and *full* incomes are equalized across state lines. This is important, for it implies that the effects of state fiscal policies on state personal income will be contemporaneous.

The empirical results indicate that there may be several states for which the factor price equalization hypothesis may be violated. However, for most of these states the coefficient for $E(Y_{US})$ is significantly different from unity; it tends to be higher than unity for the states with a negative intercept and smaller than unity for the states with positive intercept terms.

The empirical results indicate that, with few exceptions, the government purchases and transfer payment variables were not statistically significant. One explanation for this result is that states are pursuing "optimal" spending policies. However, where substitution effects are important (and our analysis indicates that the relative tax burden appears to have a consistent negative significant effect across states), a policy of equating γ to unity may indicate excessive spending. Interpreted in this way, the empirical results indicate that the optimal amount of public programs should exceed unity in order to cover the program costs and the "excess burden" generated by the taxes levied to finance the program. Therefore, our results suggest that in most states the expenditure and transfer payment programs are larger than their optimal size. Of course, our analysis does not take into account distributional effects, which may result in different spending optima.

Although the empirical results lead one to reject the homogeneity of coefficients across states, that does not necessarily imply that the functional form [equation (8)] should differ across states. It should be noted that the empirical analysis presented in this chapter is capable of explaining differences in real per capita income across states without specific references to such regional exogenous factors such as climatic conditions and/or mineral wealth.

In 38 of the states examined, the relative tax burden was negative and significant. These results suggest that relative tax burdens distort the factors of production and work-leisure choice as well as other factors such as location. Alternatively stated, the results indicate that state tax policy influences the states' income level. Furthermore, the results indicate that the relationship is a contemporaneous one. The magnitude of the tax burden coefficient does not necessarily imply that a reduction in tax rates will bring about an increase in tax revenues (i.e., the states' tax revenues appear to be in the upward-sloping segment of the Laffer Curve as opposed to the downward-sloping segment). These results are in marked contrast to other studies that have examined the relationship between tax burden and state personal incomes.

The results presented in this chapter also have implications for the success of predatory tax policies. It should be emphasized that there is an effect on the U.S. economy resulting from the average state tax rate. Consequently, if all states engage in predatory or "beggar thy neighbor" tax policies, there may be no *relative* gain, but there would be an *absolute* gain owing to the reduced average marginal tax rates.

Although our results indicate support for the integrated economy approach, regional differences still exist. The empirical analysis of this chapter suggests the conclusion that individual state fiscal policies can and do influence relative state real per capita income levels. In contrast, federal fiscal policy mainly influences absolute or national economic performance.[19] As a result, the empirical analysis suggests that both state and federal fiscal policies matter in the determination of the overall economic performance of a state or region.

APPENDIX A: DATA SOURCES

The data used in this study came from a variety of sources reporting on aggregate U.S. annual time series from 1957 to 1977. Data for federal government purchases of goods and services, federal transfer payments, federal tax revenues, and personal income at constant prices were taken directly from the *National Income Accounts*. Population figures were obtained from the U.S. Department of Commerce, Bureau of Census *Current Population Reports*. Tax revenues and state expenditures and transfer payments were obtained from U.S. Department of Commerce *States' Government Finances*. Finally, the states' personal income figures were taken directly from the U.S. Department of Commerce, Bureau of Economic Analysis.

NOTES

This chapter is adapted from an article which originally appeared in the *Southern Economic Journal* (July 1987) and is reprinted with permission.

1. For an excellent summary of the earlier studies see Due (1961). The observation of seemingly persistent differences in nominal factor income across states, of course, ignores the possibility—pointed out by Coelho and Ghali (1971)—that such differences may merely reflect differences in price levels across states. More recent attempts to explain observed price and income differentials across political boundaries have emphasized differences in technologies (Batra and Scully 1972). The popular press has distinguished between the "Sunbelt" and the "Snowbelt" in the past and more recently between states along the East Coast and California versus the interior.

2. Earlier empirical studies (Bloom 1955) failed to find any association between state fiscal policies and relative economic performance. However, these studies failed to examine state expenditure and tax policies relative to those of other states. This model misspecification error may lead to biased results and explain the absence of a

relationship between state fiscal policies and relative economic performance reported by these studies.

3. The household commodity is assumed to be produced by the following linear, homogenous, twice differentiable production function $Z = f(H,X)$, where H denotes the amount of household time (i.e., leisure) and X the amount of market goods used in the production process.

4. Since by assumption there is no unemployment of either factor of production (i.e., they are always engaged in either market or nonmarket activity), the market reward to each factor of production represents the appropriate measure to value the factor services—both market and nonmarket.

5. Conventional accounting techniques value government services at factor costs. However, there is no reason why the value of these services should equal their costs, as pointed out by Bailey (1971). Thus, in any analysis of fiscal policy, a provision should be made for this possibility.

6. For simplicity of exposition, factors are classified as either mobile or fixed. In principle, the analysis could also be extended to allow for differing degrees of factor mobility (i.e., adjustment costs). For a two-sector model with adjustment costs, see Mussa (1978). However, if factor prices are equalized irrespective of the degree of factor mobility (e.g., through trade in goods), the degree of factor mobilty will have no qualitative effect on the basic premise of this chapter that the incidence of state and local fiscal policy will fall the most on the immobile factor. The major effect of the degree of mobility will be on the *migration* pattern—an issue that we *do not* explicitly focus on in this chapter.

7. The mobile factor full-income measure may be expressed as

$$\Omega_{Mi} = (N_{Mi}R_{Mi} + \alpha[\gamma_f G_f + \Psi_f TR_f - T_f]$$
$$+ a_i[\gamma_{Si}G_{Si} + \Psi_{Si}TR_{Si} - T_{Si}]).$$

Substituting the federal, state, and local governments' budget constraint yields the full-income measure shown in equation (4).

8. For ease of exposition, we assume that equality of the mobile factor income Ω_{mi}/N_{Mi} across states implies the equality of factor rewards RMi. A sufficient condition for this to be the case is that the mobile factor, because of its mobility, is able to avoid the state taxes. However, also because of its mobility, neither is it able to benefit from the state and local services.

9. The general conditions under which trade is sufficient to equalize factor returns are well known in the economic literature (Samuelson 1949). The effects of factor migration on factor price equalization are also well known (Mundell 1957; Samuelson 1965).

10. A formal derivation of this equation is available from the authors upon request as Appendix B.

11. The data employed in the tests below come from a variety of sources; a detailed explanation of the sources appears in Appendix A.

12. For these programs, the government may be thought of as setting the criteria governing eligibility for transfer payments rather than total expenditures. That is, the government sets the benefit package. In this sense, the eligibility criteria are analogous to a tax rate schedule and total transfer payments to tax revenues. In this case, transfer payments per person as well as the effective marginal tax rates are endogenously determined (Canto and Webb 1983).

13. The results for the simultaneous equation estimates are available from the authors upon request as Appendix D. Similarly, the seemingly unrelated results are available as Appendix C.

14. This interpretation was suggested to us by a referee.

15. Chow (1960) and Fisher (1970) have suggested the following F test for homogeneity of coefficients across equations using the sum of squared residuals: Because the estimated value of the F statistic, 12.8, exceeds the critical F value (235,7689) at the 1 percent level, one can reject the null hypothesis of homogeneous coefficients across states. Rejection of the homogeneity of coefficients across equations precludes the possibility of pooling the data and reporting the empirical analysis in a more compact manner. An alternative way to present the joint significance of the coefficients of one of the fiscal variables across all 48 equations may be obtained by using the binomial distribution. This, of course, assumes that the coefficients are independent of each other (which in the absence of any prior to the contrary may be a reasonable assumption). The binomial distribution yields the probability density function for a given number of successful outcomes (i.e., significant coefficients), X. Or,

$$\Lambda = [n!/(s!(n-s)!)]1 - q^{n-s}q^s$$

where n is the number of observations (48) and q is the probability of a success (5 percent). The null hypothesis is that the fiscal variable has no effect on economic activity. One would expect to find nq significant coefficients by chance. The mode or most likely outcome is 2.48 successes, with a probability of 0.215. Upon inspection of Table 1.1 it is apparent that the number of successful outcomes for the government purchases, transfer payments, and tax rate variables are 6, 4, and 38, respectively, with a corresponding probability of 0.220, 0.127, 2.3×10^{-40}.

Although the assumption of independent outcomes may not be entirely correct, the probability for each outcome implied by the binomial distribution is highly suggestive. The probability of outcomes for the government purchases and transfer payments variables is of the same order of magnitude as that of the null hypothesis, whereas the probability of the tax rate outcome is several orders of magnitude smaller than that expected by the null hypothesis.

16. Under a progressive tax system, an exogenous increase in a state growth rate will increase tax revenues more than proportionately. Therefore, the effective rates utilized in this study will unambiguously underestimate the true marginal tax rate. Thus, the degree of progression will induce a positive correlation between tax rates and economic growth, thus biasing the estimated coefficient against the hypothesis that tax rates discourage market sector production.

17. We estimated the correlation among the different explanatory variables and found that, in most cases, the correlation between state explanatory variables was less than 0.25. In some cases, however, the correlation was in excess of 0.5. There was a high correlation between state tax and transfer payment variables for North Carolina, Rhode Island, Virginia, Louisiana, Colorado, and Delaware. There was also high correlation between state government spending and taxes for Oregon, Missouri, California, and Colorado. Finally, there was high correlation between state transfer payments and government expenditures for North Carolina, South Carolina, Tennessee, Utah, Virginia, Washington, Missouri, Colorado, and Nebraska. In most cases, the multicollinearity issue does not present a problem. However,

the above variables may be collinear, and the equations for those states should be viewed with caution.

18. Assuming that the state tax base is equal to state personal income, the critical value of the tax burden coefficient must be larger than 10 for a tax rate reduction to generate an increase in tax revenues. This can be shown as follows: In 1977, the last year in our sample, total state and local revenue per $1,000 of personal income was $110.50; that is, the average tax burden was 11.05 percent. Thus, holding income constant, a 10 percent across-the-board reduction of state tax rates would lower the state relative tax burden from 11.00 percent to approximately 10 percent. Alternatively stated, the 10 percent reduction in tax rates reduces the tax burden by approximately 1 percentage point. Furthermore, in order to collect the same amount of revenue, the tax base has to expand by 10 percent. Therefore, abstracting from the state's progressive taxation and tax deductions and exceptions and factor migrations, it then follows that the only way the tax base will increase by this much is if the personal income in the state increases by 10 percent—that is, if the magnitude coefficient of the relative tax burden is larger than 10. The critical value of the coefficient depends on the initial conditions. However, none of the calculations performed suggested that, for any of the states, a tax rate reduction would result in higher revenues.

19. For a discussion of the impact of recent federal tax policies on the U.S. economy and tax revenues, see Canto, Joines, and Webb (1986).

REFERENCES

Alam, Alaa. "The Effects of Fiscal Policy on the Trade Balance." Ph.D. dissertation, Graduate School of Business, University of Southern California, 1981.

Bailey, Martin J. *National Income and the Price Level.* 2d ed. New York: McGraw-Hill, 1971.

Batra, R., and Scully, Gerald. "Technical Progress, Economic Growth and the North-South Wage Differential." *Journal of Regional Science* 12, no. 3 (December 1972): 375-86.

Becker, Gary. "A Theory of the Allocation of Time." *Economic Journal* 75, no. 299 (September 1965): 493-517.

Bloom, Clark. "State and Local Tax Differentials and the Location of Industry." Iowa City: Bureau of Business Research, State University of Iowa, 1955.

Borts, George. "The Equalization of Returns and Regional Economic Growth." *American Economic Review* (June 1960): 329-47.

Canto, Victor A.; Joines, Douglas; and Webb, Robert I. "The Revenue Effects of the Kennedy and Reagan Tax Cuts: Some Time Series Estimates." *Journal of Business and Economic Statistics* 4 (July 1986): 281-88.

Canto, Victor A., and Webb, Robert I. "Persistent Growth Rate Differentials Among States in a National Economy with Factor Mobility." In *Foundations of Suppy-Side Economics*, edited by Victor Canto, Douglas Joines, and Arthur Laffer. New York: Academic Press, 1983.

Chow, Gregory. "Test of Equality Between Sets of Coefficients in Two Linear Regressions." *Econometrica* (July 1960): 591-605.

Coelho, Philip, and Ghali, Moheb. "The End of the North-South Wage Differential." *American Economic Review* (December 1971): 932-37.

Due, John. "Studies of State-Local Tax Influences on Locations of Industry." *National Tax Journal* 14, no. 2 (June 1961): 167-73.

Fisher, Franklin. "Tests of Equality Between Sets of Coefficients in Two Linear Regressions: An Expository Note." *Econometrica* (March 1970): 361-66.

Genetski, Robert, and Chin, Young. "The Impact of State and Local Taxes on Economic Growth." Hanes Economic Research Office Service, November 1978.

Greenwood, Michael. "Research on Internal Migration in the United States: A Survey." *Journal of Economic Literature* (June 1975): 397-433.

Kadlec, Charles, and Laffer, Arthur. "The Jarvis-Gann Tax Cut Proposal: An Application of the Laffer Curve," in *The Economics of the Tax Revolt*, edited by Arthur Laffer and J. Seymour. New York: Harcourt Brace Jovanovich, Inc., 1979.

McLure, Charles E. "Taxation, Substitution and Industrial Location." *Journal of Political Economy* (January/February 1970): 112-32.

Mundell, Robert. "International Trade and Factor Mobility." *American Economic Review* (June 1957): 231-35.

Mussa, Michael. "Dynamic Adjustment in the Heckscher-Ohlin-Samuelson Model." *Journal of Political Economy* (October 1978): 775-92.

Newman, Robert. "Industry Migration and the Growth of the South." University of British Columbia, School of Commerce, Working Paper no. 743, November 1980.

Samuelson, Paul. "International Factor-Price Equalization Once Again." *Economic Journal* (June 1949): 181-97.

_____. "Equalization by Trade of the Interest Rate Along with the Real Wage." In *Trade, Growth and the Balance of Payments*, edited by M. Baldwin, Chicago: Rand McNally, 1965.

Zellner, Arnold. "An Efficient Method of Estimating Seemingly Unrelated Regression and Tests for Aggregation Bias." *Journal of the American Statistical Association* (June 1962): 348-68.

_____. "Causality and Econometrics." Reprinted in *Basic Issues in Econometrics*. Chicago: University of Chicago Press, 1984, pp. 35-74.

2

Practical Applications of the
State Competitive Environment

Victor A. Canto

Governors are concerned with state-specific policies and are judged by how well the state economy is performing. In 1990, 19 governors were elected. Only six incumbent governors lost in their reelection bids (Table 2.1). The four Republicans presided over significant increases in their states' tax burdens. Similarly, in the eight states where no incumbents were running and the governor's party lost, all had rising or high tax burdens.

In the coming decade, every state in the United States will be striving for its share of economic growth—some with enviable success; others with disappointing results. As states seek to attract and hold industries and workers within their borders, the winners and the losers will be separated by their ability to "read" the competitive environment and then influence events in such a way as to enhance their own state's appeal.

The forces at play in the environment touch on all the elements of competition. Climate, waterways and seaports, the location of airport facilities, and the price of energy all have differential effects on economic development among states. Other factors, such as the shift to low-sulfur coal and/or the discovery of vast new quantities of oil, have helped such states as Wyoming and Texas to post outsized gains in personal income and employment in recent years.

But fiscal policy is the most important factor common to all states, strongly influencing competitiveness and hence relative economic growth rates. Within fiscal policy, the change in a state's tax burden relative to the nation is most important. The tax burden, arrived at by dividing total tax revenue by total personal income, is a widely accepted measure used to

Table 2.1
Party Change in Governorships and Relative Tax Burdens

	Incumbents - Lost	Rank of Relative Change In Tax Burden 1991*
Florida	Bob Martinez(R)	47
Kansas	Mike Hayden(R)	30
Michigan	James Blanchard(D)	11
Minnesota	Ruddy Perpich(D)	7
Nebraska	Kay Orr(R)	48
Rhode Island	Edward DiPrete(R)	46

Non-Incumbents - Party Changed

Alaska(D)	25
Connecticut(D)	31
Massachusetts(D)	49
New Mexico(R)	41
Ohio(D)	29
Oklahoma(R)	45
Texas(R)	40
Vermont(D)	42

( ) Party of previous governor
* Change in taxes as a % of 1988 revenues,
1 = lowest increase in relative burden.

Sources: New York Times, November 8, 1990, pp. A16-17; U.S. Bureau of the Census, *Government Finances in 1987-88* (Washington, DC: GPO, 1990); National Conference of State Legislatures *State Budget and Tax Actions, 1990.*

compare tax policies across states. As such, the tax burden indicates the effective average tax rate of a particular state.

The responsiveness of the relative growth rates to changes in this tax variable plus two expenditure variables was estimated for each of the states and the District of Columbia, excluding Alaska and Wyoming. This empirical research yielded two fundamental results:

1. The impact of a change in the tax burden relative to the U.S. average was negative and significant in 22 states.[1] The chance of such a result being

random is approximately 1 in 6 billion. This result provides strong statistical support to the assertion that an increase in a state's relative tax burden subtracts from its economic growth. On average, for every 1 percent rise in a state's relative tax burden, its rate of growth declines by approximately 0.5 percent in the year of the relative tax increase.

2. The impact of a change in real per capita government purchases relative to the U.S. average was significant in 4 of the 48 states. There is approximately a 1 in 8 chance of this result being random. In three states, an increase in per capita government expenditures was associated with higher relative growth. This result indicates that state and local government expenditures on goods and services have little impact on a state's economic performance.

Just as important, this research suggests the relative importance of fiscal policy to a state's economic growth rate.

• On average, approximately 50 percent of the variation in a state's performance is associated with changes in the U.S. economy and is therefore outside the purview of state economic policies (Figure 2.1). Changes in the U.S. economy have a proportionate effect on each state's perfor-

Figure 2.1
The Relative Importance of State and Local Fiscal Policy to a State's Economic Growth

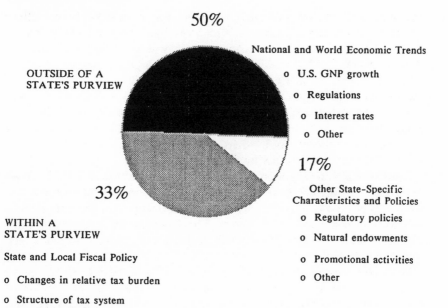

50%

OUTSIDE OF A
STATE'S PURVIEW

National and World Economic Trends

o U.S. GNP growth

o Regulations

o Interest rates

o Other

17%

33%

Other State-Specific
Characteristics and Policies

WITHIN A
STATE'S PURVIEW

o Regulatory policies

State and Local Fiscal Policy

o Natural endowments

o Changes in relative tax burden

o Promotional activities

o Structure of tax system

o Other

o Spending policies

mance, leaving unchanged each state's relative performance. The 1981/82 recession, for example, lowered growth in all states, whereas the recovery has buoyed output and employment across the nation.

Specific events outside a state's purview also can have a disproportionate effect on its growth rate. For example, employment and production in the domestic steel industry have decreased owing to a combination of factors including U.S. tax and regulatory policies, a shift in the cost advantage to foreign producers, foreign subsidies, and excess worldwide steel capacity. In states where the steel industry is a major source of manufacturing jobs, such as Pennsylvania, Maryland, Ohio, and Indiana, the economies of these states suffered.

• Changes in effective average state tax rates relative to the rest of the United States are a major determinant of a state's relative and absolute performance. On average, approximately one third of a state's overall performance (two thirds of the area affected by state policies) is associated with changes in the state and local tax burden relative to the mean for all states (Figure 2.1).

• The remaining one sixth of a state's competitiveness and relative economic performance can be attributed to other factors such as changes in natural endowments, regulatory policies, and business climate.

IMPLICATIONS

The implications are clear-cut: Every state that raises its tax burden above the national average will find it difficult to retain existing facilities and to attract new business. New business starts will unambiguously decline. Mobile capital and labor will emigrate to seek higher after-tax returns in other states, and immobile factors of production will be left behind to bear the burden of the state and local taxes. Corporations with many plants or outlets in states that are increasing their relative tax burdens will fare poorly compared with companies with facilities concentrated in states that are reducing their relative tax burdens. Business failures will increase in the states with rising relative tax burdens.

Symmetrically, a reduction in tax rates reduces the cost of doing business in a state. This increases the demand for the now-less-expensive goods and services produced within the state. The higher demand for the state's goods and services will result in an increased profitability for businesses located within the state. Business failures will decrease in states with declining relative tax burdens.

If all else remains the same, a reduction in tax rates also increases the return to capital and work effort, leading to increases in the supplies of capital and labor within the state. Declining relative tax burdens will experience an increase in business starts. Higher returns to labor and capital will also encourage the immigration of mobile factors from other states. As time horizons lengthen, the process of adjustment will incorporate the movement of plants and businesses to the state and the retention of plants and businesses that might otherwise have left the state. This migration of factors of production will continue until after-tax returns for mobile factors within the state are equalized with after-tax returns for their counterparts elsewhere in the economy. The returns of state-specific immobile factors will increase unambiguously.

Changes in tax rates have the greatest impact on the supplies of factors of production that are highly mobile. For example, consider a worker who is prepared to relocate to achieve a higher standard of living. This worker's availability to the work force within a state will be extremely sensitive to a change in state tax rates.

By contrast, the supplies of immobile factors of production and/or real estate will be affected only slightly by tax rate changes. For example, capital in the form of a new steel mill is highly immobile. Its operating level initially will be relatively unaffected by a change in a state's tax rates. The major impact of state tax rate changes will be on the mill's after-tax profits and, ultimately, whether to close down or to remain open.

Consider two identical steel mills that are located 40 miles apart: One mill is located in Kentucky; the other in Ohio. Since both steel mills sell virtually identical products in the U.S. market, competition will force them to sell their products at approximately the same price. Because the two steel facilities are only 40 miles apart, they both have to pay the same after-tax wages to their employees and the same prices to their suppliers.

Given this situation, consider what would happen if Ohio doubled its income tax rate, whereas Kentucky lowered its income tax rate. Because the steel market is highly competitive, the Ohio company would not be able to pass the tax increase on to its customers in the form of higher prices, nor would it be able to pass it backward to its suppliers or employees.

Initially, at least, the Ohio steel mill would have to absorb the tax increase through lower after-tax profits. This drop in profits would be accompanied by a fall in the Ohio mill's stock price and an increased likelihood of business failure. Clearly, the mill in Kentucky would benefit in the short run, thereby reducing its probability of failure.

The empirical results suggest that states' economies respond fairly quickly to changes in relative tax burden. Thus, in order to forecast changes in states' economic performance, a reliable estimate of changes in states' relative tax burden must be developed.

ESTIMATES OF THE TAX BURDEN

Over the years the National Conference of State Legislatures and the National Governors Association have published static revenue estimates of the impact of state tax actions. These estimates form the basis for the calculations of the changes in state tax burden.

In calculating the tax burden changes, care is made not to include any measure that leaves marginal tax rates unchanged. The estimated tax burdens are known at the beginning of the fiscal year and, hence, can legitimately be used as a forecast of the tax burden changes that will occur during the fiscal year.

Table 2.2 presents a historical summary of the changes in relative tax burden for the 1985-92 fiscal years. A distribution of the tax burden changes is reported in Table 2.3. Upon inspection, it is apparent that the bulk of the magnitude of the tax burden changes is smaller than 1 percent.

APPLICATIONS

In spite of the myriad qualifications inherent in this type of research, the results are promising. The importance of the responsiveness of a state's relative growth rate to changes in tax rates goes well beyond the changes in each state's relative position.

First, an analysis of the states' responsiveness to changes in their relative tax rates provides insight into the importance of fiscal policy to the health of a national economy. In essence, each state is being treated as a country with an open economy. Just as states compete with each other for the location of factories, offices, and jobs within the U.S. economy, the United States must compete with countries around the world for the location of economic activity. Moreover, since monetary policy is the same for all of the states, the effect of fiscal policy is isolated. In order to allow for costly adjustment and to identify the temporal precedence without ambiguity, the relation between changes in relative tax burden and relative changes in personal income were examined. The tabulated results are reported in Table 2.4. During the period in question, there were 135 relative tax burden increases; in 85 cases, the per capita personal income declined in the state with the increasing relative tax burden. Further examination of Table 2.4 indicates that the negative relation is even stronger the larger the magnitude of the tax increase.

Second, for investors and corporate planners, knowledge of a company's exposure to a state where taxes are either rising or falling relative to the nation can be an important input in investment or location decisions. Companies with production facilities concentrated in a state where relative tax rates are declining, for example, can, in general, expect to reap higher after-tax rates of return than those companies in states with rising tax burdens. The extent of the duration and magnitude of such gains or losses is tied inextricably to the mobility of each company's competitors, workers, and the sensitivity of its customers to the price of its goods. Immobile factors of production, such as residential real estate, will bear the burden of taxation.

Table 2.2

Change in Marginal Taxes as a Percent of Two Years' Previous Tax Revenues

	FY85	FY86	FY87	FY88	FY89	FY90	FY91	FY92
Alabama	0.06	0.25	0.0	0.48	0.0	0.0	0.96	0.0
Alaska	0.09	0.17	0.0	0.0	0.0	0.0	0.0	0.0
Arizona	6.85	0.37	0.0	0.0	3.52	0.5	4.5	0.0
Arkansas	9.81	2.46	0.0	2.21	0.0	0.21	0.0	5.93
California	0.0	0.0	0.0	0.0	0.0	0.0	2.26	13.19
Colorado	-2.84	-0.3	3.13	2.41	0.0	1.27	0.0	0.0
Connecticut	0.33	0.06	-1.16	0.0	1.64	10.88	0.12	17.29
Delaware	-1.12	-0.12	-1.86	-2.	0.0	0.0	2.63	2.36
D.C.	0.0	0.0	0.0	0.0	0.0	0.0	-0.8	0.0
Florida	-0.12	1.19	0.4	5.54	7.14	0.41	6.41	1.88
Georgia	0.0	0.0	0.0	0.0	1.07	7.27	0.0	0.0
Hawaii	0.0	1.87	3.62	0.0	0.0	-2.06	-0.1	0.0
Idaho	-2.38	1.01	5.94	6.	1.11	-0.24	0.0	4.52
Illinois	-3.5	0.82	0.0	0.56	0.07	5.21	0.0	-2.41
Indiana	0.0	1.96	0.0	5.3	0.64	0.0	-0.97	0.0
Iowa	0.0	2.27	1.02	1.06	1.36	-0.15	-0.14	0.84
Kansas	0.0	-1.04	5.18	4.17	-1.31	-0.22	0.38	11.27
Kentucky	3.22	1.49	7.39	1.69	1.46	0.17	12.46	5.43
Louisiana	15.4	-0.2	3.18	0.53	5.85	-1.13	5.71	0.0
Maine	-0.13	0.14	1.07	-0.24	0.57	-0.49	-1.04	1.75
Maryland	0.1	-0.64	0.0	2.65	-0.05	-0.38	0.0	0.0
Massachusetts	-0.1	0.08	0.0	0.0	0.93	3.88	8.51	12.98
Michigan	-3.15	-2.11	-3.04	0.0	0.0	0.06	0.0	0.55
Minnesota	-4.89	-5.48	-7.24	4.66	5.34	-0.09	0.04	1.38
Mississippi	2.81	3.45	0.0	0.79	0.0	0.59	0.0	0.0
Missouri	0.0	0.67	0.0	4.9	0.0	1.26	1.19	0.0
Montana	0.0	0.0	0.61	5.59	0.0	0.32	0.11	0.45
Nebraska	-3.45	1.62	0.14	0.19	-0.52	0.69	7.03	0.37
Nevada	0.0	2.19	0.0	2.27	0.0	1.73	0.0	7.9
New Hampshire	0.0	-1.5	0.0	-0.64	-0.14	1.98	3.26	0.28
New Jersey	0.09	-0.16	0.0	0.0	0.62	0.0	11.85	6.91
New Mexico	0.48	1.32	8.44	6.1	2.29	0.75	1.77	0.0
New York	0.0	-1.08	-2.65	-5.31	0.0	-1.08	2.61	1.36
North Carolina	0.0	0.0	0.95	0.93	-0.11	1.68	3.74	0.04
North Dakota	4.19	3.42	3.37	4.36	2.82	9.15	0.0	0.0
Ohio	-0.58	-2.16	-3.36	1.76	0.0	0.91	0.61	0.48
Oklahoma	8.1	11.07	0.0	9.33	-0.15	0.26	4.92	0.0
Oregon	0.0	-1.32	-0.96	0.77	0.52	0.47	0.43	1.39
Pennsylvania	-0.89	-0.61	-1.96	-0.52	0.0	3.46	0.0	4.42
Rhode Island	-1.54	-0.67	0.1	-1.14	-0.01	5.41	5.52	6.72
South Carolina	7.81	0.0	0.0	1.59	0.0	0.44	0.28	0.0
South Dakota	0.0	0.87	0.0	0.99	-0.47	0.0	0.0	0.0
Tennessee	9.29	0.94	2.11	0.0	0.45	2.51	0.31	0.0
Texas	5.66	0.0	0.0	13.24	12.78	-0.99	1.82	0.0
Utah	3.86	0.32	0.0	6.14	-2.93	0.0	0.0	0.0
Vermont	2.84	4.29	-0.74	-0.62	-0.73	4.23	3.85	7.44
Virginia	0.87	1.46	0.67	0.0	0.0	0.07	0.36	0.0
Washington	0.0	0.73	0.56	0.24	0.57	0.84	1.44	0.0
West Virginia	0.0	-3.13	0.0	0.34	5.94	12.82	0.0	0.0
Wisconsin	-1.67	-2.37	0.05	-0.53	-1.17	-0.1	-0.05	0.07
Wyoming	0.0	0.0	0.0	0.0	0.0	0.87	0.0	0.0
United States	0.54	-0.12	-0.44	1.12	1.39	0.98	2.29	3.39

Source: National Conference of State Legislatures, *State Budget and Tax Actions, 1985-1991.*

Table 2.3
Distribution of Relative Tax Burden Changes for the 50 States and the District of Columbia

Range Of Tax Change	FY85	FY86	FY87	FY88	FY89	FY90	FY91	FY92
-0.08 %								
-0.07			1					
-0.06								
-0.05		1		1				
-0.04	1							
-0.03	3	1	2					
-0.02	2	3	1		1	1		1
-0.01	3	4	3	2	2	2	1	
0>X>-.01	5	7	2	5	8	8	5	
0	18	8	23	13	19	9	16	24
0.01	7	12	8	10	8	16	10	8
0.02		8	2	4	5	5	4	5
0.03	2	3	1	4	2	1	3	1
0.04	2	2	4		1	2	3	
0.05	1	1		4		1	2	2
0.06	1		2	4	3	2	2	2
0.07	1			2			1	2
0.08	1		1		1	1	1	2
0.09	1		1				1	
0.1	2			1		1		
0.11						1		
0.12		1					1	1
0.13					1	1	1	1
0.14				1				1
0.15								
0.16	1							
0.17								
0.18								1

Source: National Conference of State Legislatures, *State Budget and Tax Actions, 1985-1991.*

Table 2.4
Relative Personal Income Growth Versus Relative Tax Increases

Year	Magnitude of Tax Increase	Number of State Tax Increases	Same Year Personal Income Changes		One Year Later Personal Income Changes	
			Same Direction	Opposite Direction	Same Direction	Opposite Direction
1985	0%	13	4	9	5	8
1986		36	18	18	15	21
1987		42	16	26	17	25
1988		19	4	15	8	11
1989		10	3	7	8	2
1990		15	5	10	na	na
Total		135	50	85	53	67
1985	2%	12	3	9	4	8
1986		8	2	6	2	6
1987		9	2	7	2	7
1988		12	1	11	6	6
1989		6	2	4	5	1
1990		9	2	7	na	na
Total		56	12	44	19	28
1985	4%	7	2	5	3	4
1986		2	1	1	1	1
1987		5	1	4	1	4
1988		8	1	7	4	4
1989		4	1	3	4	0
1990		6	2	4	na	na
Total		32	8	24	13	13
1985	6%	6	1	5	3	3
1986		1	0	1	0	1
1987		3	0	3	0	3
1988		2	0	2	0	2
1989		1	0	1	1	0
1990		4	2	2	na	na
Total		17	3	14	4	9

na = Not available.

Source: U.S. Department of Commerce.

The data reported in Table 2.5 support the maintained hypothesis. In 82 of the 135, real estate prices declined the year of a relative tax burden increase. Again, the relation becomes stronger the larger the magnitude of the increase. This relation is even stronger when one accounts for the lag time (e.g., one year) expected when changing residences.

State actions could impact the overall financial position of state and local governments in an adverse manner. States lowering their relative burdens can be expected to experience accelerated economic growth, whereas those increasing their relative tax burdens should exhibit a slower pace of economic expansion. Owing to the connection between state and local tax policy and economic performance, the values of assets located in states that alter their tax policies will fluctuate in predictable directions. Assets will tend to become more valuable in states that are cutting tax rates, whereas tax rate increases will tend to depress asset values.

The tax base will decline. The increased unemployment and business

Table 2.5
Relative Single Family Housing Price Changes Versus Relative Tax Increases

Year	Magnitude of Tax Increase	Number of State Tax Increases	Same Year Single Family Housing Price Changes		One Year Later Single Family Housing Price Changes	
			Same Direction	Opposite Direction	Same Direction	Opposite Direction
1985	0%	13	6	7	3	10
1986		36	16	20	15	21
1987		42	18	24	14	28
1988		19	5	14	5	14
1989		10	2	8	7	3
1990		15	6	9	na	na
Total		135	53	82	44	76
1985	2%	12	5	7	3	9
1986		8	3	5	4	4
1987		9	4	5	1	8
1988		12	3	9	4	8
1989		6	1	5	4	2
1990		9	3	6	na	na
Total		56	19	37	16	31
1985	4%	7	4	3	2	5
1986		2	1	1	1	1
1987		5	3	2	0	5
1988		8	3	5	3	5
1989		4	1	3	3	1
1990		6	1	5	na	na
Total		32	13	19	9	17
1985	6%	6	4	2	1	5
1986		1	0	1	0	1
1987		3	3	0	0	3
1988		2	1	1	1	1
1989		1	1	0	1	0
1990		4	1	3	na	na
Total		17	10	7	3	10

na = Not available.

Source: Federal Housing Finance Board, *Rates and Terms on Conventional Home Mortgages—Annual Summary, 1989.*

Table 2.6
General Fund Balance Changes Versus Relative Tax Increases

Year	Magnitude of Tax Increase	Number Of State Tax Increases	Same Year Ending Balance Changes		One Year Later Ending Balance Changes	
			Same Direction	Opposite Direction	Same Direction	Opposite Direction
1985	0%	13	7	5	2	10
1986		36	8	23	15	15
1987		42	18	19	28	11
1988		19	16	2	2	15
1989		10	2	6	9	1
1990		15	8	7	3	12
Total		135	59	62	59	64
1985	2%	12	7	4	1	10
1986		8	1	5	3	2
1987		9	3	6	6	3
1988		12	11	1	2	9
1989		6	1	4	6	0
1990		9	4	5	2	7
Total		56	27	25	20	31
1985	4%	7	4	2	0	6
1986		2	0	2	1	0
1987		5	2	3	3	2
1988		8	7	1	2	5
1989		4	1	3	4	0
1990		6	3	3	1	5
Total		32	17	14	11	18
1985	6%	6	4	1	0	5
1986		1	0	1	0	0
1987		3	0	3	1	2
1988		2	2	0	1	1
1989		1	0	1	1	0
1990		4	2	2	1	3
Total		17	8	8	4	11

Note: Some states had no change in General Fund ending balance.

Source: National Conference of State Legislatures, *State Budget and Tax Actions, 1985-1991.*

failures will result in higher overall government expenditures. Whether the combined effect improves or worsens the state's financial position is an empirical issue. The results reported in Table 2.6 indicate that a year after a tax burden increase the state ending balances declined in 62 of 135 cases.

NOTE

1. The binomial distribution may be used to estimate the probability of having 22 independent outcomes exceed the 5 percent significance level.

3

State Economic Environment: Business Starts and Business Failures

Victor A. Canto and John E. Silvia

How much of the decline in a state's economic performance is attributable to the state's tax policy is open for debate. Our own research suggests that state tax policies play a major role in a state's competitive environment and affect the returns to state-specific factors of production.[1]

The evidence presented here uncovers a link between state and local relative tax burdens and business starts and business failures. The connection between state fiscal policy and state economic performance is particularly important at this stage, when the U.S. economy is in a recession. The states' actions may exacerbate the downturn and result in predictable regional differences. Similarly, the limitation of state and local deductions will also alter the states' competitive environment.

THE FRAMEWORK

Every state that raises its tax burden above the national average will find it difficult to retain existing facilities and to attract new business. New business starts will unambiguously decline. Mobile capital and labor will emigrate to seek higher after-tax returns in other states, and immobile factors of production will be left behind to bear the burden of the state and local taxes. Corporations with many plants or outlets in states that are increasing their relative tax burdens will fare poorly compared with companies with facilities concentrated in states that are reducing their relative tax burdens. Business failures will increase in the states with rising relative tax burdens.

Symmetrically, a reduction in tax rates reduces the cost of doing business in a state. This increases the demand for the now-less-expensive goods and services produced within the state. The higher demand for the state's goods and services will result in an increased profitability for businesses located within the state. Business failures will decrease in states with declining relative tax burdens.

If all else remains the same, a reduction in tax rates also increases the return to capital and work effort, leading to increases in the supplies of capital and labor within the state. Declining relative tax burdens will experience an increase in business starts. Higher returns to labor and capital will also encourage the immigration of mobile factors from other states. As time horizons lengthen, the process of adjustment will incorporate the movement of plants and businesses to the state and the retention of plants and businesses that might otherwise have left the state. This migration of factors of production will continue until after-tax returns for mobile factors within the state are equalized with after-tax returns for their counterparts elsewhere in the economy. The returns of state-specific immobile factors will increase unambiguously.

THE DATA

This theoretical framework provides for an alternate test of the state competitive environment portfolio strategy. Insofar as state and local policies alter a state's competitive environment, a direct relation between changes in a state's relative tax burden and business starts and business failures will be observed.

Over the years, we have calculated changes in states' relative tax burdens based on state actions for the coming fiscal years.[2] Independent of our research, Dun & Bradstreet has published statistics on business starts for the years 1985, 1986, and 1987.[3] Business failure data are available for the 1985-90 years.

THE EVIDENCE

The limited sample for business starts of 1985-87 and the wide sample for business failures of 1985-90 may be used to examine the relation between business starts and business failures and relative tax burdens. To allow for a gradual adjustment to the changes in tax rates, we identified the states for which the relative tax burden declined during the 1985/86 period (Table 3.1). The screen yielded 14 states. The group of states with declining tax burdens experienced a 0.31 percent increase in business starts and a 14.11 percent decrease in business failures in 1986. In contrast, in those states with

Table 3.1

State Business Starts and Business Failures in 1986 Relative to Legislated Tax Changes in 1985 and 1986

	Business Starts	Business Failures
States with declining relative tax burdens in 1985 and 1986		
Colorado	5.28%	12.15%
Kansas	-14.72	-0.80
Maryland	5.91	-4.93
Michigan	-1.56	2.71
Minnesota	-0.73	15.99
New Hampshire	4.80	-15.90
New Jersey	2.16	-15.66
New York	0.42	-27.51
Ohio	0.72	-23.86
Oregon	-4.64	-21.21
Pennsylvania	7.19	-12.55
Rhode Island	6.11	-53.02
West Virginia	-2.10	-54.95
Wisconsin	-4.47	2.01
Average	0.31%	-14.11%
States with increasing relative tax burdens in 1985 and 1986		
Arizona	-9.17%	-11.02%
Arkansas	2.99	-57.41
Kentucky	-8.59	-9.82
Mississippi	-9.20	-0.53
North Dakota	-6.02	-0.16
Oklahoma	-12.39	95.10
South Carolina	-19.58	6.44
Tennessee	0.65	-10.43
Texas	-12.51	37.43
Utah	-0.76	-9.10
Vermont	-0.31	-34.37
Virginia	4.71	-43.26
Average	-5.85%	-3.09%
United States	6.02%	7.34%

rising tax burdens, business starts decreased 5.85 percent, and they experienced a 3.09 percent decrease in business failures.

A systematic relation between relative tax burdens and business failures is also apparent in 1987 (Table 3.2). The 32 states with rising tax burdens during 1986 and 1987 experienced a 0.11 percent decline in business starts and a 5.05 percent increase in business failures, respectively, whereas states with declining relative tax burdens experienced a 1.19 percent increase in business starts and a 1.45 percent decline in business failures.[4]

Table 3.2
Average State Business Starts and Business Failures in 1987 Relative to Legislated Tax Changes in 1986 and 1987

	Business Starts	Business Failures
States with declining relative tax burdens in 1986 and 1987		
Michigan	-2.29%	12.25%
Minnesota	-0.50	7.61
New York	1.85	13.31
Ohio	2.64	-7.23
Oregon	-3.00	-33.36
Pennsylvania	8.41	-1.26
Average	1.19%	-1.45%
States with increasing relative tax burdens in 1986 and 1987		
Alabama	1.16	28.16
Alaska	-9.88	8.67
Arizona	-2.28	21.65
Arkansas	0.90	15.43
California	-9.20	-2.02
Florida	4.93	-3.19
Georgia	5.44	69.65
Hawaii	2.64	-47.40
Idaho	-3.08	35.40
Illinois	1.89	0.63
Indiana	-0.21	18.45
Iowa	-7.37	30.68
Kentucky	-11.27	1.29
Maine	9.09	0.66
Massachusetts	2.06	-10.87
Mississippi	23.00	18.03
Missouri	-5.75	-3.53
Montana	-10.72	58.17
Nebraska	2.64	61.94
Nevada	6.76	-23.25
New Mexico	-1.44	-17.05
North Carolina	-0.56	1.18
North Dakota	13.17	7.36
Oklahoma	2.64	-28.56
South Carolina	4.24	5.83
South Dakota	2.64	60.31
Tennessee	0.46	-2.87
Texas	-8.82	9.52
Utah	0.04	8.31
Virginia	5.59	22.98
Washington	-2.55	-31.54
Wyoming	-19.68	-1.49
Average	-0.11	5.05
United States	-2.64%	-0.66%

Contrary to expectations, the results for 1988 show that states with rising tax burdens have a faster declining failure rate than states with declining tax burdens (Table 3.3).

Late in 1986 the second round of Reagan tax rate cuts was adopted. The reductions in federal tax rates, through their interaction with state and local taxes, produced changes in relative marginal tax rates. In turn, these changes produced state reactions. Some states chose to return the windfall by conforming to federal codes and lowering their tax rates. Other states chose to do nothing. We calculated the estimates of the revenue impact of the potential windfall for the transition years. Usually, the two years were combined. Whenever the revenue impact of the transition was not split among the two years, we chose to allocate them equally among the two

Table 3.3
Average State Business Failure Changes in 1988 Relative to Legislated Tax Changes in 1987 and 1988

States with declining relative tax burdens in 1987 and 1988

Connecticut	37.67%
Delaware	79.48
Michigan	5.88
New York	38.79
Oregon	-26.72
Pennsylvania	-2.81
Vermont	16.89
Average	21.33%

States with increasing relative tax burdens in 1987 and 1988

Arkansas	-11.57%
Colorado	19.49
Florida	4.72
Idaho	-12.93
Indiana	--27.80
Kansas	--8.53
Kentucky	-24.98
Maryland	-7.48
Missouri	-5.59
Montana	-23.53
Nevada	21.34
New Mexico	48.55
North Dakota	45.66
Oklahoma	-83.34
South Carolina	39.55
Texas	-0.61
Utah	5.00
Average	-3.52%
United States	-6.99%

years. Clearly, if there are any feedback effects, the longer the time span, the more likely the states' revenue estimates will be off the mark.

These lead us to suspect the reliability of the estimated relative tax burden as an approximation of the true changes in state relative tax burden. Not surprisingly, the 1988 performance does not conform to the model's prediction. This failure we attribute to the transition effects. Since we use two consecutive years of tax burden changes, the 1989 screen will also be affected (Table 3.4). However, in estimating the relative tax burden for 1989, the effects will not be as severe as those of 1988. The revenue impact of the state actions are made one year ahead—not two years ahead, as they were for 1988. The more accurate static revenue data remove one potential problem. All that is left is how to deal with the effect of federal tax reform on states' relative tax burden. We estimated the potential effect by assuming that taxpayers faced the highest marginal income tax rates at the state level. Once the 1989 adjustments are made, one is left with the problem of what data to use for 1988.

An alternative way to handle the transition year is to discard completely the apportionment between the two years. The states identified as increasing their relative tax burdens during the transition as well as during 1989 experienced a 3.97 percent increase in business failures (Table 3.5). In contrast, states with declining relative tax burdens experienced a 2.45 percent decline in business failures.

The results for 1990 are equally impressive. The 22 states with increasing tax burdens experienced a 29.57 percent decline in business failures—substantially higher than the 19.51 percent increase in business failures for the United States as a whole (Table 3.6). Although states with declining tax burdens experienced an increase in business failures, the increase was significantly below the U.S. average.

The evidence shows that increasing relative tax burdens are associated with a decline in business starts and an increase in business failures. Symmetrically, declining relative tax burdens are associated with increases in business starts and declines in business failures.

THE OUTLOOK FOR 1991 BASED ON STATE TAX ACTIONS

The National Conference on State Legislatures publishes all the state tax rate increases and decreases that are slated to become effective during the next calendar year. As reported in the *Wall Street Journal*, state taxes for 1992 are the largest since 1971.[5] These legislated tax increases formed the basis of our estimates for changes in state relative tax burdens for 1991 and 1992. States experiencing a decline in tax burden during these two years should experience increased economic opportunity and growth and a below-average rate of business failures. States increasing their tax burden during

Table 3.4
**Average State Business Failure Changes in 1989 Relative to Legislated
Tax Changes in 1988 and 1989**

States with declining relative tax burdens in 1988 and 1989

Alabama	-11.71
Alaska	-57.27
California	-3.60
Delaware	-55.51
Georgia	38.71
Hawaii	6.87
Illinois	15.40
Iowa	-6.41
Maine	56.70
Massachusetts	48.80
Michigan	27.69
Mississippi	21.61
Nebraska	-8.14
New Hampshire	-16.39
New Jersey	-26.45
New York	-5.38
North Carolina	25.45
Oregon	-0.54
Pennsylvania	25.40
Rhode Island	40.77
South Dakota	8.25
Tennessee	13.89
Vermont	5.96
Virginia	37.40
Washington	-11.52
Wisconsin	-31.55
Wyoming	-42.28
Average	3.56%

States with increasing relative tax burdens in 1988 and 1989

Florida	13.71%
Kentucky	9.43
Minnesota	-37.15
New Mexico	26.87
North Dakota	-27.69
Texas	-25.34
Average	-6.70%

these two fiscal years will experience a decline in their competitive environment in the near future.

Table 3.5
Average State Business Failure Changes in 1989 Relative to Legislated
Tax Changes in 1988 and 1989 (Adjusted)*

States with declining relative tax burdens in 1988 and 1989

Alabama	-11.71%
Alaska	-57.27
California	-3.60
Delaware	-55.51
Georgia	38.71
Hawaii	6.87
Illinois	15.40
Iowa	-6.41
Maine	56.70
Massachusetts	48.80
Michigan	27.69
Nebraska	-8.14
New Hampshire	-16.39
New Jersey	-26.45
New York	-5.38
Pennsylvania	25.40
Rhode Island	40.77
South Dakota	8.25
Virginia	37.40
Washington	-11.52
Wisconsin	-31.55
Wyoming	-42.28
Average	1.35%

States with increasing relative tax burdens in 1988 and 1989

Connecticut	6.95%
Florida	13.71
Kentucky	9.43
Louisiana	10.12
Minnesota	-37.15
New Mexico	26.87
North Dakota	-27.69
Texas	-25.34
Average	-2.89%

*   The relative tax burden has been adjusted to allow for the impact of federal tax reform on the states' relative tax rates.

Table 3.6
Average State Business Changes Relative to Legislated Tax Changes, 1990

States with declining relative tax burdens in 1989 and 1990

Alabama	12.26
Alaska	-33.17
Arkansas	-34.16
California	-5.16
Delaware	72.12
Hawaii	-32.27
Idaho	12.21
Indiana	4.01
Iowa	-16.95
Kansas	-3.52
Maine	22.83
Maryland	-91.08
Michigan	-17.93
Mississippi	-34.90
Montana	-18.99
Nebraska	31.01
New Jersey	57.82
New York	32.62
Ohio	8.28
Oklahoma	5.00
Oregon	9.26
South Carolina	65.14
South Dakota	46.16
Utah	6.78
Virginia	10.42
Washington	-60.53
Wisconsin	-25.06
Wyoming	21.88
Average	8.08%

States with increasing relative tax burdens in 1989 and 1990

Connecticut	91.99%
North Dakota	12.76
West Virginia	19.10
Average	41.29%

NOTES

1. Victor A. Canto and Robert I. Webb, "The Effect of State Fiscal Policy on State Relative Economic Performance," *Southern Economic Journal* 54, no. 1 (July 1987); and Victor A. Canto, Charles W. Kadlec, and Arthur B. Laffer, "The State Competitive Environment," A. B. Laffer Associates, August 8, 1984.

2. Canto, Kadlec, and Laffer, "The State Competitive Environment"; Victor A. Canto, "The State Competitive Environment," A. B. Laffer Associates, December 20, 1985; idem, "The State Competitive Environment: 1987-88 Update," A. B. Laffer Associates, February 5, 1988.

3. Dun & Bradstreet Corporation, *Business Starts Record and Business Failure Record*, 1985 through 1987.

4. The state tax burdens have been adjusted to include the impact of federal tax rate reduction on the states' relative tax burden.

5. Timothy Noah, "States' Tax Increases for the Year Show Biggest Jump Since 1971, Survey Finds," *Wall Street Journal*, August 31, 1991, p. A16.

Part II

*Investment Implications:
Asset Prices and State
Economic Policy*

4

Either California's Housing Prices Are Going to Fall or California's in for One Helluva Rise in Personal Income

Arthur B. Laffer and Christopher S. Hammond

INTRODUCTION

California's real estate boom has been truly incredible. But as good as it has been, it is difficult to view California's housing boom as either generic or otherwise impervious to human action. Serendipity is wonderful except when it is anticipated. When anticipated, serendipity is a blueprint for catastrophe.

When viewing California's real estate market, the logical sequence from original cause to the final effect is as follows:

California's taxes affect California's business climate.

California's business climate affects California's population growth.

California's population growth affects California's home prices.

Based on historical relationships and recent changes in California politics, it is hard to visualize a continuation of California's frenetic economic prosperity, a continuation of California's population growth, and thereby a continuation of California's real estate appreciation. California has indeed been fortunate in the past 15 years. The elements that came together to provide California with this incredible prosperity don't seem to be likely to continue over the coming decade. As a consequence, natural market forces will lead to a fairly dramatic decline in California real estate prices.

On the cusp of tragedy is the fact that many in California and elsewhere have made large financial commitments predicated on California's continued real estate boom. Savings and loans, banks, and insurance companies all have large stakes in California real estate. Even a moderate redressing of California's real estate prices could result in a major reordering of finances. And while it is true that the underlying economy will be far less affected by a rebalancing of asset values, now is a time of major changes in the ownership of wealth. These times will be remembered for many years to come.

In the grand scheme of things, housing in the near and intermediate term is a relatively fixed factor. Only at great expense can houses or other forms of real estate be transported. In the very long run, however, new construction combined with depreciation can relocate enormous quantities of real estate at a relatively low cost. This long-run mobility of factors all but vanishes in the nearer term.

In the case of the real estate market, the importance of long-run forces is altogether too easy to overlook. While during any day, week, month, or year, long-run forces appear to be irrelevant, they do ultimately prevail over all else. In the long run, equivalent houses should cost roughly the same everywhere. Betting against these long-run forces is literally "betting against the house." You do win from time to time, but the odds are not in your favor.

Whether in the long or short run, adjustments to market shocks occur through changes in price and/or changes in quantity. Increases in demand result in higher price and greater quantity. If the supply curve is elastic, then the increase in price will be small and quantity great.

In the near term, changes in housing demand invariably come up against relatively inelastic supplies. Therefore, real estate prices provide a great deal of the buffer for near-term adjustments to changes in market conditions, whereas the quantity of homes accounts for less. The long-run tendency, however, is still worth keeping in mind. Over long periods of time, housing prices should equilibrate across different locations. All long-run changes in locational demand should be accommodated by changes in supply—not relative prices.

In a collection of figures, we have attempted to create a picture of California. Without having to shout or draw pictures, the prognosis for California's real estate market virtually jumps off the pages. Such a tendentious depiction is inherently risky. For a number of reasons, we are not sanguine about California's real estate market. We believe our reasons are objective and unbiased, but, nonetheless, the reader should be well aware of where we're coming from.

CALIFORNIA'S REAL ESTATE APPRECIATION

In Figure 4.1, the median current dollar price of a California house is plotted for the time period from 1968 through 1989 using annual data. The same data series is also plotted for the United States as a whole. What

Figure 4.1
Median Home Prices: California Versus United States

Median
Price ($,000's)

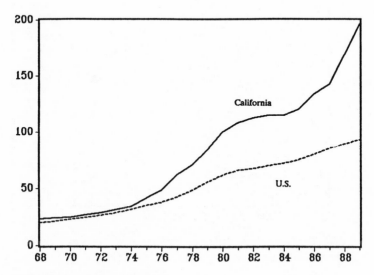

Source: California Association of Realtors.

jumps out at the viewer is how close to the rest of the country California housing prices were back in 1968 and how far they had diverged by 1989. In 1968, California's median-priced house was about 16 percent more expensive than for the United States as a whole. In 1989, California's median-priced house was well over twice that of the median-priced house for the United States as a whole.

Income differences alone don't seem to be sufficiently great to account for such a large change in relative housing prices or the magnitude of the current discrepancy.

HOUSING AFFORDABILITY: CALIFORNIA AND THE UNITED STATES

While many considerations should go into the concept of affordability, income appears to be the essential ingredient. Many measures of affordability also exist, each with its own special features and nuances. Lacking universal "truth," we have chosen to relate the median house price to per capita personal income for both California and the United States. The shortcomings of such a measure should be obvious (Figure 4.2).

Figure 4.2
Median Home Prices Relative to Per Capita Personal Income:
California Versus United States

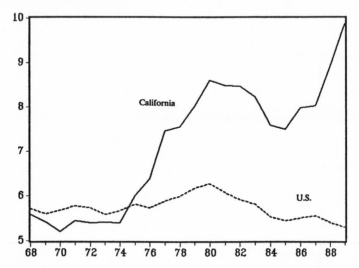

Sources: Bureau of Economic Analysis, U.S. Department of Commerce; California Association of Realtors.

In spite of the inherent data problems, the differences between California
and the rest of the nation are not ameliorated when personal income is
taken into account. When income is taken into account, California prices
no longer look "out of line" in the 1968-75 period. In fact, for most of that
period, California home prices appear a smidgeon low in relation to income.

But from 1975 on, California's median housing price relative to per
capita personal income takes off vis-à-vis the rest of the country. By 1989,
California's median house price relative to California's per capita personal
income nearly doubled in magnitude relative to the U.S. median house price
relative to U.S. per capita personal income.

Virtually all of the increase in this measure of "unaffordability" of California homes relative to the United States comes from the increase in the
price of a house in California relative to the rest of the nation. Relative per
capita personal income stayed roughly the same over the period 1968-89. In
1970, for example, California's per capita personal income was 17 percent
greater than the per capita income for the nation as a whole. In 1989, California's per capita personal income was 13 percent above the nation's.

For the United States as a whole—if our measure of affordability is
deemed appropriate—houses have become slightly more affordable over the
past 30 years. In California, housing has become less affordable by a factor
of almost two.

CALIFORNIA'S HOUSING PRICES AND
POPULATION GROWTH

Part of the change in home prices may well be accounted for by California's phenomenal population growth relative to the rest of the nation.

Because the supply of houses is relatively inelastic in the near term, immigration can reasonably be expected to have a major impact on housing prices. Immigration should affect housing prices not only in absolute terms but also relative to income.

Over the past 22 years, data show a close relationship between California's excess population growth and the price of a California home. In Figure 4.3, we have plotted the two series using annual data for the period 1968-89. Affordability is once again the median price of a California home divided by per capita personal income. For the relative demand for California homes, we use California's excess population growth, for example, the

Figure 4.3
California Median Home Price Relative to Per Capita Personal Income Versus California Excess Population Growth

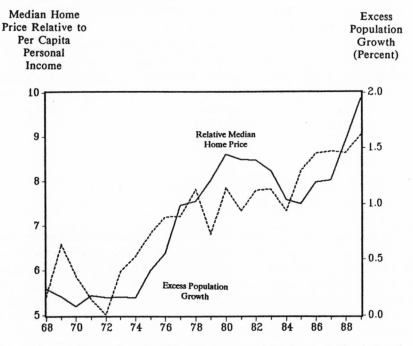

Sources: Bureau of Economic Analysis, U.S. Department of Commerce; California Association of Realtors.

annual percent change in California's population less the percent change in the population of the United States.

Given the crude nature of these data, the statistical fit is really quite exceptional. Excess population growth goes a long way in "explaining" just why California's real estate appreciation has been so awesome.

But on closer scrutiny additional interesting features become apparent. For example, California's rate of population growth has always been higher than population growth rates for the United States. But back in the late 1960s and early 1970s the differences in the growth rates were far smaller than they were in the 1980s. The leveling-off period for differences in relative population growth rates from, say, 1978 to 1985 was also a period of a flat housing price "affordability" index. The latest surge in California's population growth has been accompanied by an equivalent or even bigger surge in California's home prices. As of 1989, homes in California were *less* affordable than at any time in recent history. Ironically, for the rest of the nation, homes were *more* affordable than at any time in recent history.

So far, we have restricted the time period to 1968 through 1989 solely because earlier data on median home prices were not available. For per capita income and population growth, however, data for the entire postwar period are readily available. Unfortunately, in a readily accessible form, state and local fiscal data only go back as far as 1960. Nonetheless, even a few more data add to our analytic base.

The analysis so far shows the following observations and linkages: (1) California housing prices are a lot higher than those in the rest of the nation; (2) the excess rise in California's housing prices is of relatively recent origin—say, over the last 15-plus years; (3) even relative to income, California has experienced extraordinarily rapid housing appreciation; and (4) the extraordinary surge in California's real estate values is directly related to California's extraordinary population growth.

ECONOMIC DETERMINANTS OF CALIFORNIA'S POPULATION GROWTH

Taking our story the next step adds a new economic dimension. The question to answer now becomes, Why are people now moving to California in such great numbers? Clearly the weather, mountains, beautiful coastline, and other natural endowments should have had the same siren's lure during, say, the 1965-75 period as they did earlier and later. And yet California's excess population growth has shown a great deal of variation over the years.

There is no lemma in supply-side economics more powerful than the lemma that economic incentives motivate people to relocate. Imagine two locations, A and B. Then ask, What would happen to migration patterns if B's per capita income rose relative to A's per capita income? In the absence of other extenuating circumstances, B's population growth should increase relative to A's population growth.

In Figure 4.4, California's excess population growth and California's relative per capita income are plotted for the years 1950-89. This longer time period reveals the true variability of California's excess population growth. Back in the 1950s, California's population growth exceeded that of the nation by well over two percentage points in most years. While the average growth differential in the 1950s was high, the volatility was also very high. But some of that high volatility can be rationalized by the fact that the over-all population of California was by today's standards small. California was relatively empty, and yet the rest of the country was relatively full. Perhaps back then the operational constraints were different than they are now.

Back in 1950, if a million people had moved to California, there was plenty of room, and that million people would have resulted in a 0.71 per-

Figure 4.4
Relative California Per Capita Personal Income (CA/U.S.) Versus California Excess Population Growth

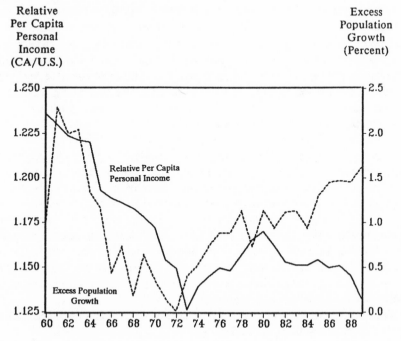

Sources: Bureau of Economic Analysis, U.S. Department of Commerce; California Association of Realtors.

cent decline in the rest of the nation's population. Therefore, in 1950 to increase California's population by 9.37 percent, the rest of the nation's population would have had to have fallen by 0.71 percent.

In 1990, California is a different world altogether. While California may not be full, it surely is not as empty as it was in 1950. With our 1990 population of over 29 million people, to increase that population now by 9.37 percent would mean an influx of 2.72 million people or a reduction in the population of the rest of the nation by 1.24 percent. Whichever way you look at it, either from the supply side of the rest of the nation or the capacity of California to absorb, percentage population growth was a lot easier in 1950 than it was in 1990. Therefore, while long-trem population comparisons are instructive, the different time periods are not strictly comparable.

The basic conclusion must be that it will be harder and harder for California to maintain its relative population growth advantage over the rest of the nation. California is fuller, and the rest of the nation is relatively smaller.

Figure 4.4 does show a strong corroboration of the basic supply-side lemma that people tend to move for economic reasons. The lemma simply makes sense, and it's always nice when the data confirm common sense. Higher per capita incomes in California relative to the United States are closely associated with more rapid population growth in California.

Figure 4.5 displays yet another version of the basic supply-side lemma that people tend to move for economic advantage. There are two differences between Figure 4.4 and Figure 4.5: (1) the time periods covered are different—1950-89 in Figure 4.4 as opposed to 1960-89 in Figure 4.5; (2) the economic advantage variable is California's relative per capita income in Figure 4.4 and California's excess unemployment rate in Figure 4.5.

Unemployment being a disadvantage, there should be an inverse relationship between California's excess population growth and California's excess unemployment The numbers once again confirm supply-side economic logic. Simple common sense, once again, vanquishes complex error.

Whether one uses relative per capita income or California's excess unemployment, economics does have a role to play. No one need ever deny that noneconomic factors also play roles in determining California's population growth. They do. But what we have established is the simple proposition that California's relative population growth, in part, depends on California's economic climate. The more jobs California has and the higher the pay for those jobs relative to the United States as a whole, the more California's population will increase.

When added to the other propositions, the logical linkages are almost complete. We now have the following:

Relative per capita incomes affect relative home prices (Figure 4.2).

Figure 4.5
California Excess Unemployment Versus California Excess
Population Growth

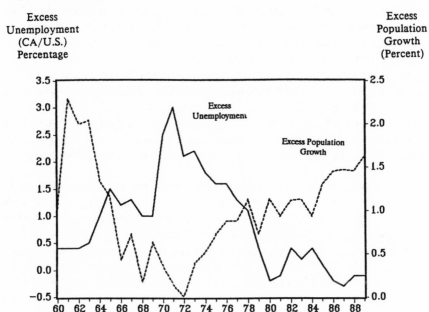

Excess
Unemployment
(CA/U.S.)
Percentage

Excess
Population
Growth
(Percent)

Sources: U.S. Bureau of the Census; U.S. Department of Labor Statistics.

Relative population growth raises relative home prices (Figure 4.3).
People move for relative economic advantage (Figures 4.4 and 4.5).

TAXES AND ECONOMIC GROWTH: CALIFORNIA AND THE UNITED STATES

We have everything now in place, save for the original cause. Economic conditions do cause migration, and migration and economic conditions together do cause changes in housing prices. But what causes changes in economic conditions?

Again, it is clear that a lot of factors come into play when it comes down to the economy—whether on a national, state, or local level. And even though a policy may be a national policy, it still may have different regional effects. And California arguably could be near one extreme when it comes to defense spending, troop deployment, gas taxes, and so on. But still it's a good bet that state and local policy differences will affect the relative performance of the different states.

Take, for example, two similar companies—one in California and one elsewhere. If these two companies compete in the U.S. market, then a tax increase in California not shared by the company outside of California will damage the California company's ability to compete. Whether the California company tries to pass the tax increase forward on its customers or backward on its workers and suppliers or just lowers its return on capital, the California company will be damaged.

Higher prices will make the California company less competitive. Lower factor prices and lessened returns on capital will precipitate a withdrawal from the now higher-taxed California-based company. Whichever of the effects takes place, or in what combination, doesn't change the basic fact that higher California taxes render California-based companies less competitive in the grand scheme of economics. California-based companies will lose business.

With lost business, there soon will be lower wages, lower profits, and higher unemployment. The incentives for people and capital to migrate into California will be diminished. As a consequence, migration into California will diminish. The logical sequence is now complete.

In Figure 4.6, California's tax burden (total state and local tax receipts divided by the state's personal income) is compared with the state and local tax burden for the nation as a whole from 1960 through 1988. The reason

Figure 4.6
Tax Burden for California and United States: Tax Revenues per $1,000 of Personal Income

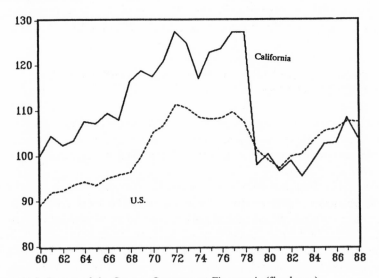

Source: U.S. Bureau of the Census, *Government Finances in* (fiscal year).

for the 1960-88 time interval is simply that prior to 1960 state and local tax data had not been compiled on a consistent basis and 1989's tax data have not yet been made available.

Figure 4.6 is incredibly revealing about California's past and present. With only a little additional information, California's future unfolds before our very eyes. From the early 1960s to the early 1970s, California and the sum of all states increased taxes as a share of personal income by enormous amounts. From 1960 to 1972, California increased total state and local tax receipts as a share of personal income from 10.0 percent to 12.7 percent. In the vernacular, that is not "chopped liver" by any stretch of the imagination. During that same time period, the sum of all states raised their tax burden from 8.9 percent to 11.1 percent. California once again was right at the forefront.[1]

To keep everything in its proper perspective, the 1960s and early 1970s were the eras of the go-go sixties followed by the Johnson/Nixon meltdown.

The mid-1970s was a period of massive tax indigestion following the tax binge. The economy stank everywhere but was especially bad in California. From 1960 until 1978, California and the sum of all states moved together, with California always having much higher taxes. In 1977, for example, California ranked as the third highest taxed state in the nation. In 1960, California was way up there on the tax charts, too. From 1960 through 1977, California remained one of the very highest taxed states in the nation—a dubious honor, to be sure. But prior to the end of the 1960s, even though California's taxes were relatively very high, they had been rising sharply from a much lower base.

From the standpoint of a state's economics, a state's absolute tax burden should be important in addition to its relative tax burden. Using an extreme hypothetical illustration, if California's state tax burden were twice that of other states and yet amounted to only $0.02 per $1,000 income, the relative tax burden should have only a minimal impact on anything. The absolute tax burden would be so small as to dilute the relative tax effect.

In the very early 1960s, California relative tax burden was quite high, but its absolute tax burden was much less than it was in the mid-1970s. As a result of a lower absolute tax burden, California's relative tax burden should have weighed less heavily on California's economy in the early 1960s than in the mid-1970s.

In 1978, a force that had been building strength for several years finally brought a huge and dramatic change to the California economy. In June 1978, Proposition 13 rolled the entrenched political establishment. Proposition 13 was a constitutional amendment that (1) set property taxes not to exceed 1 percent of a property's value, (2) allowed the base value to grow no more than 2 percent per year unless the property changed hands, and (3) required that all new or increased taxes be voted in by a supermajority of the electorate. Proposition 13 won in a landslide.

Following on Proposition 13's heels was an elimination of the state's inheritance tax, an indexing of the state's income tax, and an elimination of the state's business inventory tax. In 1979, Proposition 4 passed, locking the tax gains into place by requiring (1) spending to grow no faster than the sum of population growth and inflation and (2) all surplus revenues to be returned to the taxpayers.

Figure 4.6 shows just how dramatic Proposition 13, and others, has been to California's relative tax burden. It was amazing! But two points do need to be emphasized. First, while Proposition 13—and others that followed—did occur in and around 1978, a lot of political buildup had been apparent in California well before 1978. Second, while Proposition 13 was global in its impact, other states had similar measures, a few of which even preceded the passage of Proposition 13.

But knowing that antecedents to Proposition 13 existed in California and that other states had similar measures does not negate the "taxquake from California." Without Proposition 13, there would not have been the Reagan tax revolt, and Margaret Thatcher surely would not have been the Margaret Thatcher we know and love.

In Figure 4.7 and 4.8, California's tax burden is directly related to the

Figure 4.7
California Tax Burden Versus Excess Unemployment (CA/U.S.)

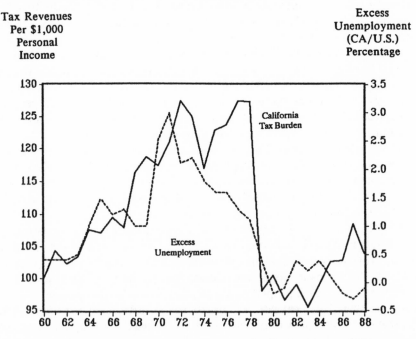

Sources: U.S. Bureau of the Census, *Government Finances in* (fiscal year); U.S. Department of Labor Statistics.

Figure 4.8
California Tax Burden Versus Relative Per Capita Personal Income

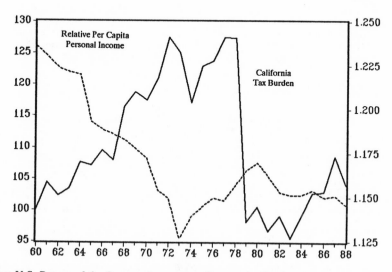

Source: U.S. Bureau of the Census, *Government Finances in* (fiscal year).

state of California's economic well-being. In Figure 4.7, California's tax burden is plotted against California's excess unemployment over the period 1960-88.

As charts of this genre go, this is a good fit. Over the broad sweep of time California's excess unemployment is definitely correlated with California's tax burden. When one realizes just how little is included in this analysis, the relationship is much more impressive.

Throughout all the buildup of the Vietnam War, California's unemployment rate was rising relative to the rest of the nation. Now how's that for a surprise? During the Vietnam and defense wind-down, California's excess unemployment rate was falling. Even the large defense buildup of the 1980s is scarcely visible in California's excess unemployment rate. On this scale of analysis, it's hard to uncover the California effect of the defense budget.

Figure 4.8 is not meant as new evidence independent of Figure 4.7. In fact, Figure 4.8 is a different perspective on the relationship between California's tax policies and the performance of the California economy. Figure 4.8 plots California's relative per capita personal income against the same tax burden series.

Diagram 4.1
Linkage Established Between California Economic Conditions,
Population Growth, and California Home Prices and Affordability

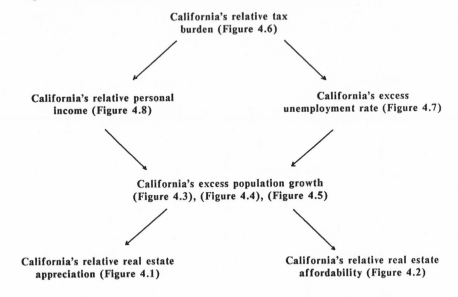

California's relative tax
burden (Figure 4.6)

California's relative personal
income (Figure 4.8)

California's excess
unemployment rate (Figure 4.7)

California's excess population growth
(Figure 4.3), (Figure 4.4), (Figure 4.5)

California's relative real estate
appreciation (Figure 4.1)

California's relative real estate
affordability (Figure 4.2)

Combining Figures 4.7 and 4.8 closes the logical structure. Diagram 4.1 illustrates the logical sequence and the relevant figures.

WHITHER THE VALUE OF CALIFORNIA REAL ESTATE?

As this chapter is being written, the 485-acre parcel of land immediately to the east of Laffer's property is undergoing a massive transition. The Japanese acquired the property from the bankrupt Southmark Corporation and have started to develop the property in earnest. Close to 800 homes are anticipated over the next five or so years, and right now five huge "Cats" and many more giant trucks are building the infrastructure on a six-day-per-week basis.

Immediately to the west of the property, a 50-acre development has just been readied for 22 new homes. The development was started some three years ago, and while all the lots are ready to begin construction, only four houses are in different stages of production. Another neighbor's house has been "on the market" for about nine months. In this neighborhood, at least, the pipeline is pretty full.

The early Keynesians liked to think of business cycles in a rather mechanistic fashion. A key element of their theory of the business cycle was the concept called *the accelerator*. The accelerator was simply the relationship between changes in demand and changes in some specific investment category. For inventories—an investment of short durability—the accelerator was small. But when investment capital was long-lived, the accelerator could be huge.

To illustrate this concept, imagine a static population of some 1,000 people where 10 people live in each house. If houses depreciate at 1 percent per year, then the construction industry will have to produce one house per year to offset depreciation. Now, if population were to grow at 1 percent per year, then the construction industry would have to produce two houses per year, one to offset depreciation and one for the additional 10 people.

In this example, a 1 percent increase in population has led to a 100 percent increase in the size of the construction industry. Because construction is both on the demand and supply side of the equation, the accelerator may be magnified even more. Construction personnel not only build homes but live in them as well.

California's relative housing prices from their low around 1974 have risen by an incredible amount. At first, and for quite some time thereafter, California's construction industry just couldn't catch up. Construction was incessantly behind the power curve. The stories are now legend of lotteries in Orange County giving people the right to make offers on houses the ground for which had just been broken. Those were the days. "The Keynesian accelerator" was alive and well and big.

Even today, construction is a huge component of the California economy. But it would be hard to argue that the construction industry is in arrears like it was at the end of the 1970s. If anything, California's construction industry has caught up with the pent-up demand and may even be a little ahead.

In June of 1990, California voters passed Proposition 111, which raised the gas tax and the truck weight tax. Proposition 111 also weakened the Gann spending limits passed in 1979. Over the past several years, numerous ways have been found to circumvent Proposition 13. By all accounts, a new era is at hand.

This new era is far from a complete return to the pre–Proposition 13 era. Senator Pete Wilson defeated Diane Feinstein for governor, which is clearly a plus. Some of the most antibusiness initiatives were badly defeated by the California voters in November as well.

From the standpoint of California politics, the outlook is far better today than it was at the end of June 1990. Being far better, however, is a far cry from being good.

With the state of California politics and the nation as a whole, the conditions just aren't there to justify California's ever-increasing home values. The long and short of it is that California is in for a serious housing slump.

NOTE

1. In fact, a little digression appears apropos. Ronald Reagan was elected governor of California in 1966 by a plurality of almost 1 million votes over incumbent governor Edmund G. "Pat" Brown, Sr. Reagan was reelected in 1970 by a 500,000-vote margin over assembly speaker Jesse Unruh.

When Reagan took office, the highest marginal personal income tax rate in California was 7 percent. When he left office, the highest marginal personal income tax rate was 11 percent. The year in which Reagan took office (1967), taxes as a share of personal income were 10.8 percent. The year in which he left office (1975), taxes as a share of personal income were 12.3 percent.

Reagan also spearheaded efforts to void the state's antiabortion statutes, successfully led the battle for a state equal rights amendment, and instituted the first criminal furlough program. How's that for egg in your beer?

5

The State Competitive Environment: An Ebb Tide Lowers All Boats

Victor A. Canto

The 1990 budget agreement was hailed by President George Bush and his budget director, Richard Darman, as a breakthrough that would reform the budget process and finally bring the budget deficit under control. According to their estimates, the deficit was to decline by $50 billion the first year and $500 billion over five years. There were two new features introduced into the budget process: In addition to the flexible spending target, the pay-as-you-go feature would further restrain spending. These were hailed by Darman as innovations in the budget process that would bring spending and the deficit under control.[1]

Our view was not as optimistic as the views of Darman and President Bush. We argued that the Bush administration fell into the age-old budget trap. On its surface, there is seeming symmetry between spending and taxes and the resultant deficit. The appearance of symmetry is an illusion, however, with immense significance. Tax increases and spending cuts became equally attractive options to deal with the budget deficit. In addition, the president agreed to the famous pay-as-you-go provision. It required that revenue increases be found to make up for the "static" revenue losses generated by a tax rate cut. Since any tax rate cut must be accompanied either by a spending cut or by a tax rate increase, the agreement effectively blocks any tax rate cuts. This, at least, locks the economy into the current overall "average tax rate." The focus will no longer be on reducing overall disincentives but will be on raising one group's marginal tax rate to lower that of another group.[2] Furthermore, at that time, we also argued that elimination of the "bubble," by raising tax

rates at the upper end, and other features of the tax rate changes would
further slow the economy. The slower growth rate would, in turn, result in
lower-than-expected tax revenues. These effects, and the inability to control
spending, would lead to larger deficits.[3]

Much of what we feared has come to pass. The static revenue increase did
not materialize. The economic downturn was sharper than expected, and
the budget deficit has worsened.[4] Budget Director Richard Darman
attributed the worsened deficit projections to technical corrections.

The significant underestimations are easily explained in terms of the
substitution effects generated by the higher tax rates resulting from the
budget agreement. The higher tax rates create incentives to avoid and evade
taxes. This reduces the taxable base and results in smaller revenue collections than those forecast by economic models that do not fully account for
feedback or substitution effects.

The tax increase was a major cause for the worsening economic conditions
during the last few months. At present, no major actions are being contem-
plated to close the federal budget deficit. Perhaps Office of Management
and Budget (OMB) data manipulations finally created an apathy for the
numbers so that the public does not care nor does it trust the official
figures and estimates. Even if the budget deficit is of no concern and no
action is taken at the federal level, there are reasons to be concerned. States
have enacted numerous tax increases; the accounts in the press point out
that the state tax increases, in percentage terms, are the largest since 1971.[5]
Previously legislated tax increases, combined with increases enacted
throughout the year, add significantly to this record figure (Table 5.1). The
magnitude of the increase, $24 billion, is slightly smaller than the sum of
last year's federal tax increase of $17.9 billion plus state and local increases
of $10.7 billion.[6]

THE U.S. ECONOMY AND STATES'
RELATIVE PERFORMANCE

The implications for the U.S. economy are quite clear. Collectively, the
state actions will have an impact on the U.S. economy similar to federal
budget actions. The increased tax rates will reduce the level of economic
activity. The state actions will lengthen the U.S. recession. Insofar as the
residents of a state anticipate a tax increase, they will try to avoid the taxes
by accelerating purchases. Since most state actions take place in July, it
seems reasonable to assume the bulk of anticipation effects would take
place during the second quarter.

The press interpreted as encouraging news the fact that real gross national
product (GNP) increased at a 0.4 percent annual rate during the second
quarter. This may be a harbinger of a future slowdown if the acceleration of

Table 5.1
State Tax Actions for Fiscal Year 1992
Ranked by Tax Increases as Percent of 1989 Taxes (in millions)

	Fiscal '92 Tax Revenue Increases*	Fiscal '92 Increases as % of '89 Taxes	Personal Income as % of U.S. Total	Cumulative % of Personal Income
Wisconsin	$1,700.0	17.33%	1.85%	1.85%
Connecticut	1,300.0	16.03	1.80	3.65
Pennsylvania	3,000.0	14.37	4.79	8.44
Massachusetts	1,764.9	12.98	2.94	11.38
Kansas	478.4	11.08	0.96	12.34
California	6,700.0	11.04	13.36	25.70
Tennessee	703.0	10.83	1.66	27.36
New Jersey	1,900.0	10.10	4.17	31.53
Idaho	126.0	8.90	0.33	31.86
Arkansas	245.0	8.55	0.72	32.58
Vermont	88.0	8.37	0.21	32.79
Nevada	157.2	7.90	0.50	33.30
New Hampshire	130.0	7.29	0.50	33.79
North Carolina	698.0	6.76	2.32	36.11
Minnesota	607.0	6.45	1.77	37.88
Kentucky	280.7	5.43	1.19	39.07
Missouri	385.0	5.11	1.93	41.00
Louisiana	298.0	4.79	1.31	42.31
Illinois	700.0	3.21	5.01	47.32
New York	1,484.0	2.71	8.53	55.86
Maine	64.0	2.68	0.46	56.31
Delaware	32.0	2.36	0.29	56.60
Rhode Island	40.0	2.11	0.41	57.01
Texas	500.0	1.88	6.15	63.15
Florida	303.0	1.46	5.19	68.34
Oregon	71.0	1.39	1.05	69.40
Washington	96.4	1.06	1.98	71.38
Maryland	90.0	0.87	2.26	73.63
Iowa	28.0	0.56	1.03	74.67
Michigan	101.0	0.55	3.68	78.35
Ohio	98.0	0.53	4.09	82.44
Montana	5.7	0.45	0.26	82.70
Nebraska	10.0	0.37	0.59	83.29
Utah	3.0	0.12	0.52	83.81
Arizona	0.0	0.00	1.29	85.10
North Dakota	0.0	0.00	0.21	85.31
Indiana	0.0	0.00	2.02	87.33
South Dakota	0.0	0.00	0.24	87.57
Alaska	0.0	0.00	0.26	87.83
Georgia	0.0	0.00	2.37	90.20
Colorado	0.0	0.00	1.34	91.53
Mississippi	0.0	0.00	0.71	92.24
Alabama	0.0	0.00	1.29	93.53
West Virginia	0.0	0.00	0.53	94.07
South Carolina	0.0	0.00	1.14	95.20
New Mexico	0.0	0.00	0.47	95.67

Table 5.1 (continued)

	Fiscal '92 Tax Revenue Increases*	Fiscal '92 Increases as % of '89 Taxes	Personal Income as % of U.S. Total	Cumulative % of Personal Income
Hawaii	$ 0.0	0.00%	0.48%	96.15%
Oklahoma	0.0	0.00	1.05	97.20
Virginia	0.0	0.00	2.64	99.84
Wyoming	0.0	0.00	0.16	100.00
United States	24,187.3	5.19%	100.00%	

*Includes legislation enacted in 1990.

Sources: National Governors Association, *Fiscal Survey of the States*, April 1991; U.S. Bureau of the Census; Federation of Tax Administrators.

purchases took place so as to avoid state taxes. In short, state actions will contribute to the likelihood of a "double-dip."

States whose tax actions raise tax revenue, on a static basis, by more than 2 percent of 1989 taxes account for 57.01 percent of U.S. personal income (Table 5.1). Those with rising relative tax burdens account for 39.07 percent. The impact of state actions on the states' economies, and thereby on U.S. GNP, should not be ignored.

Our research on the state competitive environment suggests that the recovery will be uneven regionally. California, Connecticut, Idaho, Kansas, Kentucky, Massachusetts, New Jersey, Nevada, Pennsylvania, and Vermont—the states with rising absolute and relative tax burdens—will have tougher times. In contrast, Alabama, Arizona, Colorado, Georgia, Hawaii, Mississippi, New Mexico, North Dakota, Indiana, Oklahoma, South Carolina, South Dakota, and Wyoming will tend to have stronger economies.

WHO SUFFERS THE BURDEN OF STATE TAXATION?

This part of the analysis recognizes that the person upon whom the tax is levied is not necessarily the person paying the tax. In short, the incidence of a tax may be different from the burden of a tax. The ability to pass a tax forward to one's customers or backward to one's suppliers depends on the demand and supply elasticities for the product and the factors of production.

Ronald Reagan's economic policies were predicated, in part, on the concept that the incidence of a tax was different from the burden of a tax. To borrow an expression from President John F. Kennedy, "a rising tide lifts all boats." This truly captures the incidence model implicit in Reagan's economic policies. The tax rate cuts increased opportunities for all. Opponents ridiculed the Reagan incidence model and caricatured it and presented it in a different light. They called it "trickle-down" economics.

Although Reaganomics had some trickle-down elements, insofar as we believed that lowering the tax rates on the rich would help the poor, *trickle-down* implied only a vertical movement where the bulk of the benefits remained at the upper-income level. The trickle-down characterization missed much of what we may call lateral expansion of opportunities that the rising-tide image captured. We believe the rising-tide image is more appropriate than trickle-down. The former encompasses the latter and much more. Trickle-down goes a long way to explain the effect of certain taxes.

One only needs to consider the famous luxury tax. The intent was to collect additional revenue from wealthy individuals who were making frivolous expenditures. However, contrary to expectations, the impact of the luxury tax has been to reduce the purchase of luxury items significantly. Boat sales are down, employment in that industry is down, and the tax revenues are well below projection. The negative image could only be reversed by eliminating the luxury tax. Employment opportunities would be increased.[7] The boat industry example is a clear illustration of trickle-down: a tax on the wealthy hurting the poor.

It is also quite interesting that people who think about the luxury tax do not extend the analysis beyond the boat and do not consider the possibility that other taxes may affect people other than the ones upon whom the tax was levied. Trickle-down is only one illustration that the incidence of a tax is different from the burden of a tax. This, however, is not an all-encompassing concept. There are other incidence models. The lateral effects may be greatly affected by mobility. Absent movement costs, factors of production will migrate to arbitrage differences in after-tax income. In a small state economy, after-tax returns will be determined in the national economy, and state tax increases will only result in higher pre-tax salaries that leave the after-tax salaries unchanged. The logic applies not only to people but also to businesses. Recent stories in the press document how "back offices" are moving offshore.[8]

The lateral incidence model suggests that mobile factors will emigrate from states increasing their relative tax burdens, and some factors that are unable to migrate may adjust their utilization rate. The overall result of the emigration and lower utilization rate will be a lower level of economic activity and lower after-tax income for the factors that can neither move nor adjust their hours of work. The states raising tax rates will underperform the national average because income and fixed asset values decline, as does the amount of the mobile factor. Neighboring states without tax actions will experience an above-average performance owing to the increased activity generated by the mobile factors that migrated into the state.

This is a case where an ebb tide (i.e., tax increase) lowers every boat. Clearly, the rising tide is a broader, more encompassing incidence model than the more narrow trickle-down model, which implies that higher incomes get a disproportionate share of the benefits.

PERSONAL FINANCES: SINGLE FAMILY HOUSE PRICES

The burden of state taxation will fall disproportionately on those who cannot adjust their hours of work (utilization rate) or those who cannot migrate. The net value of income generated by the immobile factors will unambiguously decline. Insofar as the tax gets passed backward to suppliers, it may very well be called trickle-down. It is quite possible, also, for a tax to be passed laterally. We feel comfortable saying that our incidence model shows that general taxes will fall disproportionately on the immobile factors.

Traditionally, real estate is considered the quintessential fixed factor. It follows that the value of real estate should fluctuate in a predictable direction with changes in state and local policies. This is an empirically testable implication that, as shown in this chapter, is supported by the data.

The Contemporaneous Relation

A summary of state and local tax increases and changes in single family house prices relative to the U.S. average is reported in Table 5.2 and clearly supports our hypotheses. There have been 136 increases in state relative tax burdens during 1985-90, of which 82 resulted in declines in single family house prices relative to the United States in the same year of the tax increase.

Table 5.3 reports the relation between a state's tax changes in a fiscal year and the average change in single family housing prices during the same calendar year. Prior to discussing the results, it may prove worthwhile to point out that tax data are available only on a fiscal year basis, whereas single family house prices are available on a calendar year basis.[9] The fiscal year will lead the calendar year by six months. For example, fiscal year 1985 began on July 1, 1984, in most states, whereas the calendar year began on January 1, 1985. In effect, any calendar year will span two fiscal years. The fiscal and calendar years coincide only during half the year. The contemporaneous relation obtained mixing the fiscal and calendar years will be weakened by the nonoverlapping components. Given the patterns identified in Table 5.2, Table 5.3 suggests that the lack of data synchronization significantly masks the contemporaneous relation. In three of the six years (1985, 1986, 1988), states with increasing tax burdens outperformed states with declining relative tax burdens.[10] Yet in every one of those years, the numbers of states behaved according to the hypothesis. Single family house prices were below the national average in states with rising relative tax

Table 5.2

Single Family Housing Prices and State Tax Increases, 1985-90

Year	Magnitude of Tax Increase	Number of State Tax Increases	Number of Single Family Housing			
			Same Year		One Year Later	
			Increase	Decrease	Increase	Decrease
1985	Greater than	13	6	7	3	10
1986	0%	35	16	19	15	20
1987		39	17	22	11	28
1988		21	5	16	6	15
1989		13	4	9	8	5
1990		15	6	9	na	na
Total		136	54	82	43	78
1985	Greater than	12	5	7	3	9
1986	2%	8	3	5	4	4
1987		10	5	5	1	9
1988		12	3	9	4	8
1989		8	3	5	6	2
1990		9	3	6	na	na
Total		59	22	37	18	32
1985	Greater than	7	4	3	2	5
1986	4%	2	1	1	1	1
1987		6	3	3	0	6
1988		10	3	7	4	6
1989		5	2	3	3	2
1990		6	1	5	na	na
Total		36	14	22	10	20
1985	Greater than	6	4	2	1	5
1986	6%	1	0	1	0	1
1987		4	3	1	0	4
1988		3	1	2	1	2
1989		2	2	0	1	1
1990		4	1	3	na	na
Total		20	11	9	3	13

The state tax burdens have been adjusted to include the impact of the Tax Reform Act of 1986 on state relative tax burdens.

Sources: National Governors Association, *Fiscal Survey of the States*; National Conference of State Legislatures, *State Budget and Tax Actions in* (fiscal year); U.S. Bureau of the Census, *Government Finances in* (fiscal year); Federal Housing Finance Board, *Rates and Terms on Conventional Home Mortgages*.

burdens, and single family house prices were above the national average in states with declining relative tax burdens.

One factual explanation for the apparent contradiction of the relation reported in Tables 5.2 and 5.3 is that the average for the years is dominated by large fluctuations in single family house prices. An obvious question is whether these "large fluctuations" are systematic and largely attributable to the fact that the fiscal and calendar years do not fully coincide.

Table 5.3
Effect of Relative State Tax Changes in a Fiscal Year on Single Family Housing Prices During the Same Calendar Year

	1985	1986	1987	1988	1989	1990
States with increasing tax burdens:						
Number of states	13	35	39	21	13	15
Average % change in home prices	-2.15	1.18	-1.75	-5.51	-3.69	-5.80
States with decreasing tax burdens:						
Number of states	37	15	11	29	37	35
Average % change in home prices	-6.04	0.59	-0.10	-5.82	-0.97	4.51

Sources: National Governors Association, *Fiscal Survey of the States*; National Conference of State Legislatures, *State Budget and Tax Actions in* (fiscal year); U.S. Bureau of the Census, *Government Finances in* (fiscal year); Federal Housing Finance Board, *Rates and Terms on Conventional Home Mortgages.*

A One-Year Lag Relation

Examining the impact of the state actions during a fiscal year and comparing it with the change in single family house prices during the following calendar year yield even better results. With the level of mobility varying between factors, a lag response can be expected since less mobile factors respond more gradually. Some 120 instances that resulted in state and local relative tax burden increases were accompanied by 76 decreases in single family house prices relative to the U.S. average.[11] The results reported in Table 5.4 are quite impressive. The group of 13 states increasing their tax burdens in a fiscal year, say, 1985, experienced a decline in single family house prices relative to the United States, an average of 4.53 percent in 1986. Symmetrically, the 37 states with a declining relative tax burden experienced a 2.95 percent increase above the national average in single family house prices. In every single year, the group of states with declining tax burdens experienced a greater appreciation in single family house prices than states with rising relative tax burdens.

A More Stringent Screen

In order to learn the robustness of the relation and to reduce the effect of asynchronous data, we developed a more stringent screen. We examined the performance of single family house prices on states with rising relative tax burdens during two consecutive years versus states that experienced declines in their relative tax burden during two consecutive years.

Table 5.4

Effect of Relative State Tax Changes in a Fiscal Year on Single Family Housing Prices During the Following Calendar Year

	1986	1987	1988	1989	1990
States with increasing tax burdens in previous year:					
Number of states	13	35	39	21	13
Average % change in home prices	-4.53	-2.20	-6.74	-3.19	-4.86
States with decreasing tax burdens in previous year:					
Number of states	37	15	11	29	37
Average % change in home prices	2.95	0.51	-1.95	-0.58	3.62

Sources: National Governors Association, *Fiscal Survey of the States*; National Conference of State Legislatures, *State Budget and Tax Actions in* (fiscal year); U.S. Bureau of the Census, *Government Finances in* (fiscal year); Federal Housing Finance Board, *Rates and Terms on Conventional Home Mortgages.*

Table 5.5

Effect of Two Consecutive Fiscal Year Changes in Tax Burdens on Single Family Housing Prices in Second Calendar Year

	1986	1987	1988	1989	1990
States with increasing tax burdens for 2 consecutive years:					
Number of states	12	31	19	7	5
Average % change in home prices	-4.11	-2.37	-5.54	0.46	-4.62
States with decreasing tax burdens for 2 consecutive years:					
Number of states	14	7	9	23	27
Average % change in home prices	1.31	0.34	-1.23	1.49	4.94

Sources: National Governors Association, *Fiscal Survey of the States*; National Conference of State Legislatures, *State Budget and Tax Actions in* (fiscal year); U.S. Bureau of the Census, *Government Finances in* (fiscal year); Federal Housing Finance Board, *Rates and Terms on Conventional Home Mortgages.*

Twelve states experienced consecutive years of rising relative tax burdens in 1986. Single family house prices in those states declined 4.11 percent (Table 5.5). In contrast, the 14 states experiencing a decline in their relative tax burdens experienced an increase of 1.31 percent above the national average. In every single year, the portfolio of states with consecutive declines in relative tax burdens outperformed the portfolio of states with rising relative tax burdens.

IMPLICATIONS

Last year's budget agreement was reported to close the budget deficit gap by some $50 billion, of which $17.9 billion constituted federal tax increases. State and local taxes were also increased an additional $10.7 billion. Contrary to the administration's assumptions, the budget agreement has resulted in slower economic growth (i.e., a recession) and lower-than-expected tax revenues.

The states' combined actions for fiscal year 1992 will, on a static revenue basis, raise $24 billion in taxes. The magnitude of the state actions is similar to that of last year's federal, state, and local actions. Our economic analysis suggests that the combined actions will, in effect, ease the tide of economic activity, thereby lowering all boats (i.e., all states will suffer). Our view is that the recession will last longer than expected. In addition, there will be some trickle-down regional effects.

Five states—Kentucky, Massachusetts, New Jersey, Rhode Island, and Vermont—have enacted above-average tax increases during fiscal years 1991 to 1992 and are thus included in our list of states most likely to underperform the economy.[12] Six other states—Alaska, California, Connecticut, Kansas, Nevada, and Pennsylvania—have enacted significant tax increases and should be included in a watch list.

Investment Implications

The return to fixed factors located in the states increasing their relative tax burden will be below their national average counterpart. A clear implication directly out of this chapter is that the average price of single family houses in those states will be below the U.S. average.

The analysis may be easily extended to other factors. For example, small-cap stocks located in the states increasing their relative tax burden will perform in a similar manner. The recent above-average performance of small-cap stocks implies that portfolio managers will downsize the average capitalization of their stock holdings. In doing so, they could be inadvertently increasing their regional exposure. This may be remedied quite easily through underweighting companies located in the states with rising relative tax burdens and overweighting small-cap stocks located in states with falling relative tax burdens.

The analysis may be used to identify other potential fixed factors. One that immediately comes to mind is that of small regional banks. Their deposits, commercial loans, and real estate loans will, in most cases, be local. Therefore, a slower pace of economic activity will reduce the volume of business done by the banks. Insofar as bankruptcies and business failures increase and single family house prices decline, the quality of the small banks' portfolios will also decline, producing a negative effect on the bank's earnings and stock prices.

In contrast, small banks located in areas with declining relative tax burdens will experience an improvement in the quality of their loan portfolios.

NOTES

1. David Wessel, "Congress Is Shifting More Power over Spending to the President," *Wall Street Journal*, October 29, 1990, p. A7.

2. Victor A. Canto, "Behind the 1991 Outlook: How Economic Policy Affects Secular Changes," A. B. Laffer, V. A. Canto & Associates, February 1, 1991.

3. Arthur B. Laffer, "Let Bush Be Bush," A. B. Laffer, V. A. Canto & Associates, November 1, 1990; Victor A. Canto, "The Credit Crunch Revisited," A. B. Laffer, V. A. Canto & Associates, November 16, 1990.

4. See Matthew B. Kibbe, "The Laffer Curve in Reverse," *Wall Street Journal*, July 22, 1991, p. A8.

5. Timothy Noah, "States' Tax Increases for Year to Show Biggest Jump Since 1971, Survey Finds," *Wall Street Journal*, August 13, 1991, p. A16.

6. Jeffrey H. Birnbaum and Jackie Calmes, "Wrenching Battle on Deficit Reduction Points to More Contests in Years Ahead," *Wall Street Journal*, October 29, 1990, p. A3.

7. What is interesting is that, in a recent TV interview, a salesman of luxury items accused the rich of calculatedly not purchasing the luxury item (i.e., luxury automobile), as if all the wealthy individuals got together and conspired not to purchase the items.

8. Bernard Wysocki, Jr., "American Firms Send Office Work Abroad to Use Cheaper Labor," *Wall Street Journal*, August 14, 1991, p. 1.

9. The state tax burden is reported annually in our state competitive environment papers. The housing data are available from the Federal Housing Finance Board.

10. During 1989, both groups underperformed the U.S. average. This result is due to the fact that the U.S. average is a weighted average, whereas the state averages give equal weight to the states.

11. Since 15 of the 136 relative tax burden increases occurred during 1990, the data on single family house prices for the year after are not yet available.

12. Although Governor William Weld of Massachusetts is lowering taxes, increases for fiscal year 1992 have been legislated in previous years. See Janet Novak, "The Boston Supply-Side Party," *Forbes*, August 5, 1991, pp. 81-83.

6

The Determinants and Consequences of State General Obligation Bond Rating Changes

Victor A. Canto, Christopher Charles, and Arthur B. Laffer

In terms of the number of issuers, the American municipal bond market is probably the world's largest securities universe. More than 80,000 governmental entities exist, of which a majority have issued debt from time to time. As of 1989, total state and local debt outstanding exceeded $800 billion. While the municipal market has never had the high profile of its corporate and governmental peers, the growing investor attention focused on tax policy and competitive factors warrants a look at municipals in that context.

Municipal bonds issued by state and local governments are, in many cases, rated by one or more of the investment service companies (Moody's and Standard & Poor's [S&P]). These ratings represent a basic assessment of the relative credit quality of the issue.[1] To the issuer, a higher rating means a lower cost of capital through reduced interest costs and lower underwriting spreads. To the investor, a higher rating means, in theory, reduced nonsystemic risk (i.e., default risk). While a multitude of considerations go into the assignment of a bond rating, it can be argued that ratings of general obligation (GO) municipal bonds may be viewed as a crude indicator of the issuer's relative economic standing. The determination of a municipal bond rating rests heavily on four factors: the issuer's capital structure (exiting debt and the assets available), its current position (fiscal and budgetary), its governmental status (state, city, or district), and its general economic and competitive position. However, only the latter focuses on the outlook for the state.

A clear illustration of the importance of dynamic considerations is the debate that centers around state tax initiatives. Opponents of tax rate cuts argue that the rate cuts will lower the state's bond ratings and, as a consequence, will raise interest costs by tens of millions of dollars. Conversely, those in favor of raising tax rates argue that the tax increase will improve bond ratings and lower a state's interest costs.

The starting point in any discussion of a possible bond rating change that might result from a tax rate change is the determination of the static revenue impact of the state tax action. It is calculated by applying the tax rate change to the corresponding tax base. However, the tax rate changes will affect migration patterns, business location decisions, business starts and failures, real estate values, and overall economic activity.[2] The changes in the tax base resulting from these feedback effects will always be in the opposite direction to the tax rate changes. Thus, a tax rate increase will result in a lower taxable base, whereas a tax rate reduction will result in an increase in the taxable base.

The experience during the 1985-91 period shows that of the 46 credit rating changes, 19 of the 26 credit rating upgrades occurred in states lowering their relative tax burden, and 12 of the 20 downgrades occurred in states raising their tax burden. The correlation clearly lends support to the view that the dynamic effects generated by state tax action more often than not will more than offset the static revenue effect.

Changes in state GO bond ratings occur infrequently and thus are likely to represent significant changes in perceived economic and financial conditions. The distribution of the changes clearly indicates that state competitiveness is related to their timing and direction.

THE CONSEQUENCES OF GO RATING CHANGES

Changes in credit ratings often provide the public and the local press with their most unambiguous warning that their hometown might be going through fiscal turmoil. An immediate topic of discussion is whether a change in the bond's rating increases borrowing costs. Cities and states universally dread the trauma of a change in their bond rating. Local politicians and financial advisers take it as an article of faith that a reduction in ratings assigned by Moody's or Standard & Poor's will raise their cost of borrowing and place an additional burden on the taxpayer.

During the 1980s, the spread between Aaa and Aa municipal GO bonds averaged 24 basis points; the spread between Aa and A averaged 28 basis points; and the spread between A and Baa averaged 36 basis points. The spread between the different quality bonds illustrates the potential increase in interest rates that may result from a ratings downgrade. Whether a bond's rating change affects a state's borrowing costs is an empirical issue addressed in this chapter.

The data available on GO yields include weekly observations of transaction prices for 13 states—California, Virginia, New Jersey, Minnesota, Pennsylvania, New York, Wisconsin, Illinois, Florida, Texas, Washington, Massachusetts, and Louisiana—spanning 1985 to 1991.[3] Combining the limited samples for which yields on state GO bonds were available with the credit rating changes (Table 6.1), we identified 15 events. Four of these events consisted of upgrades: California in 1989, Louisiana in 1990, Massachusetts in 1988, and Washington in 1990. The remaining events were downgrades: Louisiana in 1988; Texas in 1987; New York, twice in 1990; and Massachusetts, seven times during the 1989-90 period.

One way to analyze the impact of ratings changes on GO yields is to estimate how the municipal market might have performed in the absence of the ratings change. There are several ways to obtain such estimates. One may look at the historical performance of the state GO yields relative to an aggregate market index. The historical differential between the GO yield and the market index is then used as the expected yield differential. The differential performance between the historical average (expected value) and

Table 6.1
Changes in Moody's Credit Rating of State GO Debt Since 1985 (fiscal year)

	1985	1986	1987	1988	1989	1990	1991
Arkansas		A1 7/11/85					A1 to Aa 9/19/90
California					Aa to Aaa 10/6/89		
Connecticut		Aa to Aa1 10/18/85				Aa1 to Aa 4/9/90	
Louisiana	Aa to A1 4/4/85	A1 to A 4/24/86	A to Baa1 2/10/87				
Massachusetts				A1 to Aa 2/9/88	Aa to A 6/21/89	A to Baa1 11/15/89 Baa1 to Baa 3/19/90	
Michigan		A to A1 4/24/86					
Montana	Aa1 to Aa 6/28/85						
New Hampshire	A1 to Aa 1/21/85				Aa to Aa1 11/9/88		
New Mexico	Aa1 to Aa 2/22/85						
New York		A to A1 5/27/86				A1 to A 6/6/90	
Oklahoma			Aaa to Aa 6/3/87				
Oregon						A1 to Aa 1/8/90	
Pennsylvania		A to A1 3/6/86					
Texas			Aaa to Aa 3/10/87				
Washington		A to A1 7/28/86				A1 to Aa 1/8/90	

actual differential between the state GO and the aggregate GO yield index is attributed to the ratings change.

Since there is no definitive procedure for selecting a time period to calculate the cumulative excess returns, five different intervals were chosen within the event period. The first interval begins 12 months prior to and ends with the event month (the month in which a ratings change takes place). The second interval begins six months prior to and ends with the event month. The third interval begins with the event month and ends three months after the event month. The fourth interval begins with the event month and ends six months after the event month. The fifth interval encompasses the previously mentioned intervals; it begins 12 months before the event month and ends 6 months following the event month.

The Upgrades

In three of the four events where a state GO bond was upgraded, the result was a decline in the state bond yield relative to the historical average. It appears that the market anticipated the 1990 upgrade of Louisiana's GO bonds. The decline in yield, however, continued even after the announcement of the upgrade (Table 6.2). In the six months following the event, the yield declined an average of 27 basis points relative to its historical differential.

Massachusetts's 1988 upgrade yields similar results. The only difference in the pattern is that the biggest decline in yield differential relative to its historical trend occurred in the three months after the event. In the quarter following the event, the yield on Massachusetts's general obligation bonds declined 34 basis points relative to its historical average.

Washington's 1990 upgrade resulted in a decline in yield of 10 basis points relative to its historical average during the six months following the upgrade. California proved to be the exception to the pattern. The data show that the yield of California GO bonds decreased 2.6 basis points three months after a downgrade but increased within six months.

The Downgrades

The 11 downgrades point to an increase in the yield of the states' general obligation bonds relative to their historical averages (Table 6.2). In line with other results, it appears that the market anticipated Louisiana's 1988 downgrade. The yield differential started widening before the downgrade. The widening differential trend continued after the event, and it peaked in the three months after the event when it averaged a 45 basis points increase in the yield differential.

New York's 1990 Moody's and S&P downgrades occurred at different times during the year, thereby giving us two event dates. Both dates show a pattern of increasing differential yield relative to the historical average, peaking at an average increase of 10 to 11 basis points in the six months following the event date (Table 6.2). Texas's 1987 downgrade yields somewhat similar results. The more interesting case study is that of Massachusetts. During 1989 and 1990, Massachusetts GOs were downgraded four times by S&P and three times by Moody's. In all cases, the downgrades resulted in an increase in the yield differential of Massachusetts's GOs relative to their historical average.

At the time of the first downgrade, Massachusetts was still enjoying its "Massachusetts miracle" image, and as a consequence, yields were still low relative to the national average. Massachusetts GOs had been upgraded in 1988. Examination of the Massachusetts events shows that the yield differential increased in every subsequent downgrade, peaking at an average excess of 25 basis points during the six months following the March 1990 downgrade by Moody's.

THE DETERMINANTS OF GO RATING CHANGES

Portfolio managers able to anticipate rating changes would significantly improve their portfolio performance. A downgrade in GO bond ratings raises a state's borrowing costs anywhere from 8.5 basis points to 25 basis points, thereby reducing the GO bond price. Conversely, an upgrade will lower yield up to 26.5 basis points, thereby increasing the price of the GO. The probability of a rating change by either one of the rating agencies can be quantified based on the expected economic performance of the state relative to the rest of the nation.

Knowledge of the way municipal bonds are rated may allow analysts to anticipate bond rating changes and position their portfolios to take advantage of the anticipated yield changes resulting from the ratings change.

Initially, four economic variables were used as indicators of a state's economic performance: the change in the state relative tax burden, the percent change in single family house prices relative to the U.S. average, the percent change in the state personal income relative to the U.S. average, and the state unemployment rate relative to the national average. Largely because of the number of variables and possible overlaps of information contained in the explanatory variables, few of the variables are statistically significantly related to the ratings change. Sequential elimination of the less significant variables allowed us to obtain a final model for the upgrades (Table 6.3) and the downgrades (Table 6.4). A description of the sample selection and of the statistical technique used is reported in the Appendix.

The model for GO rating upgrades finds a negative and significant rela-

Table 6.2
Average Excess Yield on State Bonds During a Bond Rating Change Event*

State	Event Date	Grade Change	52 Weeks Up to Rating Change	26 Weeks Up to Rating Change	13 Weeks After Rating Change	26 Weeks After Rating Change	52 Weeks to 26 Wks After Rating Change
California	10/6/89	Up-Moody's	0.043% (5.807)	0.052% (4.890)	0.025% (1.652)	0.014% (1.345)	0.034% (5.568)
Louisiana	2/12/88	Down-S&P	0.147 (4.598)	0.293 (6.365)	0.452 (6.741)	0.353 (7.665)	0.216 (8.302)
Louisiana	12/19/90	Up-S&P	-0.185 (-5.777)	-0.211 (-4.590)	-0.262 (-3.906)	-0.265 (-5.747)	-0.211 (-8.128)
Massachusetts	2/9/88	Up-Moody's S&P	-0.296 (-6.004)	-0.317 (-4.474)	-0.338 (-3.271)	-0.326 (-4.596)	-0.306 (-7.649)
Massachusetts	5/17/89	Down-S&P	-0.242 (-4.903)	-0.187 (-2.635)	-0.050 (-0.481)	-0.009 (-0.132)	-0.163 (-4.077)
Massachusetts	6/21/89	Down-Moody's	-0.225 (-4.555)	-0.161 (-2.270)	0.018 (0.175)	0.068 (0.956)	-0.127 (-3.184)
Massachusetts	6/27/89	Down-S&P	-0.219 (-4.438)	-0.152 (-2.149)	0.021 (0.204)	0.077 (1.081)	-0.121 (-3.013)
Massachusetts	7/19/89	Down-S&P	-0.199 (-4.044)	-0.125 (-1.765)	0.030 (0.290)	0.103 (1.449)	-0.099 (-2.479)
Massachusetts	11/15/89	Down-Moody's	-0.097 (-1.961)	-0.009 (-0.132)	0.222 (2.148)	0.221 (3.112)	0.009 (0.233)

Massachusetts	12/13/89	Down-S&P	-0.057 (-1.154)	0.053 (0.746)	0.201 (1.943)	0.224 (3.158)	0.036 (0.887)
Massachusetts	3/19/90	Down-Moody's	0.047 (0.943)	0.155 (2.188)	0.246 (2.381)	0.254 (3.577)	0.115 (2.877)
New York	3/26/90	Down-S&P	-0.028 (-1.135)	-0.031 (-0.865)	0.153 (2.981)	0.102 (2.890)	0.014 (0.691)
New York	6/6/90	Down-Moody's	0.011 (0.436)	0.066 (1.861)	0.040 (0.771)	0.117 (3.318)	0.047 (2.340)
Texas	8/14/87	Down-S&P	NA NA	0.058 (3.766)	0.097 (4.315)	0.085 (5.538)	NA NA
Washington	1/8/90	Up-Moody's	-0.008 (-0.457)	-0.017 (-0.656)	-0.085 (-2.214)	-0.099 (-3.773)	-0.038 (-2.579)

* t-statistics in parentheses.

Table 6.3
The Determinants of State GO Bond Rating Upgrades Results of the Logit Estimation*

Independent Variable	Coefficient	Standard Error	Significance Level
Constant	-3.195	0.450	0.000
Relative change in state tax burden	-0.330	0.179	0.065
Relative change in state tax burden lagged one year	-0.221	0.148	0.136
Relative change in state tax burden lagged two years	0.026	0.155	0.869
Relative change in state tax burden lagged three years	-0.223	0.142	0.117
Relative change in state unemployment rate lagged two years	-0.329	0.464	0.478

* The dependent variable is the rating change, and equals 1 when there is an upgrade and zero whenre there is no change. Downgrades are excluded.

Sources: U.S. Bureau of Labor Statistics; National Conference of State Legislatures.

tionship between increases in relative tax burden and rating changes (Table 6.3). The coefficient for the relative unemployment rate is also negative but not statistically significant at the usual significance level (i.e., 10 percent). Taken at face value, the coefficient for the tax burden suggests that a 1 percent increase in relative tax burden reduces the chances of an upgrade of 33 percent during the year of the reduction, 22 percent the following year, no impact two years later, and a 22 percent change three years later. The relative unemployment rate does not appear to have a significant effect.

In contrast, the model for GO rating downgrades finds a positive and significant relation between a state's relative unemployment rate and a ratings downgrade (Table 6.4). The state tax burden does not appear to exert a significant effect on rating downgrades. The exception is the relative tax burden lagged two years, which appears to be marginally significant. Our research shows that the relative tax burden and relative unemployment rate are inversely related. Therefore, it will be a mistake to interpret each of the coefficients separately.

It is reassuring to know that the coefficients of the explanatory variables have opposite signs in the two models (i.e., upgrades versus downgrades). It is interesting to note that the pattern of significant coefficients also alternates.

Table 6.4
The Determinants of State GO Bond Rating Downgrades Results of the Logit Estimation*

Independent Variable	Coefficient	Standard Error	Significance Level
Intercept	-3.426	0.470	0.000
Relative change in state tax burden	0.042	0.095	0.655
Relative change in state tax burden lagged one year	0.024	0.119	0.840
Relative change in state tax burden lagged two years	-0.192	0.154	0.213
Relative change in state tax burden lagged three years	0.004	0.104	0.966
Relative change in state unemployment rate lagged two years	1.299	0.506	0.010

* The dependent variable is the rating change and equals 1 when there is a downgrade and zero when there is no change. Upgrades are excluded.

Sources: U.S. Bureau of Labor Statistics; National Conference of State Legislatures.

ELEMENTS OF A GO PORTFOLIO STRATEGY

States that raise taxes relative to the national average risk a future increase in their cost of capital, whereas those lowering their tax rates relative to the U.S. average have an increased chance of reducing their future cost of capital. The implied impact of a proposed state tax action on the issuer's cost of capital should play a part in the decision-making process.

Rating agencies traditionally underestimate the dynamic effects of tax rate changes. This error leads the rating agencies to miss turning points in the state's competitive environment, giving rise to potential forecasting mistakes.

The credit agencies could unnecessarily put a state on a credit watch or change the credit rating. Initially, the yield may be adversely affected. Ultimately, the economic conditions will determine the rating. In this case, the forecast error will be reversed in time by restoring the original credit rating. The Puerto Rican tax reform of the late 1970s and California's Proposition 13 in 1978 are two preeminent examples where the rating agencies missed their mark and had to revise their rating.[4] In both cases, our framework predicted the rating agencies' mistakes.

If a more accurate estimate of the dynamic effects can be made, then one may be able to anticipate credit rating changes as well as state credit rating forecast errors. These may be used to develop a state GO bond portfolio strategy.

The empirical evidence reported in Table 6.2 indicates that GO rating changes will alter the yields of the affected states' general obligation bonds. Increasing the weights of the bonds whose ratings have been upgraded and decreasing the weights of the bonds whose ratings have been downgraded will improve the GO portfolio's performance. Although the market participants appear to anticipate rating changes, the evidence reported in Table 6.2 indicates that the GO yields of the states affected by rating changes will continue to change even after the rating change is announced. The gains of the portfolio strategy may be increased by correctly anticipating rating changes. Our research suggests that the data on the relative tax burden and the state unemployment rate are useful for forecasting rating changes (Tables 6.3 and 6.4).

Prior to identifying the buy and sell portfolios, we need to develop a way to measure the impact of the economic environment on GO yields. Earlier in the chapter, we discussed the difficulties in obtaining transaction and not matrix prices. We were able to obtain a limited sample of GO for 13 states. In order to control for differences in risks, we estimated the differential between the state GO and the average for the 13 states. In addition, we also subtracted the historical average yield differential. What remained is our estimate of the state GO yield that results from changing economic conditions (Table 6.5). For example, during fiscal year 1988, California's GO bonds improved relative to the national average (i.e., had a 2 basis point lower yield relative to the historical average) and deteriorated in the

Table 6.5
Selected Average Excess State GO Bond Yields by Fiscal Year

	1987*	1988	1989	1990	1991
California	-0.013	-0.02	0.033	0.007	-0.014
Virginia	-0.016	-0.019	0.032	0.005	-0.011
New Jersey	-0.027	-0.017	0.029	0.013	-0.01
Minnesota	0.029	-0.032	0.024	0.004	-0.01
Pennsylvania	0.013	-0.036	0.009	0.017	-0.001
New York	-0.096	-0.155	-0.054	0.016	0.231
Wisconsin	0.077	-0.044	0.027	0.016	-0.033
Illinois	0.049	0.043	0.003	-0.015	-0.056
Florida	0.136	0.11	-0.024	-0.044	-0.108
Texas	0.034	0.072	0.023	-0.014	-0.095
Washington	0.127	0.12	0.048	-0.056	-0.172
Massachusetts	-0.284	-0.316	-0.217	0.151	0.518
Louisiana	-0.029	0.295	0.067	-0.101	-0.239

* Fiscal year 1987 from December 31, 1986.

following year (i.e., had a 3.3 basis point excess in yield relative to the historical average). Having developed an estimate of the change in yield differential resulting from a changing economic environment, all that remains to be determined is whether, in fact, the change in yields was related to the economic environment and whether the change in environment was anticipated.

The estimated logit function may be used to construct probability estimates of a rating upgrade or a rating downgrade for each of the states. Since the data used in the estimation of these probabilities are readily available at the beginning of each fiscal year, the estimated probabilities may be legitimately used in constructing a portfolio strategy.

Appendix A reports the estimated probabilities of a GO rating upgrade and/or downgrade for each state during the fiscal years 1988 through 1991. The probabilities are then used to construct a buy and a sell portfolio. If the economic environment is related to the relative yields of state general obligation bonds, the portfolio strategy can yield significant results even if rating changes do not occur. The buy portfolio may include GO bonds for all states that simultaneously rank in the top half of the estimated range of probabilities of upgrades as well as in the bottom half of the range of estimated probabilities of a downgrade. A more stringent cutoff, such as a ranking in the top 30 percent, may be employed. The sell portfolio would consist of the mirror image of the buy portfolio.

Applying the portfolio strategy to the available data sets yields interesting results. For three of the four years, the buy portfolio yield declined relative to the average, whereas that of the sell portfolio increased in every year (Table 6.6). The buy portfolio outperformed the sell portfolio in three of the four years. When more stringent requirements are applied, the buy portfolio out-

Table 6.6
Average Relative Excess Yield for State GO Bonds Based on Probabilities of Downgrades and Upgrades in Fiscal Year*

	1988	1989	1990	1991
Buy portfolio	-0.048	0.016	-0.012	-0.083
	(6)	(8)	(3)	(3)
Sell portfolio	0.184	0.008	0.040	0.097
	(2)	(3)	(4)	(4)

* Number of states in parentheses.

The buy portfolio includes the states that simultaneously rank in the top half of the probability of upgrade and the bottom half of the probability of downgrade. The sell portfolio is the mirror image of the buy portfolio.

Sources: Moody's Corporation; Standard & Poor's Corporation.

Table 6.7
**Average Relative Excess Yield for State GO Bonds Based on Probabilities
of Downgrades or Upgrades in Fiscal Year***

	1988	1989	1990	1991
Buy portfolio	-0.040	-0.014	0.010	N.A
	(2)	(2)	(2)	(0)
Sell portfolio	0.184	0.008	0.151	0.254
	(2)	(3)	(1)	(2)

* Number of states in parentheses.

The buy portfolio includes the states that simultaneously rank in the top 15 of probability of upgrade and the bottom 15 of the probability of downgrade. The sell portfolio is the mirror image of the buy portfolio.

Sources: Moody's Corporation; Standard & Poor's Corporation.

performed the sell portfolio in each of the four years (Table 6.7). Given the estimated sample size, the results are only suggestive. Nevertheless, they are quite encouraging, for they suggest a differential of up to 23 basis points may be realized using the strategy outlined in this chapter.

Using data on legislated state actions, we have estimated the likelihood of rating changes for fiscal 1992, which began July 1, 1991 (Table 6.8). The estimated probabilities provide the necessary information to develop the different portfolios as outlined in this chapter.

APPENDIX A: SUMMARY OF
ANALYSIS METHODOLOGY

The Mean Value Model

The "event time methodology" pioneered by E. Fama, M. Fisher, M. Jensen, and R. Roll requires an equilibrium model of the expected change in equity value (i.e., the rate of return).[5]

R. Merton[6] and S. LeRoy[7] have suggested alternative models to estimate the expected rate of return of aggregated equity indexes. One commonly used model, a variant of which will be adopted in this chapter, is the mean value model.

The expected return on an index is estimated by taking the mean value of the returns over a prespecified time length prior to the event period. Then the mean value is applied outside the event period. Any deviation from the expected return is attributed to the event. Therefore, these forecast errors

Table 6.8
Probabilities of State GO Bond Rating Changes, FY1992

Probability of Downgrade		Probability of Upgrade	
West Virginia	0.13%	Illinois	50.40%
North Dakota	0.23	Utah	42.07
Illinois	0.25	Colorado	32.43
Louisiana	0.35	Wyoming	31.35
Washington	0.35	South Dakota	30.32
Georgia	0.47	Wisconsin	29.24
Colorado	0.52	Washington	25.02
Wyoming	0.56	Mississippi	24.87
Nebraska	0.70	Alaska	23.72
South Dakota	1.11	Georgia	22.08
New Mexico	1.16	South Carolina	21.13
Mississippi	1.29	Indiana	20.39
Montana	1.39	Alabama	20.31
Utah	1.42	Montana	19.35
Texas	1.49	Hawaii	19.28
Tennessee	1.52	Iowa	19.13
Oregon	1.61	Virginia	19.07
Alabama	1.68	Maryland	18.51
Arkansas	1.78	Michigan	17.94
Nevada	1.87	Missouri	17.65
South Carolina	1.97	Tennessee	16.84
Iowa	1.98	Ohio	16.82
Kentucky	2.09	North Dakota	16.16
Wisconsin	2.15	Maine	13.79
Missouri	2.22	Oregon	12.94
Oklahoma	2.27	New Mexico	11.37
Ohio	2.38	West Virginia	10.42
Arizona	2.47	North Carolina	9.65
Alaska	2.72	Oklahoma	9.19
New York	3.31	New York	9.07
Connecticut	3.37	Nebraska	7.67
Virginia	3.50	New Hampshire	6.65
Michigan	3.55	Pennsylvania	5.65
North Carolina	3.61	Minnesota	5.47
Florida	3.70	Arizona	4.35
Hawaii	4.00	Arkansas	4.24
Pennsylvania	4.14	Idaho	3.67
Minnesota	4.37	Louisiana	3.62
Indiana	4.42	Delaware	3.40
Kansas	5.75	Nevada	2.59
Maryland	6.17	Texas	1.45
Idaho	6.42	Kansas	1.11
California	7.09	Florida	0.80
Vermont	7.65	Rhode Island	0.64
Maine	8.38	Kentucky	0.25
New Jersey	11.08	California	0.22
New Hampshire	19.87	New Jersey	0.15
Massachusetts	22.79	Connecticut	0.05
Rhode Island	25.30	Vermont	0.05
Delaware	42.72	Massachusetts	0.03

(i.e., deviations from the mean) are used as a proxy for the event-related abnormal return.

Applying the model to general obligation bonds requires some modification. If the maintained hypothesis is that the average yield is related to the bond ratings, it follows that a differential will be observed between two bonds that have different ratings. A simple application of the mean value model would incorrectly attribute that differential to a rating change (i.e., an event). A simple way to correct for such a possible problem is to estimate historical (i.e., average) interest rate differentials between the GO bonds in question and an index. Any deviation of the interest rate differential from the historical trend is then attributed to the ratings change.

The Mean Value Model Test

The length of the event period is usually chosen arbitrarily. For purposes of this study, the event period spans 12 months preceding the announcement of the action (EM − 12) and the 6 months following the announcement of the action (EM + 6). The average excess return (*AER*) for each event is calculated as follows:

$$AER_t = \frac{1}{J_t} \sum_{J=1}^{J=k} ER_{jt},$$

(1)

where J_t is the number of rating changes selected, and t denotes time relative to the event period. ER_{jt} denotes the excess return for the particular event in the t-month relative to the event time. The statistical significance of the abnormal performance is determined by constructing a statistic for the cumulative average excess return (*CAER*), where

$$CAER_{t1, t2} = \sum_{t=t1}^{t=t2} AER_t.$$

(2)

Significance of the *CAER* is determined by the "*t*-test" statistics calculated from the ratio of the cumulative excess return to its estimated standard deviation.[8] The standard deviation is estimated from the time series of the state GO yield. The major problem with the estimation of the *t*-statistic is the time series dependency of the data used to estimate the variance. Most event studies have ignored this issue. However, if the prediction errors exhibit first-order autocorrelation, the variance of the *CAER* will be undervalued. In cases where there is first-order autocorrelation, the variance of the *CAER* will be undervalued. In cases where there is a first-order auto-correlation, the following formula will be used to estimate the variance:[9]

$$\text{Var} (CAER_{t1, t2}) = t \text{ Var} (AER_t) + 2 \frac{t-1}{t} COV (AER_t, AER_{t+1}).$$

(3)

A second major problem arising from the estimation of the variance in event studies is the evidence that the variance of the return increases around the event announcement.[10] This will result in an underestimation of the true *t*-test values. We shall use the event period—a high-variance period—to estimate the variance of the *CAER*. This will cause our results to be on the conservative side. Another problem may arise if an incorrect universal event period is imposed for all the events selected. It has been argued that an arbitrary choice of event period may lead to suboptimal results.[11] Despite the possibility of bias in parameter estimations due to a misspecified event period, most even time studies have used an arbitrary universal event period for estimating event-related effects.

In order to minimize the problem, one should ideally use maximum likelihood techniques for each of the policies or events selected. One possible reason for a change in event period length is that speed of information dissemination and efficiency of adaptation to events for a state may be changing over time. Although we are imposing a universal event period, the impact of a possible misspecification of the event period, if any, is being minimized by examining the effect of the event (rating change) over four different intervals in the event period.

The Logistic Probability Curve: Sample Selection and Estimation Technique

Our analysis of GO upgrades and downgrades employs a time series analysis. The rates of change are studied using a mixture of cross section and time series analysis. To examine rates of change, annual data on changes in the state general fund ending balances, state unemployment relative to the nation, the percent change in personal income relative to the percent change in the United States, percent change in single family house prices relative to the United States, and change in relative tax burdens were collected. The rating changes are reported in Table 6.A-1.

A rating change in a given year is the event to be explained. In the case of an upgrade, the dependent variable takes a value of unity when an upgrade occurs; otherwise, it is zero. Similarly, in the analysis of downgrades, the dependent variable takes a value of unity when a downgrade occurs; otherwise, it is zero. The period of analysis is from 1985 to 1991.

The described objective is to predict bond rating changes. Care must be taken to ensure that all the necessary data to be used are available at the time of the prediction. For example, most state fiscal years begin on July 1. Thus, July 1, 1991, marks the beginning of the state's fiscal 1992. On July 1, we have knowledge of the state actions enacted for fiscal 1992. The static revenue impact of the actions is widely available; hence, we are able to construct the changes in relative tax burden for 1992.

Data on economic variables are available with a lag. However, by July, numbers for the state's personal income and unemployment rates for the previous calendar year (i.e., 1990) are readily available. Therefore, inclusion of this year-end variable approximates the data availability at the beginning of the state's fiscal year.

The historical data from the affected states and the matching sample were used to produce observations where no rating changes occurred. The dependent variable in both the upgrade and downgrade analysis was the qualitative variable indicating nonintervention or the imposition of a rating change. Given the qualitative nature of the dependent variable, logit analysis was chosen to predict a rating change. The use of logit analysis is consistent with the use of this procedure in other applications. Logit makes only minimal requirements concerning the statistical properties of error terms in the regression.

Logit analysis estimates a logistic probability curve as a function of the explanatory variables. Since the dependent variables are binary and the function is nonlinear, maximum likelihood estimation techniques are used. Our estimates are based on times series processor (TSP) logit routines. The model is then used to develop estimates of the likelihood of a rating downgrade or a rating upgrade (Tables 6.A-1 through 6.A-4).

NOTES

The helpful comments and suggestions of Charles Parker and Walter Blasberg are gratefully acknowledged. Andrew Schaeffer, Alan MacEachern, and Russell Silberstein provided helpful assistance.

1. Ratings of state GO bonds, as published by Moody's Investor's Service, range from Baa to Aaa. There are seven possible ratings within this range. In order of increasing quality, they are Baa, Baa1, A, A1, Aa, Aa1, and Aaa.

2. Victor A. Canto and Robert I. Webb, "The Effect of State Fiscal Policy on State Relative Economic Performance," *Southern Economic Journal* 54, no. 1 (July 1987); Victor A. Canto, Charles W. Kadlec, and Arthur B. Laffer, "The State Competitive Environment," A. B. Laffer Associates, August 8, 1984; Victor A. Canto and Arthur B. Laffer, "A Not-So-Odd Couple: Small Cap Stocks and the State Competitive Environment," A. B. Laffer Associates, June 24, 1988; Victor A. Canto and John E. Silvia, "The State Competitive Environment: Business Starts and Business Failures," A. B. Laffer, V. A. Canto & Associates, October 16, 1990;

Table 6.A-1
Probabilities of State GO Bond Rating Changes, FY1988

Probability of Downgrade		Probability of Upgrade	
Nevada	0.21%	New York	56.85%
Indiana	0.72	Minnesota	24.57
Iowa	0.80	Michigan	23.00
Pennsylvania	0.86	Delaware	20.23
Connecticut	0.94	Nebraska	19.92
Delaware	0.97	West Virginia	18.76
Illinois	1.05	Pennsylvania	15.82
Hawaii	1.08	Rhode Island	14.25
New Hampshire	1.24	Illinois	12.10
Michigan	1.29	Ohio	9.49
Rhode Island	1.29	New Hampshire	7.67
West Virginia	1.31	Connecticut	6.85
Nebraska	1.38	Wisconsin	6.73
Vermont	1.40	Vermont	6.51
Virginia	1.41	New Jersey	6.06
New Jersey	1.64	Nevada	5.72
Georgia	1.83	Georgia	5.34
South Dakota	2.01	Colorado	5.29
Ohio	2.03	South Dakota	5.01
South Carolina	2.03	Massachusetts	4.90
California	2.14	Oregon	4.82
New York	2.50	Washington	4.80
Florida	2.62	Alaska	4.13
Arkansas	2.84	California	4.06
Missouri	2.89	Virginia	4.05
Kentucky	2.97	Maine	3.33
Oklahoma	3.02	Wyoming	3.25
Massachusetts	3.37	Alabama	2.97
Oregon	3.43	Hawaii	2.81
Maine	3.49	North Carolina	2.64
Tennessee	3.59	Iowa	2.62
North Carolina	3.68	Maryland	1.98
Washington	3.81	Indiana	1.44
Minnesota	4.13	Mississippi	1.36
Maryland	4.30	Florida	1.07
Wisconsin	4.63	Missouri	1.02
North Dakota	5.04	Arizona	0.80
Utah	5.49	South Carolina	0.55
Arizona	6.23	Montana	0.43
New Mexico	8.03	Tennessee	0.37
Montana	8.32	Kentucky	0.28
Kansas	10.31	Kansas	0.27
Alabama	11.24	Arkansas	0.25
Mississippi	11.85	Utah	0.23
Idaho	12.60	Idaho	0.18
Alaska	13.66	North Dakota	0.07
Colorado	22.76	New Mexico	0.06
Louisiana	28.54	Louisiana	0.04
Wyoming	31.60	Oklahoma	0.03
Texas	45.37	Texas	0.01

Table 6.A-2
Probabilities of State GO Bond Rating Changes, FY1989

Probability of Downgrade		Probability of Upgrade	
Oregon	0.48%	New York	34.28%
Alabama	0.57	Wisconsin	18.17
Iowa	0.86	Rhode Island	13.90
Tennessee	0.87	Delaware	12.15
North Dakota	1.05	Pennsylvania	10.44
Hawaii	1.05	Michigan	9.73
Kentucky	1.06	New Hampshire	9.34
Mississippi	1.11	Oregon	8.78
Idaho	1.14	Alabama	8.35
New Mexico	1.24	Kansas	8.34
Louisiana	1.26	Colorado	8.02
Kansas	1.36	Ohio	7.85
Maine	1.78	Wyoming	7.81
New York	2.05	California	7.28
Wisconsin	2.05	Maine	7.21
New Jersey	2.10	Alaska	6.68
California	2.15	New Jersey	6.64
North Carolina	2.22	South Dakota	6.34
Virginia	2.32	Nebraska	5.92
Delaware	2.38	Washington	5.77
Pennsylvania	2.58	Illinois	5.49
Montana	2.96	North Carolina	5.26
Illinois	3.06	Virginia	4.82
Washington	3.20	Massachusetts	4.65
West Virginia	3.23	Hawaii	4.41
Oklahoma	3.39	Tennessee	4.24
Arizona	3.40	South Carolina	4.06
South Carolina	3.47	Georgia	4.03
Massachusetts	3.51	Maryland	3.84
Arkansas	3.56	West Virginia	3.52
Ohio	3.64	Iowa	3.51
Vermont	3.78	Utah	3.43
South Dakota	3.92	Mississippi	3.41
Wyoming	4.41	Connecticut	2.62
Georgia	4.51	Nevada	2.44
New Hampshire	4.77	Kentucky	2.22
Connecticut	5.10	Arkansas	2.08
Maryland	5.19	Arizona	1.66
Rhode Island	5.19	Minnesota	1.65
Indiana	5.83	Montana	1.43
Michigan	5.95	Missouri	1.41
Florida	6.23	Louisiana	1.09
Nebraska	6.81	Indiana	1.00
Alaska	7.20	Idaho	0.91
Colorado	7.47	New Mexico	0.52
Texas	8.75	North Dakota	0.29
Missouri	9.99	Florida	0.18
Nevada	10.89	Oklahoma	0.08
Utah	11.10	Vermont	0.06
Minnesota	33.82	Texas	0.01

Table 6.A-3
Probabilities of State GO Bond Rating Changes, FY1990

Probability of Downgrade		Probability of Upgrade	
Idaho	0.15%	Utah	17.23%
Texas	0.24	Minnesota	16.43
Utah	0.33	New York	14.60
Wyoming	0.50	Wisconsin	11.21
Oklahoma	0.58	Michigan	10.96
New Mexico	0.64	Ohio	10.38
Mississippi	0.74	Alaska	8.88
Indiana	0.80	Wyoming	8.70
Minnesota	0.82	Delaware	7.34
Wisconsin	0.83	Mississippi	7.12
Montana	1.22	Nebraska	7.09
Alaska	1.35	South Dakota	6.96
South Carolina	1.49	Oklahoma	6.91
Washington	1.54	Indiana	6.74
Nevada	1.58	California	6.00
Missouri	1.59	Alabama	5.86
Iowa	1.60	South Carolina	5.76
Ohio	1.92	Maine	5.48
Colorado	1.99	Maryland	5.30
Louisiana	2.02	Washington	5.29
Kentucky	2.03	Iowa	5.25
Nebraska	2.14	Arkansas	5.05
North Carolina	2.29	Nevada	4.87
North Dakota	2.31	Oregon	4.81
Florida	2.65	New Jersey	4.70
Kansas	2.89	Hawaii	4.56
Arkansas	3.19	Virginia	4.37
Tennessee	3.40	Montana	4.37
Alabama	3.52	Missouri	4.26
Maine	3.54	Colorado	4.03
Hawaii	3.59	Kansas	3.52
California	3.79	Pennsylvania	3.20
Michigan	4.02	North Carolina	3.01
Oregon	4.48	New Hampshire	2.68
Illinois	4.50	Idaho	2.33
South Dakota	5.05	Arizona	1.69
Pennsylvania	5.14	Rhode Island	1.45
Virginia	5.54	Louisiana	1.37
Rhode Island	5.59	Tennessee	1.25
Vermont	6.50	Florida	1.23
New Jersey	6.57	Illinois	1.18
Maryland	7.08	Massachusetts	1.09
West Virginia	8.33	Texas	0.98
Connecticut	8.53	Kentucky	0.89
New Hampshire	8.59	New Mexico	0.52
Arizona	9.45	Georgia	0.32
Massachusetts	10.70	Vermont	0.12
Delaware	11.20	Connecticut	0.12
New York	12.04	North Dakota	0.06
Georgia	15.01	West Virginia	0.03

Table 6.A-4
Probabilities of State GO Bond Rating Changes, FY1991

Probability of Downgrade		Probability of Upgrade	
Louisiana	0.04%	Alaska	23.52%
Alaska	0.18	New York	19.57
Texas	0.23	Hawaii	18.75
West Virginia	0.36	Maine	13.23
Kentucky	0.65	Michigan	12.64
Arizona	0.66	Colorado	11.57
New Mexico	0.76	Wisconsin	10.50
Montana	1.33	Wyoming	9.74
Oklahoma	1.45	Mississippi	9.47
Idaho	1.46	Virginia	9.12
Tennessee	1.50	South Dakota	8.58
North Dakota	1.57	Maryland	8.36
Vermont	1.66	Iowa	7.97
Maryland	1.66	Oregon	7.57
Indiana	1.82	Alabama	7.52
Hawaii	1.82	Pennsylvania	7.41
Illinois	1.93	Tennessee	7.15
Mississippi	2.16	Arkansas	7.11
Arkansas	2.35	Ohio	6.66
Michigan	2.43	Delaware	6.43
Pennsylvania	2.43	Washington	6.10
Ohio	2.44	Indiana	6.03
Colorado	2.48	Louisiana	5.79
Minnesota	2.90	South Carolina	5.71
Georgia	2.96	Minnesota	5.56
Kansas	2.96	Nevada	5.43
Oregon	3.45	California	4.74
Iowa	3.49	Kansas	4.43
Nebraska	3.51	Illinois	4.29
Alabama	3.66	Idaho	3.46
Florida	3.77	Montana	3.41
Missouri	3.81	Arizona	3.36
Nevada	4.06	Utah	2.70
California	4.31	Georgia	2.52
Virginia	4.52	West Virginia	2.21
North Carolina	4.76	Missouri	2.04
Washington	4.82	New Hampshire	2.01
Wyoming	5.05	Vermont	1.91
South Carolina	5.72	North Carolina	1.84
Utah	6.15	New Mexico	1.80
Maine	6.59	Nebraska	1.58
Wisconsin	6.74	Connecticut	0.79
Delaware	7.69	Texas	0.78
South Dakota	7.80	Rhode Island	0.58
Connecticut	8.87	North Dakota	0.45
New Jersey	9.53	Florida	0.41
Massachusetts	13.37	Oklahoma	0.38
New York	13.78	Massachusetts	0.24
New Hampshire	19.55	Kentucky	0.22
Rhode Island	24.66	New Jersey	0.22

Victor A. Canto, "The State Competitive Environment: An Ebb Tide Lowers All Boats," A. B. Laffer, V. A. Canto & Associates, August 23, 1991.

3. Data sources are from the Merrill Lynch municipal bond data base. Given the vast number of municipal issues, most of which are not traded on a daily basis, actual daily prices are obviously not available for the majority of bonds. To overcome this problem, the industry often uses "matrix pricing," in which bonds of comparable quality, coupon, maturity, type, and special features are all priced consistently. In constructing a matrix, the pricer may create dozens of such groupings, each of which will then have a unique 30- to 50-year yield curve assigned to it and regularly maintained. Once a specific bond has been assigned to a peer group in the matrix, it is priced at the appropriate point on that group's yield curve on that day.

4. Victor A. Canto and Arthur B. Laffer, "Report to the Governor: Recommendations for Economic Reform in Puerto Rico," H. C. Wainwright & Co., *Economics* (April 20, 1979); Arthur B. Laffer and Charles W. Kadlec, "The Jarvis-Gann Tax Cut Proposal: An Application of the Laffer Curve," H. C. Wainwright & Co., *Economics*, June 27, 1978.

5. E. Fama, M. Fisher, M. Jensen, and R. Roll, "The Adjustment of Stock Prices to New Information," *International Economic Review* 10, no. 19 (1969): 1-21.

6. R. Merton, "On Estimating the Expected Return in the Market: An Exploratory Investigation" (National Bureau of Economic Resources, Working Paper no. 444, Cambridge, Mass., February 1980).

7. S. LeRoy, "Expectation Models of Cost Prices: A Survey of Theory," *Journal of Finance* 37 (March 1982): 185-214.

8. R. Ruback, "The Effect of Price Controls on Equity Values" (Working Paper, University of Rochester, December 1979).

9. S. Brown and G. Warner, "Using Daily Stock Returns in Event Studies" (Working Paper, University of Rochester, February 1983).

10. William Beaver, "Econometric Properties of Alternative Security Return Methods," *Journal of Accounting Research* 19, no. 1 (Spring 1981): 163-83.

11. K. Brown, C. Lockwood, and S. Summer, "On Examinations of Event Dependency and Structural Change in Security Price Models" (Presented at the Present Westford Financial Meeting, June 1983).

7

Portfolio Strategy Based on Size, Location, and Industry Classification

Victor A. Canto, Arthur B. Laffer, and Robert I. Webb

Theory and common experience postulate that general economic factors impact stock prices in the aggregate. These same factors can have substantially different effects, depending on the size, location, and the industry groups being considered.

Over the past decade, research at A. B. Laffer, V. A. Canto & Associates has focused on developing a portfolio strategy that would identify differential performance based on overall economic environment, location, and size. Given our published work, a superior portfolio strategy is one that takes into account the investment implications of the following:

- *Capitalization.* Selection of small-capitalization rather than large-capitalization stocks will take advantage of the empirically documented differential return between small and large firms.

- *Location.* The location of plant facilities will identify companies most likely to be affected by state and local policies.

- *The overall economic environment.* The capital assets tax sensitivity (CATS) strategy will aid in the selection of industry groups that are favored by the economic environment.

A natural question addressed in this study is whether the three independent strategies can be combined into a single strategy. In order to determine the incremental performance added by the combination of the strategies, the first step in the analysis is to review the individual strategies.

SIZE-RELATED EFFECTS: THE SMALL CAPS

It has long been conventional wisdom that investments in small firms
yield greater returns than investments in the largest companies listed on the
New York Stock Exchange (NYSE) and the American Stock Exchange
(AMEX).[1] This understanding can be applied in a systematic way to earn
above-average rates of return. These are the major implications of this
research:

- The smaller the average capitalization of firms in a portfolio, the better
  that portfolio's performance. This result holds even after adjustments are
  made for risk differences as measured by betas.
- This result differs strongly from findings of the 1960s efficient market
  research that indicated that active trading strategies could not beat buy-
  and-hold strategies.

The rate of return from a portfolio consisting of small-capitalization
companies was outstanding. For example, $1 invested in a small-capitaliza-
tion portfolio for the period 1963-84 increased to more than $115. For the
same period, a portfolio consisting of companies with the largest average
capitalization grew to only $6. Superior results were found to exist at each
size gradation. In general, the smaller the firms in a portfolio, the better it
performed. While the superior performance of the size effect is not guaranteed, it was present in 17 out of 22 years of studies. Therefore, it should be
considered an important part of an overall investment strategy.

The Reagan tax cut of 1981 and the gradual movement of the Federal
Reserve toward deemphasizing money growth targets in favor of price
targets have resulted in the lowest inflation rates since the early 1960s. In
addition, (1) the modified flat tax with lower marginal tax rates that took
effect January 1, 1988, (2) changes in the regulatory environment, and (3)
continued commitment by the Fed to price rather than quantity targets have
resulted in low inflation.

The lower inflation outlook, lower tax rate, and reduced regulation during the Reagan administration reduced the advantages of companies adept
at avoiding taxes and regulations and at hedging against inflation. In short,
the Reagan policies favored larger caps over small-cap stocks. Not surprisingly, the small caps underperformed for most of the 1980s.[2]

In 1989, the small-cap selection procedure identified 125 firms in the
AMEX and 285 in the NYSE. The cutoff market capitalization was $11.09
million for the AMEX and $108.54 for the NYSE (Table 7.1). The small-
cap portfolio declined 5.68 percent versus the Dow Jones Industrial Average (DJIA) (Table 7.2). The underperformance continued during 1990,
when the small-cap portfolio declined 15.91 percent versus a 4.5 percent

Table 7.1

Number of AMEX or NYSE Listed Firms in Bottom Quintile of Market Capitalization and Cutoff Market Capitalization Value*

Year	AMEX Number of Firms	Cutoff Value (millions)	NYSE Number of Firms	Cutoff Value (millions)
1989	125	11.09	285	108.54
1990	131	6.35	294	67.28
1991	143	7.73	305	89.01

* Companies not headquartered in a U.S. state were deleted from the sample. Companies for which total return data were not available from Compustat were also excluded. The number of stocks included above were subsequently further reduced to eliminate stocks with returns of 200 percent or more. Data for 1991 are as of September 5. 1991.

Table 7.2

Average Returns of Small-Cap Portfolio*

	1989	1990	1991**
Small-cap portfolio	-5.68	-15.91	19.80
Number of stocks	405	422	418
S&P 500	27.3	-6.0	19.8
DJIA	26.0	-4.5	15.6

* Based on one year total return data as reported by Compustat for the 1989-90 period.

** Data for 1991 cover the period 1/1/91 to 9/5/91. The percentage change in the stock price during the 1/1/91 to 9/5/91 period was used as a proxy for total return. Stocks with returns of 200 percent or more were deleted from the sample.

decline for the DJIA. During the last two years, the U.S. economy has been moving toward a higher tax rate and increased regulation, an environment favorable to small caps. As of September 5, 1991, the small-cap portfolio appreciated 19.8 percent versus 15.6 percent for the DJIA.

The underperformance of the small-cap stocks during 1989 and during 1990 clearly illustrates the importance of being able to correctly apply the size screen. Our analysis and research at the time correctly predicted the underperformance of the small-cap stocks during the 1980s. Our portfolio strategy based on size recommended the large-cap stocks. The pendulum is swinging the other way. Our current outlook is for a return of the small-cap stocks.

Table 7.3
Small-Cap Portfolio Returns

	1989	1990	1991
Equal weight is given to each stock (Unconstrained)	-5.68	-15.91	19.80
Equal weight to individual state (3 or more firms)	.25	-10.34	27.56
Equal weight to individual industries (5 or more firms)	-6.37	-15.82	24.07

IS THERE A LOCATION OR INDUSTRY BIAS?

The portfolio strategy, as described, gives equal weight to each of the stocks in the portfolio. However, the composition of the bottom quintile of the NYSE and AMEX is not equally representative of the respective states and/or industry groups. The larger states and/or industry groups will, on average, tend to have more companies in the portfolio. In order to control for the potential systematic bias related to a state's size and/or industry group, we have reestimated the portfolio performance to give equal weight to each state's portfolio. We also have reestimated the performance to give equal weight to the industry groups.

In 1989, the unconstrained small-cap portfolio declined 5.68 percent, whereas the portfolio given an equal weight to each state's portfolio yielded a 0.25 percent increase (Table 7.3). The differential is present in both 1990 and 1991. Clearly, controlling location may significantly enhance the portfolio performance. Recalculating the portfolio performance by giving equal weight to each industry group also suggests the presence of an industry effect.

LOCATION: THE STATE COMPETITIVE ENVIRONMENT

The operations of small companies are more likely to be concentrated in one or a few states. As a result, the small-cap strategy may introduce a systematic regional bias. Thus, the small-cap portfolio returns could be significantly affected by state and local economic policies.

The rationale for the regional bias is easily established. Small companies typically are less able to pass tax rate changes forward to consumers or backward to suppliers. Thus, changes in states' relative tax burdens may have more pronounced effects on the after-tax returns and stock market performances of small corporations. The effect is best illustrated by the following example. Consider two identical steel mills that are located 40 miles apart. One mill is located in Kentucky; the other in Ohio. Since both steel mills sell virtually identical products in the U.S. market, competition will force them to sell their products at approximately the same price. Because the two steel facilities are only 40 miles apart, they both have to pay the same after-tax wages to their employees and the same prices to their suppliers.

Given this situation, consider what would happen if Ohio does what it did several years ago: Ohio doubles its income tax rate, whereas Kentucky lowers its income tax rate. Because the steel market is highly competitive, the Ohio company would not be able to pass the tax hike on to its customers in the form of higher prices. Likewise, the Ohio company would not be able to pass the tax hike backward on to its suppliers or employees.

Initially, at least, the Ohio steel mill would have to swallow the tax hike through lower after-tax profits. This drop in profits would be reflected by a fall in the Ohio mill's stock price. Clearly, the mill in Kentucky would benefit in the short run.

The investment implications of these observations are straightforward: Buy the stocks of companies located in states that are lowering tax rates and sell the stocks of companies in states that are raising tax rates. As simple as this strategy is, it is difficult to apply in practice because most major corporations operate in many states and, perhaps, in several countries. Thus, the impact of a particular state's tax changes on the values of the stocks of multistate corporations may be relatively minor. An investment strategy based on changes in the state competitive environment may be more rewarding if it is applied to small companies.

STATE-SPECIFIC PORTFOLIOS

Estimates of the changes in states' relative tax burden are published annually by A. B. Laffer, V. A. Canto & Associates.[3] Legislated tax changes then are used to forecast changes in states' relative tax burdens and relate them to a portfolio of small-cap companies located in the individual states. A simple average of the stock returns was calculated for each state.[4] The deviation of individual state average stock returns from the average stock return for all states in the sample was calculated for each year of the study.

The number of states with at least one NYSE or AMEX listed firm ranged from 40 in 1989 and 1990 to 41 in 1991 (Table 7.4). Because the results may be sensitive to the average return per state, subsets of the sample with two or more and three or more NYSE or AMEX listed firms were also examined.[5] For example, the number of states having two or more NYSE or AMEX listed firms ranged from 29 in 1989 and 1991 to 30 in 1990. Similarly, in 1989, 25 states consistently had three or more companies that were listed on

Table 7.4
States with One, Two, Three, or More NYSE or AMEX Listed Firms in Bottom Quintile of Market Capitalization Included or Excluded from Sample

Year	Number of States With 1 Firm	Number of States With 2 Firms	Number of States With 3 or more Firms*	Total Number of States
1989	11 AL, AK, AR, HI KY, ME, NE, NM OR, SC, UT	4 LA, NV, NH, RI	25	40
1990	10 AL, AR, HI, IA, KY NE, NM, OR, SC, UT	5 LA, ME, NV RI, VT	25	40
1991	12 AK, AR, DE, HI MD, NE, NV, OR SC, UT, VT, WV	6 NH, RI	23	41

* The following 23 states had 3 or more listed firms across all 3 years: AZ, CA, CO, CT, FL, GA, IL, IN, MA, MI, MN, MO, NC, NJ, NY, OH, OK, PA, TN, TX, VA, WA, and WI. MD and VT had 3 or more firms listed in 1989. Finally, MD and NH had 3 or more firms listed in 1990.

Table 7.5
Listing by State of Successes and Failures in the Relationship Between Changes in Relative State Tax Burdens for Selected Fiscal Years and Deviations of State Stock Returns from the Average for the Corresponding "Preceding" Calendar Year

	Successes (A negative relation)	Failures (A positive relation)
1989	24 AK, CA, CO, CT, GA, HI, IL, IN, KY, MD, MA, MI, MN, MO, NC, NE, NH, NM, NY,RI, TX, VA, VT, WI	15 AL, AZ, AR, FL, LA, ME, NV, NJ, OK, OR, PA, SC, TN, UT, WA
1990	25 AL, CO, FL, GA, HI, IA, IN, LA, MD, MA, MI, MN, MO, NH, NV, NJ, NY, NC, OH, PA, RI, TN, TX, VA, VT	15 AZ, AR, CA, CT, IL, KY, MA, NE, NM, OK, OR, SC, UT, WI, WA
1991	20 AR, CO, CT, DE, KY, MD, MI, MN, MD, NH, NY, NC, OH, OK, RI, TN, TX, VT, VA, WA	21 AL, AK, AZ, CA, FL, GA, HI, IL, IN, LA, MA, ME, NE, NV,NJ, OR, PA, SC, UT, WV, WI,

The 1991 data cover the period January 1, 1991 to September 5, 1991. Excess stock returns for 1991 were related to FY1991 changes in relative tax burdens. Because Ohio's change in relative tax burden was zero for FY1990 it was excluded for purposes of calculating successes and failures.

either the AMEX or NYSE and in the bottom quintile of market capitalization. For 1990 and 1991, 25 and 23 additional states met the criterion, respectively.

A negative relationship between changes in relative state tax burdens and deviations from the average stock return across states in the sample is clearly identified (Table 7.5). For example, in 1989, in 24 out of 39 cases a negative relation between a state's relative tax burden and state stock return was observed. In 1990, 25 cases out of 40 possible states resulted in a negative relation. The worst results occurred in 1991, when only 20 out of 41 cases showed a negative relation between state relative taxes and a state stock return.[6] The question naturally arises as to how likely these outcomes are. Under certain conditions, one can use the binomial distribution to calculate the probability that the results occurred by chance.[7] Using a one-tailed test, the above results are significant at the 17.5 percent level for 1989, at the 5.7 percent level for 1990, and at the 43.6 percent level for 1991 (Table 7.6). When the analysis is limited to the somewhat smaller subset of states with three or more listed firms in the bottom quintile of market capitalization, the results are much better, ranging from 1 percent in 1989 and 1990 to 26 percent in 1991.

Table 7.6
Number of Successes in the Relationship Between Changes in Relative State Tax Burdens for Selected Fiscal Years and Deviations of State Stock Portfolio Returns from the Average for the Corresponding "Preceding" Calendar Year and the Probability That the String of Successes Occurred by Chance When the Probability of Success for Each Outcome is Equal to 0.5

Calendar Year	States With Listed Firms of	Number of Successes	Sample Size	Probability
1989	1 or more	24	39	.0749
	2 or more	19	29	.0475
	3 or more	17	25	.0146
1990	1 or more	25	40	.0571
	2 or more	22	30	.0054
	3 or more	18	25	.0139
1991	1 or more	20	41	.4364
	2 or more	16	29	.2877
	3 or more	13	23	.2643
1989-91	1 or more	69	120	.0505
	2 or more	57	88	.0028
	3 or more	48	73	.0036

1991 data cover the period 1/1/91 to 9/5/91. Excess stock returns for 1991 were related to FY 1991 changes in relative tax burdens. Because Ohio's change in relative tax burden was zero for FY 1990 it was excluded for purposes of calculating successes and failures.

Using a large sample approximation to the one-tailed binomial test, the probability of achieving 69 successes out of 120 drawings over the three-year period by chance can be determined.[8] It is approximately 5 percent. The probability of achieving 48 successes out of 73 outcomes (in states with three or more firms) is 0.0036.

The decision rule used to determine whether to accept or reject the null hypothesis that the negative relationship between changes in a state's relative tax burden and a state's stock return occurred by chance is whether the test statistic from the large sample approximation equals or exceeds some standardized normal variable, z, at the chosen significance level. At the 10 percent significance level, the z value is 1.28, whereas the test statistic in the latter case is 2.69, leading one to reject the null hypothesis that the negative relation between states' relative tax burden and states' stock returns occurred by chance.

LOCATION-RELATED EFFECTS: THE STATE COMPETITIVE ENVIRONMENT

For investors and corporate planners, knowledge of a company's exposure to a state where taxes are either rising or falling relative to the nation can be an important input in investment or location decisions. Companies with production facilities concentrated in a state where relative tax rates are declining can, in general, expect to reap higher after-tax rates of return than those companies in states with rising tax burdens. Small-cap companies headquartered in those states should be included in the "buy" portfolio. Symmetrically, companies based in states with rising relative tax burdens should be in the "sell" portfolio. The extent of the duration and magnitude of such gains or losses is tied inextricably to the mobility of each company's competitors, workers, and the sensitivity of its customers to the price of its goods.

Aggregating the portfolios to give equal weight to each state in the falling relative tax burden (i.e., the buy portfolio) and also giving equal weight to each of the states in the rising relative tax burden (the sell portfolio) may increase diversification by reducing the risk of individual states being misclassified.

The performance of the portfolio strategy is encouraging. In 1989, the buy portfolio appreciated 5.3 percent compared with the sell portfolio, which depreciated 9.26 percent (Table 7.7). The differential performance continued during 1990. The buy portfolio declined 6.72 percent, whereas the sell portfolio declined 13.52 percent. In 1991, where small-cap stocks rallied significantly, the buy portfolio rose 30.08 percent, whereas the sell portfolio rose 19.38 percent.

The performance results for 1989-91 are suggestive of the value of the portfolio strategy of buying small-cap stocks of companies located in states with falling relative tax burdens and selling stocks of small-cap companies

Table 7.7
Average Return on Small-Cap Portfolios Located in States with Rising and Falling Relative Tax Burdens, 1989-91* (equal weight is given to each state)

Year	1989	1990	1991
Portfolio of stocks located in states with falling relative tax burdens	5.30	–6.72	30.08
Number of stocks	211	254	246
Portfolio of stocks located in states with rising relative tax burdens	–9.26	–13.52	19.38
Number of stocks	161	149	150
Overall (unweighted)	–5.68	–15.91	19.80
Number of stocks	405	422	418
Overall (equal weight to each state)	.25	–10.34	27.56
Number of stocks	272	403	396

* Stocks with returns of 200 percent or more were deleted from the sample. The number of stocks used to calculate the overall return for 1989 differs from the sum of the number of stocks in the other portfolios because the stocks of 14 companies located in Ohio were excluded because there was no change in relative tax burdens in Ohio.

Data for 1991 cover the period 1/1/91 to 9/5/91. The percentage change in the stock price during the 1/1/91 to 9/5/91 period was used as a proxy for total return. Stocks with returns of 200 percent or more were deleted from the sample.

located in states with rising relative tax burdens. These differences are significant. The state screen improved the performance of the small-cap portfolio in every year.

THE INDUSTRY EFFECTS

The evidence reported identifies a negative relationshp between changes in relative tax burdens and deviation in stock returns from the average for small firms across industry groups. The question naturally arises as to whether the average returns on a portfolio of stocks of firms in the same industry differ if the portfolio is formed from firms located in states that are raising their relative tax burdens or formed from firms located in states that are lowering their relative tax burdens. In order to test this hypothesis, the sample of NYSE and AMEX listed small-capitalization stocks used in the preceding analysis was rearranged by major industry group using the first two digits of each firm's Standard Industrial Classification (SIC) code number. Only major industry groups having five or more firms were se-

Table 7.8
Successes and Failures in the Relationship Between the Average Return on a Portfolio of Small Company Stocks in a Given Major Industry Group for Firms Located in States with Rising Relative Tax Burdens and the Average Return on a Portfolio of Small Company Stocks in the Same Major Industry Group for Firms Located in States with Falling Relative Tax Burdens for the Period 1989-91

	1989	1990	1991	1989-91
Successes	20	17	14	51
Failures	5	10	14	29
Total	25	27	28	80
Probability*	.0003	.0885	.500	.0069

* Probability of a string of successes occurring by chance using the binomial test with equal probability of success or failure.

lected for analysis.[9] Next, the firms in each major industry group were put in one of two portfolios, depending on whether the location of their corporate headquarters was in a state with a falling relative tax burden or in a state with a rising relative tax burden.

The average annual return on an investment in the stocks of the companies in the various major industry groups that compose the sample for the 1989-91 period is reported in Appendix A. In addition, the average return on both subset portfolios (i.e., stocks located in states with rising or falling relative tax burdens) is reported. In 1989, the average return on the portfolio of stocks of firms in industry groups located in states with falling relative tax burdens exceeded the return on the portfolio of stocks of firms in the same major industry group located in states with rising relative tax burdens. Where the contrary is true, the result is classified as a failure. In 1989, there were 20 successes out of 25 possible cases (Table 7.8). The estimated probability of the outcome being random is 0.0003. As is readily apparent, the results in Table 7.8 provide evidence that changes in state relative tax burdens are significant across industry groups. All that is needed now is a procedure for taking advantage of the industry effects. Our choice is based on our CATS strategy.

The CATS Strategy

The CATS approach proceeds directly from the theory of the firm and the household to establish the principle as to how any market returns to equilibrium following a macroeconomic shock. In principle, equilibrium is restored by some combination of price and quantity adjustment. Whether the alteration in the market operates through the industry's demand schedule or supply schedule, price and quantity will be the rebalancers. Quite clearly, from the standpoint of any specific firm within an industry, the greater the impact of macroeconomic shocks and the greater the role played by price in the adjustment process, the greater will be the sensitivity of that industry's profits and stock price.

While rooted in economic theory, both the conception and the measurement of equity responses to macroeconomic events are straightforward. Pillaging data from the recent past has allowed us to establish links between macroeconomic events and the returns of equities by industry. From all we are able to uncover, the market's reassessment of equity values is far from haphazard. There are distinct patterns that emerge. Some are focused with great resolution, whereas others are only dimly visible through the vast array of numbers. The CATS strategy overlays the vector of more traditional macroeconomic events on the matrix of asset relatives. If data patterns recumbent in our past observances can be presumed to extend into the future, then knowledge of what is to be for the economy can readily be translated into what is to be for stock returns. As a guide for asset managers, such linkages may prove quite valuable. Asset managers are one group with the curse to be always fully committed. Whether in or out of the market, their performance is continuously at risk. They have no choice.

Selecting among the CATS is based on our previous research.[10] Throughout most of 1989, the High-CATS were recommended, and in 1990, the Low-CATS were the preferred group.[11] In the first half of 1991, the strategy was in the High-CATS groups. The portfolio performance indicates that the industry (CATS) screen does improve the performance of the small-cap portfolio. In 1989, the portfolio that gives equal weight to the High-CATS groups decreased 5.58 percent versus 12.82 percent for the Low-CATS portfolio (Table 7.9). In 1990, the Low-CATS portfolio declined 17.22 percent

Table 7.9
Small-Cap Stocks and Industry Performance Screen (equal weight by industry)

	1989	1990	1991
HC	-5.58	-16.72	25.25
Number of stocks	247	255	294
LC	-12.82	-17.22	16.9
Number of stocks	95	100	59
Small-cap (unweighted)	-5.68	-15.91	19.80
Number of stocks	405	422	418
Small-cap (equal weight by industry	-6.37	-15.82	24.07
Number of stocks	342	355	353

The number of firms in the industry sample (HC + LC) does not equal the number of firms in the small-cap sample. The reason for this is that firms belonging to industry classifications with fewer than five firms were deleted from the industry sample, as were industries for which there was no record of tax sensitivity (i.e., could not be identified as HC or LC).

versus a 16.72 percent decline for the High-CATS portfolio. In 1991, the High-CATS portfolio appreciated 25.25 percent versus 16.9 percent for the Low-CATS portfolio as a whole. The differences in portfolio performance clearly suggest that the industry screen identifies systematic differences in the industry groups. The performance difference between the High-CATS and Low-CATS portfolios in 1990 may be attributable to a new year rotation from the High-CATS group to the Low-CATS group.

THE COMPLETE STRATEGY

The three portfolio strategies discussed earlier provide three screens for separating industries and stocks that will, on average, outperform the market. Since the screens are not mutually exclusive, the possibility exists that by combining these screens one can develop a portfolio strategy that may yield a performance that will exceed that of each of the individual portfolio strategies.

In the process of selecting the various screens, the location and/or industry classification of a particular stock may not be readily available. That is why one cannot aggregate the various subgroups into a combined broad category. Similarly, since there are stocks being excluded from the grand averages, it is possible for all the subgroups included to be below average or above average in a particular year.

The detailed performance for each of the three years illustrates the power of the strategy. Our strategy recommended large-cap stocks both in 1989 and 1990, switching to small caps in 1991. The High-CATS were recommended in 1989 and 1991.

Based on these recommendations, the best performers in 1989 would be the large-cap High-CATS stocks located in states with falling relative tax burdens. The data on large-cap stocks are not reported here. However, an indirect test is readily available. The worst-performing group should be small-cap stocks located in states with rising tax burdens in the Low-CATS group. That portfolio declined 23.59 percent (Table 7.10). In 1991, the strategy recommended a small-cap High-CATS portfolio of stocks located in states with a declining relative tax burden. Similar results are obtained in 1990 as shown in Table 7.11. This portfolio increased 31.01 percent (Table 7.12).

It should be pointed out that the portfolio performance is under-estimated—the reason being that the exclusion of stocks that had returns in excess of 200 percent biases the empirical analysis against acceptance of our approach. A portfolio manager would want to have those stocks in his or her portfolio, and the strategy performance would have been even better. An analysis of the 25 excluded stocks with returns in excess of 200 percent shows that 15 were stocks of firms located in states with decreasing relative tax burdens. The probability of that occurring by chance is estimated to be 22 percent.

Table 7.10
The Complete Portfolio Strategy for 1989
Size, Location, and Industry Groups

	High-CATS	Low-CATS
States with falling tax burden	-.25	-5.22
Number of stocks	119	59
States with rising tax burden	-14.44	-23.59
Number of stocks	128	36

Table 7.11
The Complete Portfolio Strategy for 1990
Size, Location, and Industry Groups*

	High-CATS	Low-CATS
States with rising tax burden	-17.00	-30.27
Number of stocks	151	69
States with falling tax burden	-15.58	-13.63
Number of stocks	104	31

* Includes all stocks in industry groups with five or more firms. Stocks with returns of 200 percent or more are excluded.

Table 7.12
The Complete Portfolio Strategy for 1991
Size, Location, and Industry Groups*

	High-CATS	Low-CATS
States with falling tax burden	31.01	21.43
Number of stocks**	138	75
States with rising tax burden	24.12	18.05
Number of stocks**	101	39

* 1991 data cover the period 1/1/91 to 9/5/91.

** Includes all stocks in industry groups with five or more firms. Stock with returns of 200 percent or more are excluded. Consequently, the return for all states all industries category differs from the overall retun on the small cap portfolio reported above. In addition, the all industries sample includes firm without a record of tax sensitivity.

CONCLUSIONS

An examination of the data for the last three years indicates a strong negative relationship between changes in state tax burdens relative to other states and deviations from the average stock return across states. Simply put, the stock prices of companies located in states that decreased their tax burdens relative to other states outperformed the stock prices of companies located in states that increased their tax burdens relative to other states. Similar results were found for stocks grouped by industry (Table 7.A.1). The evidence suggests that investment strategy should explicitly take into account size, location, and changes in state economic policy (i.e., industry classification). Each of the screens individually and collectively adds value to the portfolio strategy.

The question naturally arises as to which stocks are recommended to perform best for 1992. Using the above three screens, the answer lies in Tables 7A.2 through 7A.10, which break down the bottom quintile of NYSE and AMEX stocks in terms of market value (as of September 5, 1991) into various subportfolios.

NOTES

1. Marc R. Reinganum, " 'Excess' Returns in Small Firm Portfolios," *Economic Study*, A. B. Laffer Associates, April 25, 1980; idem, "Does Beta Matter? Another Look at the Capital Asset Pricing Model," *Economic Study*, A. B. Laffer Associates, November 20, 1980; idem, "Portfolio Strategies Based on Market Capitalization," *Investment Strategies*, A. B. Laffer Associates, November 10, 1981; idem, "The January Effect," *Investment Study*, A. B. Laffer Associates, November 17, 1982; idem, "Small Cap Stock Update," *Investment Observations*, A. B. Laffer Associates, July 5, 1983; Truman A. Clark, "Are Small Cap Stocks Still Alive?" *Economic Study*, A. B. Laffer Associates, October 31, 1985.

2. In order to determine the small-cap performance during more recent times, the bottom quintile of AMEX and NYSE listed companies, ranked in terms of market value for each year from 1989 through 1991, was selected for analysis.

3. Victor A. Canto, "The State Competitive Environment: 1988-89 Update," *Economy in Perspective*, A. B. Laffer Associates, December 15, 1988; Victor A. Canto and Arthur B. Laffer, "The State Competitive Environment: 1989-90 Update," *Economic Study*, A. B. Laffer, V. A. Canto & Associates, November 14, 1989; Victor A. Canto, "The State Competitive Environment: 1990-91 Update," *Economic Study*, A. B. Laffer, V. A. Canto & Associates, November 28, 1990.

4. A simple average is used rather than a market value weighted average because macroeconomic events may have a differential effect across industries.

5. The average return across all states with at least one NYSE or AMEX listed firm is used as the average return for all states. Companies with returns in excess of 200 percent are excluded from the sample for purposes of calculating the overall return.

6. A complete record spanning the fiscal year was not used. Instead, the state return data include only the January 1, 1991, to September 5, 1991, period.

7. The conditions are: All outcomes are assumed to be independent; to be dichotomous (i.e., fall into one of two possible classifications, success or failure); and to face the same probability of success (a *negative* relationship between changes in relative state tax burdens and deviations of state stock returns from the average is considered a success).

8. M. Hollander and D. Wolfe, *Nonparametric Statistical Methods* (New York: Wiley, 1973), point out that when a large sample approximation to the binomial test is used, the following equation for the test statistic, S^*, is appropriate:

$$S^* = \frac{S - np_o}{[np_o\,(1 - p_o)]^{1/2}}$$

where S = the number of successes; n = the number of outcomes, and P_o = the constant probability of success. As n increases, the statistic S^* asymptotically approaches a normal distribution with zero mean and unit variance.

9. Given data limitations, it was not possible to obtain a sufficient sample of industries when three or four digits of SIC code numbers were used or when 10 or more firms were required for each industry.

10. Victor A. Canto, "The CAT'S Meow: A Portfolio Strategy for a Modified Flat Tax," *Economic Study*, A. B. Laffer Associates, May 17, 1985; idem, "The CAT'S Meow: The Historical Record of the Fat CATS Strategy," *Investment Study*, A. B. Laffer Associates, February 13, 1986; idem, "The CAT's Meow: Sharpening Our Claws," *Economic Study*, A. B. Laffer Associates, July 18, 1986.

11. Victor A. Canto, "The CATS Behind the Bush," *Investment Study*, A. B. Laffer, V. A. Canto & Associates, August 8, 1991.

Table 7A-1
Average Returns on Portfolios of Small-Capitalization
Stocks Classified by Major Industry Group and by Location

Major Industry Group	SIC Code	Averages 1989 Industry	Rising Tax States	Falling Tax States
Oil & Gas Extraction	1300-1399	-18.63%	-59.94%	-12.73%
Builders	1500-1599	-9.90	-20.70	2.70
Food & Kindred Products	2000-2099	-16.32	9.61	-42.25
Textile Mill Products	2200-2299	-0.59	-0.59	N.A
Apparel & Other Finished Products	2300-2399	-21.90	-50.24	15.89
Lumber & Wood Products (excl. Furniture)	2400-2499	-15.94	11.24	-22.73
Chemicals & Allied Products	2800-2899	-22.20	-35.34	-2.50
Rubber & Misc. Plastic Products	3000-3099	-37.57	-74.56	-12.92
Primary Metal Industries	3300-3399	-24.91	NA.	-24.91
Fabricated Metal, Excluding Machinery, Transportation Equip.	3400-3499	13.96	-4.97	45.51
Industrial Commercial Machinery, Computer Equipment	3500-3599	-7.91	-14.04	-2.39
Construction, Mining Materials Handling Equipment	3600-3699	-3.35	-3.73	-2.52
Transportation Equip.	3700-3799	-10.01	-1.60	-15.06
Measuring Instruments, Photography Goods, Watches	3800-3899	16.00	3.67	30.10
Misc Manufacturing Industries	3900-3999	3.21	3.21	N.A
Electric, Gas, Sanitary Services	4900-4999	.75	-3.87	4.21
Durable Goods - Wholesale	5000-5099	-12.18	-20.67	-0.51
Nondurable Goods - Wholesale	5100-5199	-2.31	-17.97	10.75

Table 7.A-1 (continued)

| | | Averages 1989 | | |
Major Industry Group	SIC Code	Industry	Rising Tax States	Falling Tax States
Eating & Drinking Places	5800–5899	4.08	8.73	-0.56
Miscellaneous Retail	5900–5999	-6.10	-5.80	-10.12
Depository Institutions	6000–6099	-19.79	-32.25	-7.32
Security & Commodity Brokers	6200–6299	8.32	6.30	11.56
Insurance	6300–6399	7.24	5.28	9.20
Real Estate	6500–6599	-40.29	-45.76	-38.24
Holding, Other Investment Offices	6700–6799	-1.24	-12.48	4.89
Business Services	7300–7399	-2.28	-16.61	3.87
Health Care	8000–8099	53.51	-50.00	18.91
Engineering, Accounting, Research, Management, Relations Services	8700–8799	30.25	16.79	35.63
		Averages 1990		
Oil & Gas Extraction	1300–1399	-24.41%	-20.21%	-26.09%
Builders	1500–1599	-23.76	-15.36	-33.56
Food & Kindred Products	2000–2099	-35.41	-35.07	-35.75
Textile Mill Products	2200–2299	24.34	34.33	4.38
Apparel & Other Finished Products	2300–2399	-19.16	-40.19	15.89
Chemicals & Allied Products	2800–2899	-18.02	-42.76	-8.13
Rubber & Misc. Plastic Products	3000–3099	-35.54	-37.70	-34.68
Leather & Leather Products	3100–3199	-25.63	-22.76	-27.55
	3200–3299	.86	NA	.86
Primary Metal Industries	3300–3399	-23.97	-44.48	-18.11

Table 7.A-1 (continued)

Major Industry Group	SIC Code	Averages 1990 Industry	Rising Tax States	Falling Tax States
Fabricated Metal, Excluding Machinery, Transportation Equip.	3400-3499	1.33	4.51	-12.42
Industrial Commercial Machinery, Computer Equipment	3500-3599	-23.69	-23.86	-23.64
Construction, Mining Materials Handling Equipment	3600-3699	-5.86	-8.67	.77
Transportation Equip.	3700-3799	-10.40	-22.92	-8.31
Measuring Instruments, Photography Goods, Watches	3800-3899	12.60	-4.27	21.06
Misc Manufacturing Industries	3900-3999	-5.82	12.50	-11.92
Durable Goods - Wholesale	5000-5099	-16.08	-17.08	-15.38
Nondurable Goods - Wholesale	5100-5199	-13.33	-10.47	-8.41
Eating & Drinking Places	5800-5899			
Miscellaneous Retail	5900-5999	-33.57	-28.72	-38.43
Depository Institutions	6000-6099	-36.44	-44.87	-30.65
Security & Commodity Brokers	6200-6299	-7.65	-31.23	1.19
Insurance	6300-6399	-9.35	36.39	-20.79
Real Estate	6500-6599	-43.32	-58.78	-20.12
Holding, Other Investment Offices	6700-6799	-19.80	-27.28	-16.75
Hotels-Motels	7000-7099	-53.04	-91.67	-43.38
Business Services	7300-7399	-13.66	-7.92	-18.25
Entertainment	7800-7899	-31.50	NA	-31.50
Health Care	8000-8099	18.17	16.67	19.08
Engineering, Accounting, Research, Management, Relations Services	8700-8799	13.22	-4.12	47.88

Table 7.A-1 (continued)

Major Industry Group	SIC Code	Averages 1991 Industry	Rising Tax States	Falling Tax States
Oil & Gas Extraction	1300-1399	19.79%	35.91%	14.42%
Builders	1500-1599	35.66	-8.31	90.63
Food & Kindred Products	2000-2099	10.37	23.27	5.02
Textile Mill Products	2200-2299	26.70	27.72	13.36
Apparel & Other Finished Products	2300-2399	47.23	16.31	126.36
Chemicals & Allied Products	2800-2899	17.63	-1.56	24.52
Rubber & Misc. Plastic Products	3000-3099	17.75	-9.09	26.70
Primary Metal Industries	3300-3399	-2.47	-14.59	1.17
Fabricated Metal, Excluding Machinery, Transportation Equip.	3400-3499	22.46	14.18	28.68
Industrial Commercial Machinery, Computer Equipment	3500-3599	20.50	17.04	21.57
Construction, Mining Materials Handling Equipment	3600-3699	17.97	14.74	24.15
Transportation Equip.	3700-3799	33.49	100.80	22.99
Measuring Instruments, Photography Goods, Watches	3800-3899	51.46	79.35	34.03
Misc Manufacturing Industries	3900-3999	55.38	68.33	45.66
Communications	4800-4899	15.71	55.73	-10.96
Durable Goods - Wholesale	5000-5099	27.64	41.02	20.20
Nondurable Goods - Wholesale	5100-5199	14.98	34.87	3.05
Variety Stores	5300-5399	53.25	60.66	48.31
Consumer Electronics Stores	5700-5799	-23.55	-50.83	-9.91
Miscellaneous Retail	5900-5999	10.70	.31	18.50

Table 7.A-1 (continued)

Major Industry Group	SIC Code	Averages 1991 Industry	Rising Tax States	Falling Tax States
Depository Institutions	6000-6099	-4.67	-18.92	5.78
Security & Commodity Brokers	6200-6299	52.95	19.70	75.11
Insurance	6300-6399	-0.85	NA	-0.85
Real Estate	6500-6599	12.53	14.72	17.40
Holding, Other Investment Offices	6700-6799	15.40	14.55	15.82
Hotels-Motels	7000-7099	46.21	69.21	40.46
Business Services	7300-7399	32.44	45.41	20.91
Health Care	8000-8099	30.54	-13.65	74.72
Engineering, Accounting, Research, Management, Relations Services	8700-8799	40.77	46.21	19.05

* The percentage change in the stock price for the period 1/01/91 to 9/05/91 is used as a proxy for total return on the stock. The number of observations in the industry sample is smaller than in the preceding tests because industries with fewer than 5 firms were deleted from the sample.

Table 7.A-2

Bottom Quintile of NYSE and AMEX Stocks Classified by Market Capitalization, as of September 5, 1991

ABC	nyse	BIS	amex	DIO	amex	FMR	amex	HWL	nyse	LQP	nyse
ABG	nyse	BKP	nyse	DJI	nyse	FNL	amex	HXL	nyse	LRT	nyse
ACC	amex	BLI	nyse	DLT	nyse	FPO	nyse	IBL	amex	LVI	amex
ACE	nyse	BMC	nyse	DMC	nyse	FRA	nyse	ICL	nyse	LVX	nyse
ACR	nyse	BML	amex	DNA	amex	FRL	nyse	INT	amex	MAR	nyse
ADD	nyse	BNS	nyse	DPT	nyse	FTK	nyse	IOT	nyse	MAX	amex
ADL	amex	BOM	amex	DR	amex	FVF	nyse	IS	nyse	MBC	nyse
ADP	nyse	BPC	amex	DRE	amex	FWF	nyse	ISS	nyse	MCC	nyse
ADU	nyse	BQC	nyse	DRI	nyse	GA	amex	IT	amex	MCO	nyse
ADV	nyse	BRT	nyse	DSG	nyse	GAL	amex	ITG	nyse	MDC	nyse
AEE	nyse	BTX	nyse	DSO	nyse	GBE	nyse	ITI	nyse	MDD	nyse
AFN	amex	BZ	nyse	DVL	nyse	GDC	nyse	IVT	nyse	MDK	amex
AHH	amex	CCM	nyse	DWW	nyse	GEN	nyse	IX	nyse	MDW	amex
AHR	nyse	CCX	nyse	DYA	nyse	GES	nyse	J	amex	MH	nyse
AIM	amex	CEQ	amex	EA	amex	GHW	nyse	JEM	nyse	MJR	amex
AIZ	nyse	CFI	nyse	EB	nyse	GHX	amex	JET	nyse	MLC	amex
AM	nyse	CGE	nyse	ECC	nyse	GNL	nyse	JII	amex	MLE	nyse
AMK	amex	CHF	nyse	ECI	nyse	GPI	amex	JMY	nyse	MMO	nyse
AMM	nyse	CHI	nyse	EDO	nyse	GPO	nyse	JOB	nyse	MMS	amex
AMT	nyse	CHS	nyse	EFG	nyse	GRE	nyse	JOL	nyse	MOR	amex
AND	amex	CHT	nyse	EKO	nyse	GRG	nyse	JPS	nyse	MRT	amex
AOI	amex	CHY	nyse	EKR	nyse	GRH	nyse	KES	nyse	MSB	nyse
AP	nyse	CKP	nyse	ELJ	nyse	GTA	nyse	KGM	nyse	MTR	nyse
APR	nyse	CLU	amex	ELK	amex	GV	nyse	KNO	amex	MTY	amex
ARB	nyse	CME	nyse	EME	nyse	GX	nyse	KNT	nyse	MUN	nyse
ART	amex	CMN	nyse	ENV	nyse	H	amex	KOA	amex	MUS	amex
ARX	nyse	CMP	nyse	EPI	nyse	HAD	nyse	KOG	nyse	MW	nyse
ASB	nyse	CN	nyse	EQK	nyse	HBJ	nyse	KOL	nyse	MYR	nyse
ATA	nyse	CNB	amex	EQM	amex	HBW	nyse	KPI	amex	NBI	nyse

Table 7.A-2 (continued)

ATH	nyse	CNO	amex	EQP	nyse	HCF	amex	KUH	nyse	NCS	nyse
ATL	nyse	COA	nyse	ESE	nyse	HDS	nyse	KVN	nyse	NEG	amex
AVA	nyse	COM	amex	ESG	amex	HFD	nyse	KVU	amex	NEI	nyse
AXR	nyse	COW	nyse	ESI	amex	HFL	nyse	KWN	amex	NHR	nyse
AZ	nyse	CRI	nyse	ESL	nyse	HHC	nyse	KZ	nyse	NIC	nyse
BBE	amex	CRL	nyse	EYE	nyse	HII	amex	LBC	nyse	NLI	amex
BDL	amex	CT	nyse	FBT	nyse	HMG	amex	LCE	nyse	NM	nyse
BET	amex	CUC	nyse	FCH	nyse	HOL.A	amex	LFA	amex	NSB	nyse
BFC	amex	CVI	nyse	FCI	nyse	HOT	nyse	LFC	nyse	NSD	nyse
BFL	nyse	CXV	amex	FE	amex	HPX	nyse	LHC	nyse	NSS	nyse
BFX	amex	CYS	nyse	FFP	nyse	HRA	amex	LI	amex	NTK	nyse
BGL	nyse	CYT	nyse	FFS	nyse	HRE	nyse	LMS	nyse	NTM	nyse
BHA	amex	DC	amex	FGI	nyse	HSI	nyse	LOM	nyse	NUT	nyse
BHY	nyse	DDL	nyse	FLP	nyse	HUG	nyse	LPH	amex	OAK	nyse
BI	nyse	DII	nyse	FLY	amex	HWG	nyse	LPO	amex	OEH	nyse
OFP	nyse	RSI	nyse	TDX	amex	VOT	amex				
OJ	nyse	RTH	nyse	TEL	nyse	VRE	amex				
OPC	nyse	RTI	nyse	TFC	nyse	VS	nyse				
OSI	nyse	RTS	nyse	TG	nyse	VTC	amex				
PAR	amex	RXN	nyse	THK	nyse	VTX	amex				
PAT	nyse	RYR	nyse	THM	nyse	WAX	amex				
PDA	amex	SAI	amex	THO	amex	WBC	amex				
PDQ	nyse	SBM	amex	THP	nyse	WCP	nyse				
PDS	nyse	SBP	nyse	THR	nyse	WDG	nyse				
PFP	amex	SCT	nyse	TI	amex	WHT	amex				
PFS	nyse	SCZ	nyse	TIS	nyse	WID	nyse				
PKE	nyse	SEH	amex	TKA	amex	WJ	nyse				
PLR.A	amex	SEI	nyse	TLX	nyse	WLD	amex				
PLS	amex	SEO	amex	TMR	amex	WN	amex				
PMP	nyse	SF	nyse	TNI.B	nyse	WND	amex				
PMR	amex	SFE	amex	TNY	nyse	WOC	amex				

POR	nyse	SFM	amex	TOD	nyse	WPB	amex
PPC	nyse	SFY	nyse	TOF	amex	WRS	amex
PPI	amex	SIA	nyse	TOK	nyse	WS	nyse
PR	amex	SIZ	nyse	TPL	nyse	WU	nyse
PRT	nyse	SJS	amex	TRG	amex	WWW	nyse
PRX	nyse	SL	nyse	TSK	nyse	ZMX	nyse
PRZ	amex	SLT	nyse	TSY	nyse	ZOS	nyse
PS	nyse	SMG	amex	TT	nyse		
PSO	amex	SMX	nyse	TTN	nyse		
PSX	nyse	SNI	amex	TUG	nyse		
PTC	nyse	SOD	nyse	TXF	nyse		
PTG	amex	SPA	nyse	TYL	nyse		
PTR	nyse	SRE	nyse	UAC	amex		
PUL	nyse	STB	nyse	UFF	nyse		
PWR	amex	STG	amex	UFN	nyse		
PYF	amex	STL	amex	UH	nyse		
QASI	amex	SVB	amex	UI	nyse		
QCHH	nyse	SWL	amex	ULT	nyse		
RAY	nyse	SWV	nyse	UMB	nyse		
RB	nyse	SY	nyse	UNC	nyse		
REC	nyse	SZD	amex	UNT	nyse		
RGC	nyse	SZF	amex	UPK	nyse		
RGL	nyse	TAC	nyse	URS	nyse		
RHH	nyse	TAL	nyse	UTR	nyse		
RHT	amex	TBK	amex	VCC	nyse		
RLI	nyse	TBO	nyse	VCR	amex		
RMK.A	amex	TCC	amex	VDR	amex		
RMS	amex	TCI	nyse	VER	amex		
ROI	nyse	TCR	nyse	VHT	amex		
RPB	amex	TCS	amex	VI	nyse		
RR	nyse	TDD.B	amex	VII	amex		
RRF	nyse	TDI	nyse	VMG	nyse		

Table 7.A-3
Bottom Quintile of NYSE and AMEX Stocks Classified by Market Capitalization Located in States with Increasing Relative Tax Burdens

ADD	nyse	FLY	nyse	MTY	amex	TNI.B	amex
ADV	nyse	FPO	amex	MUN	nyse	TNY	amex
AHR	nyse	FVF	nyse	NEG	amex	TOF	amex
AIM	amex	FWF	nyse	NIC	nyse	TRG	amex
AP	nyse	GA	amex	NM	nyse	TT	nyse
ART	amex	GAL	nyse	NSB	nyse	TTN	nyse
ATH	nyse	GBE	nyse	NSS	nyse	TXF	nyse
BET	amex	GDC	nyse	OAK	nyse	UFF	nyse
BGL	nyse	GEN	nyse	OSI	nyse	UFN	nyse
BI	nyse	GES	amex	PAR	amex	UI	nyse
BKP	nyse	GNL	amex	PAT	nyse	ULT	nyse
BLI	nyse	GRE	nyse	PDA	amex	UMB	nyse
BMC	nyse	GRG	nyse	PDQ	nyse	URS	nyse
BQC	nyse	GTA	nyse	PLR.A	amex	UTR	nyse
CCM	nyse	GX	nyse	PLS	amex	VCC	nyse
CCX	nyse	H	amex	PMP	nyse	VRE	amex
CEQ	amex	HDS	nyse	PRT	nyse	VTC	amex
CFI	nyse	HFD	nyse	PRZ	amex	WCP	nyse
CHT	nyse	HFL	nyse	PSX	nyse	WDG	nyse
CLU	amex	HOT	nyse	PTG	amex	WID	nyse
CME	nyse	HXL	nyse	PUL	nyse	WJ	nyse
CN	nyse	ICN	nyse	PYF	amex	WLD	amex
CT	nyse	IS	nyse	QCHH	nyse	WN	nyse
CXV	amex	IX	amex	RAY	nyse	WOC	nyse
CYT	nyse	J	nyse	RHH	nyse	WU	nyse
DC	amex	JET	amex	RMS	amex	ZMX	nyse
DDL	nyse	JMY	nyse	SAI	amex		
DIO	amex	JOL	amex	SBP	nyse		
DNA	nyse	JPS	amex	SEO	amex		
DVL	nyse	KGM	nyse	SFE	nyse		
DYA	nyse	KOA	amex	SIA	nyse		
EA	nyse	KOL	nyse	SL	nyse		
ECC	nyse	KUH	nyse	SMG	amex		
ECI	amex	KVU	amex	SVB	nyse		
EFG	nyse	LCE	nyse	SZD	amex		
EKO	nyse	LI	amex	SZF	amex		
EME	nyse	LPH	amex	TBK	amex		
EQK	nyse	LPO	amex	TCC	amex		
EQP	nyse	LVX	nyse	TCS	amex		
ESI	amex	MAX	amex	TDD.B	amex		
EYE	nyse	MCC	nyse	TDI	nyse		
FCH	nyse	MCO	nyse	TDX	amex		
FCI	nyse	MLE	nyse	TIS	nyse		
FE	amex	MOR	nyse	TKA	nyse		
FGI	nyse	MRT	nyse	TLX	amex		

Table 7.A-4

Bottom Quintile of NYSE and AMEX Stocks Classified by Market Capitalization Located in States with Decreasing Relative Tax Burdens

ABC	nyse	CHS	nyse	FRL	amex	KWN	amex
ABG	nyse	CHY	nyse	FTK	nyse	KZ	nyse
ACC	amex	CKP	nyse	GHW	nyse	LBC	nyse
ACE	nyse	CMN	nyse	GHX	nyse	LFA	amex
ACR	nyse	CMP	nyse	GPI	nyse	LFC	nyse
ADL	amex	CNB	amex	GPO	nyse	LHC	nyse
ADP	nyse	CNO	amex	GRH	nyse	LMS	nyse
ADU	nyse	COA	nyse	GV	amex	LOM	nyse
AEE	nyse	COM	amex	HAD	nyse	LQP	nyse
AFN	amex	COW	nyse	HBJ	nyse	LRT	nyse
AHH	amex	CRI	nyse	HBW	amex	LVI	nyse
AIZ	nyse	CRL	nyse	HCF	amex	MAR	nyse
AM	nyse	CUC	nyse	HHC	nyse	MBC	nyse
AMK	amex	CVI	nyse	HII	amex	MDC	nyse
AMM	nyse	CXV	amex	HMG	amex	MDD	nyse
AMT	nyse	CYS	nyse	HOL.A	amex	MDK	amex
AND	amex	DII	amex	HPX	nyse	MDW	nyse
AOI	amex	DJI	amex	HRA	amex	MH	nyse
APR	nyse	DLT	nyse	HRE	nyse	MJR	nyse
ARB	nyse	DMC	nyse	HSI	nyse	MLC	nyse
ARX	nyse	DPT	nyse	HUG	nyse	MMO	nyse
ASB	nyse	DR	nyse	HWG	nyse	MMS	amex
ATA	nyse	DRE	nyse	HWL	nyse	MSB	nyse
ATL	nyse	DRI	amex	IBL	amex	MTR	nyse
AVA	nyse	DSG	amex	ICL	nyse	MUS	nyse
AXR	nyse	DSO	nyse	ICM	nyse	MW	amex
AZ	nyse	DWW	nyse	IK	nyse	MYR	nyse
BBE	amex	EB	amex	IMR	nyse	NBI	nyse
BDL	amex	EDO	nyse	INT	nyse	NCS	nyse
BFC	amex	EKR	nyse	IOT	amex	NEI	nyse
BFL	nyse	ELJ	nyse	ISS	nyse	NHR	nyse
BFX	amex	ELK	nyse	IT	nyse	NLI	amex
BHA	amex	ENV	amex	ITG	nyse	NSD	nyse
BHY	nyse	EPI	nyse	ITI	amex	NTK	nyse
BIS	amex	EQM	nyse	IVT	amex	NTM	nyse
BML	amex	ESE	nyse	JEM	amex	NUT	nyse
BNS	nyse	ESG	amex	JII	nyse	OEH	nyse
BOM	amex	ESL	nyse	JOB	amex	OFP	nyse
BPC	amex	FBT	nyse	JPS	amex	OJ	nyse
BRT	nyse	FFP	amex	KES	nyse	OPC	nyse
BTX	nyse	FFS	amex	KNO	nyse	PDS	nyse
BZ	nyse	FLP	nyse	KNT	nyse	PFP	amex
CGE	nyse	FMR	nyse	KOG	nyse	PFS	nyse
CHF	nyse	FNL	nyse	KPI	amex	PKE	nyse
CHI	nyse	FRA	nyse	KVN	nyse	PMR	amex

Table 7.A-4 (continued)

POR	nyse	SWV	nyse
PPC	nyse	SY	nyse
PPI	amex	TAC	nyse
PR	amex	TAL	nyse
PRX	nyse	TBO	nyse
PS	nyse	TCI	nyse
PSO	amex	TCR	nyse
PTC	nyse	TEL	nyse
PTR	nyse	TFC	nyse
PWR	amex	TG	nyse
QASI	amex	THK	nyse
RB	nyse	THM	amex
REC	nyse	THO	nyse
RGC	nyse	THP	amex
RGL	nyse	THR	amex
RHT	amex	TI	amex
RLI	nyse	TMR	amex
RMK.A	amex	TOD	nyse
ROI	nyse	TOK	nyse
RPB	amex	TPL	nyse
RR	nyse	TSK	nyse
RRF	nyse	TSY	nyse
RSI	amex	TUG	nyse
RTH	nyse	TYL	nyse
RTI	nyse	UAC	amex
RTS	nyse	UH	nyse
RXN	nyse	UNC	nyse
RYR	nyse	UNT	nyse
SBM	amex	UPK	nyse
SCT	nyse	VCR	amex
SCZ	nyse	VDR	amex
SEH	amex	VER	amex
SEI	nyse	VHT	amex
SF	nyse	VI	nyse
SFM	amex	VII	amex
SFY	nyse	VMG	nyse
SIZ	nyse	VOT	amex
SJS	amex	VS	nyse
SLT	nyse	VTX	amex
SMX	nyse	WAX	nyse
SNI	amex	WBC	amex
SOD	nyse	WHT	nyse
SPA	nyse	WND	nyse
SRE	nyse	WPB	amex
STB	nyse	WRS	amex
STG	nyse	WS	nyse
STL	nyse	WWW	nyse
SWL	amex	ZOS	nyse

Table 7.A-5
Bottom Quintile of NYSE and AMEX Stocks Classified in High-CATS
Industry Groups

ABC	nyse	CHY	nyse	FLY	nyse	KNT	nyse	OSI	nyse
ACC	amex	CKP	nyse	FPO	amex	KOA	amex	PDA	amex
ACE	nyse	CLU	amex	FRA	nyse	KOG	nyse	PDQ	nyse
ADD	nyse	CME	nyse	FRL	amex	KOL	nyse	PDS	nyse
ADP	nyse	CMN	nyse	FVF	nyse	KUH	nyse	PFP	amex
ADV	nyse	CMP	nyse	FWF	nyse	KVU	amex	PFS	nyse
AEE	nyse	CN	nyse	GA	amex	KZ	nyse	PKE	nyse
AHH	amex	CNB	amex	GAL	nyse	LBC	nyse	PLR.A	amex
AIM	amex	COM	amex	GDC	nyse	LCE	nyse	PMR	amex
AM	nyse	CRI	nyse	GEN	nyse	LFA	amex	POR	nyse
AMK	amex	CRL	nyse	GES	amex	LFC	nyse	PPI	amex
AMM	nyse	CUC	nyse	GHX	nyse	LI	amex	PR	amex
AMT	nyse	CXV	amex	GPO	nyse	LMS	nyse	PRZ	amex
AND	amex	CYS	nyse	GRG	nyse	LQP	nyse	PSO	amex
AP	nyse	CYT	nyse	GTA	nyse	LVI	nyse	PTC	nyse
APR	nyse	DC	amex	GX	nyse	LVX	nyse	PTG	amex
ART	amex	DDL	nyse	H	amex	MAR	nyse	PUL	nyse
ARX	nyse	DII	amex	HBJ	nyse	MAX	amex	PWR	amex
ASB	nyse	DIO	amex	HBW	amex	MBC	nyse	PYF	amex
ATA	nyse	DJI	amex	HCF	amex	MCC	nyse	QASI	amex
ATL	nyse	DMC	nyse	HDS	nyse	MCO	nyse	QCHH	nyse
AVA	nyse	DNA	nyse	HFD	nyse	MDC	nyse	RAY	nyse
AXR	nyse	DPT	nyse	HFL	nyse	MDD	nyse	REC	nyse
BDL	amex	DRI	amex	HHC	nyse	MDK	amex	RGL	nyse
BET	amex	DSG	amex	HII	amex	MDW	nyse	RHT	amex
BFC	amex	DWW	nyse	HRA	amex	MLC	nyse	RLI	nyse
BFL	nyse	DYA	nyse	HUG	nyse	MLE	nyse	RMS	amex
BFX	amex	EA	nyse	HWG	nyse	MMO	nyse	ROI	nyse
BGL	nyse	EB	amex	HWL	nyse	MMS	amex	RR	nyse
BHA	amex	ECC	nyse	IK	nyse	MOR	nyse	RTS	nyse
BHY	nyse	EDO	nyse	INT	nyse	MTY	amex	RYR	nyse
BI	nyse	EFG	nyse	IS	nyse	MUN	nyse	SAI	amex
BIS	amex	EME	nyse	ISS	nyse	MW	amex	SBM	amex
BLI	nyse	EQK	nyse	IT	nyse	NBI	nyse	SCT	nyse
BMC	nyse	ESE	nyse	ITG	nyse	NCS	nyse	SEH	amex
BML	amex	ESG	amex	ITI	amex	NEI	nyse	SEO	amex
BNS	nyse	ESL	nyse	IVT	amex	NHR	nyse	SF	nyse
BOM	amex	EYE	nyse	IX	amex	NIC	nyse	SFE	nyse
BQC	nyse	FBT	nyse	JEM	amex	NLI	amex	SFM	amex
BTX	nyse	FCH	nyse	JET	amex	NM	nyse	SIA	nyse
CGE	nyse	FCI	nyse	JII	nyse	NSB	nyse	SJS	amex
CHF	nyse	FE	amex	JMY	nyse	NTM	nyse	SL	nyse
CHI	nyse	FFS	amex	JOB	amex	OAK	nyse	SLT	nyse
CHS	nyse	FGI	nyse	KGM	nyse	OJ	nyse	SMX	nyse
CHT	nyse	FLP	nyse	KNO	nyse	OPC	nyse	SNI	amex
SOD	nyse	TEL	nyse	TTN	nyse	VRE	amex	WW	nyse
SPA	nyse	TFC	nyse	TXF	nyse	VS	nyse	WS	nyse

Table 7.A-5 (continued)

SRE	nyse	TG	nyse	UAC	amex	VTC	amex
STB	nyse	THM	amex	UFF	nyse	VTX	amex
STL	nyse	THP	amex	UFN	nyse	WAX	nyse
SVB	nyse	TI	amex	UH	nyse	WBC	amex
SWV	nyse	TKA	nyse	UI	nyse	WHT	nyse
SY	nyse	TLX	amex	ULT	nyse	WID	nyse
TAC	nyse	TNY	amex	UMB	nyse	WJ	nyse
TBK	amex	TOF	amex	UTR	nyse	WLD	amex
TCC	amex	TOK	nyse	VCC	nyse	WN	nyse
TCS	amex	TSK	nyse	VCR	amex	WND	nyse
TDI	nyse	TSY	nyse	VER	amex	WS	amex
TDX	amex	TT	nyse	VII	amex	W	nyse

Table 7.A-6
Bottom Quintile of NYSE and AMEX Stocks Classified in Low-CATS Industry Groups

ABG	nyse	GPI	nyse	RB	nyse
ADL	amex	GRE	nyse	RGC	nyse
ADU	nyse	HAD	nyse	RHH	nyse
AFN	amex	HMG	amex	RMK.A	amex
AHR	nyse	HOL.A	amex	RPB	amex
AIZ	nyse	HOT	nyse	RRF	nyse
AOI	amex	HPX	nyse	RSI	amex
ARB	nyse	HRE	nyse	RTH	nyse
ATH	nyse	HSI	nyse	RTI	nyse
AZ	nyse	HXL	nyse	RXN	nyse
BBE	amex	ICL	nyse	SCZ	nyse
BKP	nyse	ICM	nyse	SEI	nyse
BPC	amex	ICN	nyse	SFY	nyse
BRT	nyse	IMR	nyse	SIZ	nyse
BZ	nyse	IOT	amex	SWL	amex
CCX	nyse	JPS	amex	SZD	amex
CEQ	amex	KES	nyse	SZF	amex
CFI	nyse	KPI	amex	TBO	nyse
CNO	amex	KVN	nyse	TCI	nyse
COA	nyse	LHC	nyse	TCR	nyse
COW	nyse	LOM	nyse	THK	nyse
CT	nyse	LPH	amex	THO	nyse
CVI	nyse	LPO	amex	THR	amex
DLT	nyse	LRT	nyse	TIS	nyse
DR	nyse	MJR	nyse	TMR	amex
DRE	nyse	MRT	nyse	TOD	nyse
DSO	nyse	MSB	nyse	TPL	nyse
DVL	nyse	MTR	nyse	TRG	amex
ECI	amex	MUS	nyse	TYL	nyse
EKO	nyse	NEG	amex	UNC	nyse
EKR	nyse	NSD	nyse	UNT	nyse
ELJ	nyse	NSS	nyse	UPK	nyse
ELK	nyse	NTK	nyse	VHT	amex
ENV	amex	OEH	nyse	VI	nyse
EPI	nyse	PAR	amex	VMG	nyse
EQM	nyse	PAT	nyse	VOT	amex
EQP	nyse	PLS	amex	WDG	nyse
ESI	amex	PMP	nyse	WOC	nyse
FMR	nyse	PPC	nyse	WS	nyse
FNL	nyse	PRT	nyse		
FTK	nyse	PRX	nyse		
GBE	nyse	PS	nyse		
GHW	nyse	PSX	nyse		
GNL	amex	PTR	nyse		

Table 7.A-7
Bottom Quintile of NYSE and AMEX Stocks Classified in High-CATS
Industry Groups Located in States with Increasing Relative Tax Burdens

ADD	nyse	HDS	nyse	TCS	amex
ADV	nyse	HFD	nyse	TDI	nyse
AIM	amex	HFL	nyse	TDX	amex
AP	nyse	IS	nyse	TKA	nyse
ART	amex	IX	amex	TLX	amex
BET	amex	JET	amex	TNY	amex
BGL	nyse	JMY	nyse	TOF	amex
BI	nyse	KGM	nyse	TT	nyse
BLI	nyse	KOA	amex	TTN	nyse
BMC	nyse	KOL	nyse	TXF	nyse
BQC	nyse	KUH	nyse	UFF	nyse
CHT	nyse	KVU	amex	UFN	nyse
CLU	amex	LCE	nyse	UI	nyse
CME	nyse	LI	amex	ULT	nyse
CN	nyse	LVX	nyse	UMB	nyse
CYT	nyse	MAX	amex	UTR	nyse
DC	amex	MCC	nyse	VCC	nyse
DDL	nyse	MCO	nyse	VRE	amex
DIO	amex	MLE	nyse	VTC	amex
DNA	nyse	MOR	nyse	WID	nyse
DYA	nyse	MTY	amex	WJ	nyse
EA	nyse	MUN	nyse	WLD	amex
ECC	nyse	NIC	nyse	WN	nyse
EFG	nyse	NM	nyse	WU	nyse
EME	nyse	NSB	nyse		
EQK	nyse	OAK	nyse		
EYE	nyse	OSI	nyse		
FCH	nyse	PDA	amex		
FCI	nyse	PDQ	nyse		
FE	amex	PLR.A	amex		
FGI	nyse	PRZ	amex		
FLY	nyse	PUL	nyse		
FPO	amex	PYF	amex		
FVF	nyse	QCHH	nyse		
FWF	nyse	RAY	nyse		
GA	amex	RMS	amex		
GAL	nyse	SAI	amex		
GDC	nyse	SEO	amex		
GEN	nyse	SFE	nyse		
GES	amex	SIA	nyse		
GRG	nyse	SL	nyse		
GTA	nyse	SVB	nyse		
GX	nyse	TBK	amex		
H	amex	TCC	amex		

Table 7.A-8
Bottom Quintile of NYSE and AMEX Stocks Classified in High-CATS Industry Groups Located in States with Decreasing Relative Tax Burdens

ABC	nyse	DII	amex	LFC	nyse	SCT	nyse
ACC	amex	DJI	amex	LMS	nyse	SEH	amex
ACE	nyse	DMC	nyse	LQP	nyse	SF	nyse
ADP	nyse	DPT	nyse	LVI	nyse	SFM	amex
AEE	nyse	DRI	amex	MAR	nyse	SJS	amex
AHH	amex	DSG	amex	MBC	nyse	SLT	nyse
AM	nyse	DWW	nyse	MDC	nyse	SMX	nyse
AMK	amex	EB	amex	MDD	nyse	SNI	amex
AMM	nyse	EDO	nyse	MDK	amex	SOD	nyse
AMT	nyse	ESE	nyse	MDW	nyse	SPA	nyse
AND	amex	ESG	amex	MLC	nyse	SRE	nyse
APR	nyse	ESL	nyse	MMO	nyse	STB	nyse
ARX	nyse	FBT	nyse	MMS	amex	STL	nyse
ASB	nyse	FFS	amex	MW	amex	SWV	nyse
ATA	nyse	FLP	nyse	NBI	nyse	SY	nyse
ATL	nyse	FRA	nyse	NCS	nyse	TAC	nyse
AVA	nyse	FRL	amex	NEI	nyse	TEL	nyse
AXR	nyse	GHX	nyse	NHR	nyse	TFC	nyse
BDL	amex	GPO	nyse	NLI	amex	TG	nyse
BFC	amex	HBJ	nyse	NTM	nyse	THM	amex
BFL	nyse	HBW	amex	OJ	nyse	THP	amex
BFX	amex	HCF	amex	OPC	nyse	TI	amex
BHA	amex	HHC	nyse	PDS	nyse	TOK	nyse
BHY	nyse	HII	amex	PFP	amex	TSK	nyse
BIS	amex	HRA	amex	PFS	nyse	TSY	nyse
BML	amex	HUG	nyse	PKE	nyse	UAC	amex
BNS	nyse	HWG	nyse	PMR	amex	UH	nyse
BOM	amex	HWL	nyse	POR	nyse	VCR	amex
BTX	nyse	IK	nyse	PPI	amex	VER	amex
CGE	nyse	INT	nyse	PR	amex	VII	amex
CHF	nyse	ISS	nyse	PSO	amex	VS	nyse
CHI	nyse	IT	nyse	PTC	nyse	VTX	amex
CHS	nyse	ITG	nyse	PTG	amex	WAX	nyse
CHY	nyse	ITI	amex	PWR	amex	WBC	amex
CKP	nyse	IVT	amex	QASI	amex	WHT	nyse
CMN	nyse	JEM	amex	REC	nyse	WND	nyse
CMP	nyse	JII	nyse	RGL	nyse	WRS	amex
CNB	amex	JOB	amex	RHT	amex	WWW	nyse
COM	amex	KNO	nyse	RLI	nyse	ZOS	nyse
CRI	nyse	KNT	nyse	ROI	nyse		
CRL	nyse	KOG	nyse	RR	nyse		
CUC	nyse	KZ	nyse	RTS	nyse		
CXV	amex	LBC	nyse	RYR	nyse		
CYS	nyse	LFA	amex	SBM	amex		

Table 7.A-9
Bottom Quintile of NYSE and AMEX Stocks Classified in Low-CATS
Industry Groups Located in States with Decreasing Relative Tax Burdens

AHR	nyse	LPH	amex
ATH	nyse	LPO	amex
BKP	nyse	MRT	nyse
CCX	nyse	NEG	amex
CEQ	amex	NSS	nyse
CFI	nyse	PAR	amex
CT	nyse	PAT	nyse
DVL	nyse	PLS	amex
ECI	amex	PMP	nyse
EKO	nyse	PRT	nyse
EQP	nyse	PSX	nyse
ESI	amex	RHH	nyse
GBE	nyse	SZD	amex
GNL	amex	SZF	amex
GRE	nyse	TIS	nyse
HOT	nyse	TRG	amex
HXL	nyse	WDG	nyse
ICN	nyse	WOC	nyse

Table 7.A-10
Bottom Quintile of NYSE and AMEX Stocks Classified in Low-CATS Industry Groups Located in States with Increasing Relative Tax Burdens

ABG	nyse	KPI	amex	VHT	amex
ADL	amex	KVN	nyse	VI	nyse
ADU	nyse	LHC	nyse	VMG	nyse
AFN	amex	LOM	nyse	VOT	amex
AIZ	nyse	LRT	nyse	WS	nyse
AOI	amex	MJR	nyse		
ARB	nyse	MSB	nyse		
AZ	nyse	MTR	nyse		
BBE	amex	MUS	nyse		
BPC	amex	NSD	nyse		
BRT	nyse	NTK	nyse		
BZ	nyse	OEH	nyse		
CNO	amex	PPC	nyse		
COA	nyse	PRX	nyse		
COW	nyse	PS	nyse		
CVI	nyse	PTR	nyse		
DLT	nyse	RB	nyse		
DR	nyse	RGC	nyse		
DRE	nyse	RMK.A	amex		
DSO	nyse	RPB	amex		
EKR	nyse	RRF	nyse		
ELJ	nyse	RSI	amex		
ELK	nyse	RTH	nyse		
ENV	amex	RTI	nyse		
EPI	nyse	RXN	nyse		
EQM	nyse	SCZ	nyse		
FMR	nyse	SEI	nyse		
FNL	nyse	SFY	nyse		
FTK	nyse	SIZ	nyse		
GHW	nyse	SWL	amex		
GPI	nyse	TBO	nyse		
HAD	nyse	TCI	nyse		
HMG	amex	TCR	nyse		
HOL.A	amex	THK	nyse		
HPX	nyse	THO	nyse		
HRE	nyse	THR	amex		
HSI	nyse	TMR	amex		
ICL	nyse	TOD	nyse		
ICM	nyse	TPL	nyse		
IMR	nyse	TYL	nyse		
IOT	amex	UNC	nyse		
JPS	amex	UNT	nyse		
KES	nyse	UPK	nyse		

Part III

The Political Dimensions of State Economic Policy

8

Reapportionment and State Economic Policy

Victor A. Canto and Robert I. Webb

Under the U.S. Constitution the federal government must conduct a census of the population every 10 years. The principal purpose of the census is to reallocate political power. In particular, the results of the census are used to determine the size of each state's delegation in excess of one to the U.S. House of Representatives. States that experience net increases in population relative to other states are rewarded with larger congressional delegations. Because the number of voting U.S. representatives is fixed at 435, any increase in political representation in the House for states with relatively fast growing populations must come at the expense of states with slower growing populations.[1] Further, because each state is guaranteed at lease one representative, the maximum number of House seats "up for grabs" each decade is 385.

Economic theory suggests that people tend to move to where they can improve their standard of living. As a result, other things being equal, the states with rapidly growing economies are most likely those with rapidly growing populations. There is considerable evidence (e.g., Canto and Webb [1987]) that state economic policy can influence economic growth rates among states and, in turn, labor migration decisions. And, as Smith and Ahmed (1990) point out, labor migration is increasing in importance as an explanation of state population growth. This chapter argues that the impact of state economic policy on labor migration decisions and ultimately population growth rates means that state governments, through their economic policies, can influence reapportionment.

This chapter examines the relationship between decennial changes in relative state tax burdens and decennial changes in relative population growth rates and the net migration component of population growth among states during the time period 1950-87. In particular, it attempts to answer the question of whether decennial changes in relative population growth rates and, ultimately, changes in the size of state congressional delegations are related to state economic policies as measured by decennial changes in relative state tax burdens. The null hypothesis is that there is no consistent relationship between these variables, whereas the alternative hypothesis is that there is a negative relationship. Table 8.1 reports the changes or expected changes in state congressional delegations during the 1950-90 period.

ECONOMIC THEORY

State economic policies, particularly tax policies, influence the level of economic activity in the state by altering the incentives to produce and invest. For instance, changes in tax rates alter the relative prices of labor and leisure and influence the labor force participation decision. This, in turn, will influence the relative amounts of market and (presumably less efficient) household production. Further, state economic policies may also affect the level, timing, and composition of investment spending. Generally speaking, the lower a state's tax burden relative to other states, the greater the incentive to invest in that state.[2]

In an open economy such as ours, where factors are free to move across state political boundaries, state governments are essentially competitors with respect to their economic policies. The idea that state and local governments compete with one another in the conduct of their economic policies was first recognized by Charles Tiebout (1956). This competition results, in large part, from the ability of mobile factors of production to "vote with their feet" by relocating to political jurisdictions pursuing more favorable (to the mobile factor) economic policies.[3] Indeed, Canto and Webb (1987) argue that the observed persistent differential in factor incomes across states in the United States may be largely explained by differences in state economic policies. Moreover, the existence of different economic policies across states suggests that states are not entirely competitors in their economic policies. States are more analogous to monopolists with respect to their taxing power over fixed or relatively fixed factors of production. It is only the output of these factors of production that a state is able to influence through changes in its tax policies. The mobile factor of production is able to escape all but the lowest state tax rate in an integrated economy without internal barriers to factor migration.[4]

States where taxes are high or increasing relative to the national norm tend to experience relative population declines. Likewise, in states where taxes are low and/or falling, population growth is often above average. Congres-

Table 8.1

Changes and Expected Changes in the Size of State Delegations to the House of Representatives, 1950-90

	1950-60	1960-70	1970-80	1980-90*
Alabama	-1	-1	0	0
Alaska**	1	0	0	0
Arizona	1	1	1	2
Arkansas	-2	0	0	0
California	8	5	2	6
Colorado	0	1	1	0
Connecticut	0	0	0	0
Delaware**	0	0	0	0
Florida	4	3	4	3
Georgia	0	0	0	2
Hawaii	2	0	0	0
Idaho	0	0	0	0
Illinois	-1	0	-2	-2
Indiana	0	0	-1	0
Iowa	-1	-1	0	-1
Kansas	-1	0	0	-1
Kentucky	-1	0	0	-1
Louisiana	0	0	0	0
Maine	-1	0	0	0
Maryland	1	0	0	0
Massachusetts	-2	0	-1	-1
Michigan	+1	0	-1	-2
Minnesota	-1	0	0	-1
Mississippi	-1	0	0	0
Missouri	-1	0	-1	0
Montana	0	0	0	-1
Nebraska	-1	0	0	0
Nevada	0	0	1	0
New Hampshire	0	0	0	0
New Jersey	1	0	-1	0
New Mexico	0	0	1	0
New York	-2	-2	-5	-3
North Carolina	-1	0	0	1
North Dakota**	0	-1	0	0
Ohio	+1	-1	-2	-2
Oklahoma	0	0	0	0
Oregon	0	0	1	0
Pennsylvania	-3	-2	-2	-2
Rhode Island	0	0	0	0
South Carolina	0	0	0	0
South Dakota	0	0	-1	0
Tennessee	0	-1	1	0
Texas	1	1	3	4
Utah	0	0	1	0
Vermont**	0	0	0	0
Virginia	0	0	0	1
Washington	0	0	1	0
West Virginia	-1	-1	0	-1
Wisconsin	0	-1	0	-1
Wyoming**	0	0	0	0

* Estimated

** State has the minimum number of Representatives (1) after last apportionment.

sional seats are allocated to states according to population as measured by decadal census data. It therefore follows that state economic policies, in due course, help to determine political power.

Some states are so small that even large changes in their relative tax burdens are not sufficient to warrant a change in their congressional delegations. Likewise, some states are so close to the national norm in tax policies that they, too, experience little change. And finally, while tax policies are important, other factors also play a significant role.

In spite of the myriad qualifications inherent in this type of research, the results are promising. The state tax burden (i.e., state and local revenue collected per $100 of state personal income), as crude as that measure is, is used to gauge the level and changes in state tax policies relative to the nation.

FACTOR MIGRATION

The population of a state changes as the number of births and deaths and net migration change. State economic policy has a twofold impact on factor migration. First, the more (less) favorable the economic environment (or alternatively stated, the incentives to produce) relative to other states, the less (more) likely workers are to leave the state to relocate elsewhere. Second, the more (less) favorable a given state's incentives to produce relative to other states, the more (less) likely it will attract workers from states with less favorable economic environments to relocate there. Simply put, mobile factors will move into states that are lowering tax rates and emigrate from states that are raising tax rates.[5] Significant changes in population of individual states relative to the nation, as a whole, may, in turn, result in a reapportionment of congressional seats.

The hypothesis that state economic policies influence state relative population growth can be tested by examining the relationship between changes in the relative tax burden of a state and factor immigration or emigration.[6] The tax burden of an individual state is assumed to simply equal the ratio of total tax revenues (from all sources) to state personal income for a given calendar year. Obviously, this measure has certain drawbacks but, nevertheless, provides a rough approximation of the true tax burden. It should also be obvious that other factors may affect the factor migration decision besides changes in state relative tax rates. It is one reason why the alternative hypothesis concerns only the *direction* and not the *magnitude* of the relationship. A negative relationship between changes in state relative tax burdens and net immigration would be regarded as a success, whereas the opposite would be regarded as a failure. The binomial test, a nonparametric statistical test, is employed to determine the probability that the string of successes occurred by chance. It is assumed that the probabilities of success or failure are equally likely. These results are reported in Tables 8.2 and 8.3.

Table 8.2
Listing by State of Successes and Failures in the Relationship Between
Changes in Relative State Tax Burdens and State Net Migration for Selected
Periods Between 1950 and 1987

Period	Successes	Total	Failures	Total
1950-1960*	AL, AR, CA, CO, CT FL, GA, ID, IL, IN IA, MS, MT, NH, NJ NM, NY, NC, OH, PA RI, SC, UT, VT, VA WV, WI, WY	28	AZ, DE, KS, KY, LA NE, MD, MA, MI, MN MO, NE, NV, ND, OK OR, SD, TN, TX, WA	20
1960-1970	AZ, CA, CO, FL, GA HI, IL, IN, KY, ME MI**, MN, MO, NE NV, NH, NM, NY, OR PA, TX, UT, WA, WV WI	25	AL, AK, AR, CT, DE ID, IA, KS, LA, MD MA, MS, MT, NJ, NC ND, OH, OK, RI, SC SD, TN, VT, VA, WY	25
1970-1980	AL, AZ, AR, CO, DE FL, GA, ID, IA, KY LA, MA, MN, MO, NE NV, NH, NJ, NM, NC OH, OR, SC, TN, TX UT, VT, VA, WA	29	AK, CA, CT, HI, IL IN, KS, ME, MD, MI MS, MT, NY, ND, OK PA, RI, SD, WV, WI WY	21
1980-1987	AK, AR, CA, CO, CT FL, GA, ID, IN, IA KY, MA, MI, MN, MO NH, NM, NY, OH, OR TX, UT, WV, WI, WY	25	AL, AZ, DE, HI, IL KS, LA, ME, MD, MS MT, NE, NV, NJ, NC ND, OK, PA, RI, SC SD, TN, VT, VA, WA	25

* Excludes Alaska and Hawaii.
** Zero net migration.

It is clear from an examination of the results presented in Table 8.2 that the 1950s and the 1970s are consistent with the alternative hypothesis of a strong negative relationship between changes in state relative tax burdens and net migration. Indeed, as Table 8.3 indicates, the probability that these two strings of successes occurred by chance are 13 and 9 percent, respectively. In contrast, the 1960s and 1980s seem to be consistent with the null hypothesis of no apparent relationship between changes in state relative tax burdens and net migration.

The relatively poor results for the decade of the 1960s may be due, in large part, to de jure and de facto racial discrimination against blacks, which was especially prevalent in many southern states during this and earlier time periods. The often violent denial of basic civil, economic, and political rights restricts the perceived opportunity set of the individuals

Table 8.3
Binomial Probability that String of Successes Occurred by Chance when the Probability of Success of Each Outcome is Equal to 0.5

Period	Number of Successes	Sample Size	Probability
1950-1960*	28	48	.1322
1960-1970	25	50	.5000
(1960-1970)*	24	48	.5000
1970-1980	29	50	.0913
(1970-1980)*	29	48	.0745
1980-1987	25	50	.5000
(1980-1987)*	24	48	.5000
1950-1987	107	198	.1278
(1950-1987)*	105	192	.0744

* Excludes Alaska and Hawaii.

whose rights are denied. Like a system of high relative marginal tax rates, racial discrimination creates disincentives to produce and encourages the discriminated factor to migrate elsewhere. Not surprisingly, there was substantial migration by blacks from the South during this decade. The South, overall, experienced a net outflow of 1,380,000 blacks (or nearly 1 out of every 8) during the 1960s. (Florida, Virginia, and Georgia accounted for the vast majority of the white migrants, with 1,340,000, 206,000, and 198,000 settling in each state, respectively.) For many southern states (Arkansas, Louisiana, Mississippi, North Carolina, South Carolina, and Tennessee), net black emigration more than offset net white immigration to the state. As a result, each of these states is listed as a "failure" in the test of the relationship between changes in relative state tax burdens and state net migration during the decade of the 1960s. In the absence of racial discrimination against blacks, one would expect no difference between the migration patterns of blacks and whites—in which case, black migration to southern states would have mirrored white migration, resulting in 31 successes instead of only 25. (The probability of 31 successes out of 50 drawings is approximately 4.5 percent.)

This empirical analysis assumes that moving costs are zero. Of course, factor migration is influenced not only by the reward for moving but by the cost of moving as well. Other things being equal, the more costly a potential move is, the less likely a factor will make it. It seems reasonable to suppose that moving within the 48 contiguous states is less costly than moving to (or from) Alaska or Hawaii. Consequently, one may argue that Alaska and Hawaii should be excluded from the analysis.

As Table 8.3 indicates, when Hawaii and Alaska are excluded, the probability that the apparent negative relationship between changes in a state's relative tax burden and net migration occurred by chance is 7.4 percent during the period 1950-87. It should be noted that the determination of the probability for the overall period assumes that all the drawings are independent over time, which may not be the case.

Further, if migration costs are nontrivial there will be a gradual—rather than immediate—adjustment of the population across states, as individuals arbitrage the difference in after-tax income across localities.[7] Although trade in goods and factor migration will mitigate regional differences in income, differences in income and factor returns will remain for long periods of time owing to market imperfections. The gradual response to the changing economic conditions will generate *lagged* relationships between population growth and changes in relative tax burdens.

Differences in tax burdens may generate after-tax income differences that will, over time, cover the cost of moving from one locality to another. Empirically, we have chosen changes in state relative tax burden at a particular point in time as well as (decennial) lagged changes in state relative tax burden and state population growth as our characterization of the tax structure that may induce migrations across states. The variables as well as lagged values of population growth characterize adjustment costs.

Table 8.4 reports the estimated equation for the different time periods. In all cases, the previous decade's state population growth is useful in forecasting state population growth. The result is consistent with the partial adjustment hypothesis. If there were prior migration into a particular region, under a partial adjustment the process is expected to continue; hence, a lagged response is to be expected.

As Table 8.4 indicates, decennial changes in state relative tax burden, contemporaneous plus lagged, do have a significant and negative impact on state population growth. The results are consistent with the hypothesis that increases in tax rates will elicit a migration out of the new relatively higher tax areas.

The negative relationship between changes in relative tax burden and economic growth combined with knowledge of enacted and proposed tax legislation can be used to forecast the states most likely to gain or lose congressional seats.

Upon inspection of the empirical results reported in Table 8.4, it is clear that the responsiveness to relative tax burden changes has increased over time. There are two alternative explanations for these results relating to each of the variables used in the empirical analysis. First, one may argue that because the average tax burden has steadily increased over time, greater differences in relative tax burdens are possible. In addition, the variability of the tax burden has increased over time, thereby allowing for a more precise estimate of the coefficient. The evidence appears to be somewhat consistent with such a view, as Table 8.5 shows.

Table 8.4

Population Growth and Relative Tax Burdens (T-statistics in parentheses)

Explanatory Variable	Population Growth Between 1960 and 1970	Population Growth Between 1970 and 1980	Population Growth Between 1980 and 1987
Constant	0.069	0.119	0.018
	(2.610)	(4.630)	(2.014)
DLP560	0.229		
	(4.850)		
DLP670		0.625	
		(5.089)	
DLP780			0.424
			(9.880)
DTB560	1.588		
	(0.805)		
DTB670	-0.493	-5.310	
	(-0.327)	(-3.433)	
DTB780		0.099	-0.735
		(0.227)	(-1.483)
DTB887			-1.893
			(-2.938)
Adjusted R^2	0.315	0.452	0.725
SE	0.084	0.087	0.035
D-W	1.912	1.807	1.856
F-statistic	8.219	14.450	44.093

DLP560 = Population growth between 1950 and 1960
DLP670 = Population growth between 1960 and 1970
DLP780 = Population growth between 1970 and 1980
DTB560 = Difference in relative tax burden between 1950 and 1960
DTB670 = Difference in relative tax burden between 1960 and 1970
DTB780 = Difference in relative tax burden between 1970 and 1980
DTB887 = Difference in relative tax burden between 1980 and 1987

Table 8.5

Summary Statistics of Relative Tax Burdens Across States

Series for Relative Tax Burden	Mean	Standard Deviation	Range Maximum	Minimum
1950	0.044	0.012	0.086	0.022
1960	0.051	0.013	0.084	0.022
1970	0.061	0.012	0.089	0.033
1980	0.066	0.030	0.257	0.030
1987	0.069	0.015	0.111	0.030

A second argument can be made that when tax rates are relatively stable under a progressive tax system (such as in the 1950s) economic growth will drive the tax burden. That is, higher growth will result in a higher tax burden. This will induce a simultaneous equation bias in the estimation technique. If the growth effect is the dominant effect, a positive relationship will be observed. If, on the other hand, the disincentive effects are dominant, a negative relationship will be observed.

Table 8.6 reports the relationship between changes in a state's relative tax burden and changes (or expected changes) in the size of its congressional delegation. Keep in mind that most states will not experience a change in the size of their congressional delegation. Table 8.7 reports the probability that the observed relationship occurred by chance. The empirical evidence supports the alternative hypothesis. While there is substantial variation across decades in the size of the probability, it is clear that a negative relationship exists between changes in a given state's relative tax burden and changes in the size of its congressional delegation. Moreover, the probability that the result occurred by chance over the 40-year period is less than 2 percent. This suggests that state economic policy, by influencing factor migration decisions, ultimately influences congressional reapportionment decisions.

Table 8.6
Listing by State of Successes and Failures in the Relationship Between Changes in Relative State Tax Burdens and Changes or Expected Changes in the Size of State Congressional Delegations, 1950-90

Period	Successes	Total	Failures	Total
1950-1960*	AL, AR, CA, FL, IA MN, MI, MS, NJ, NC OH, PA, WV	13	AZ, IL, KS, KY, MA ME, MD, MO, NE, NY TX	11
1960-1970	AZ, CA, CO, FL, IA NY, PA, TX, WV, WI	10	AL, ND, OH, TN	4
1970-1980	AZ, CO, FL, MA, NV NJ, NM, OH, OR, TN TX, VT, WA	13	CA, IA, IN, MI MO, NY, PA, SD	8
1980-1987	CA, FL, GA, IA, KY MA, MN, MI, NY, OH TX, WV, WI	13	AZ, IL, KS, MT NC, PA, VA	7

* Excludes Alaska and Hawaii.

Table 8.7
Binomial Probability that String of Successes Occurred by Chance with Probability of Success of Each Outcome Equal to 0.5

Period	Number of Successes	Sample Size	Probability
1950-1960*	13	24	.4194
1960-1970	10	14	.0898
1970-1980	13	21	.1917
1980-1990 (est.)	13	20	.1316
Overall	49	79	.0162

* Excludes Alaska and Hawaii

TAX BURDEN, MIGRATION AND REAPPORTIONMENT: AN EXPLANATION

The empirical results suggest a strong link between a state's relative tax burden and a state's migration. The presence of laggerd relationships is consistent with the argument that migration is costly and adjustment to arbitrage differences in after-tax income will be a gradual one. The results identified differences in the strength of the relationship over time. These were largely attributable to the quality of the data. Objections to the quality of the data are not present during the 1970s and 1980s; hence, the equations for those periods will be used to project the congressional reapportionment by states.

The procedure is as follows: The changes in tax burden and previous population growth are used to calculate projected population growth in each state. The projected increase plus the original state population are then divided by the U.S. population, thereby obtaining the state pro rata share of the congressional delegation. The fraction multiplied by the number of congressional seats, 435, and rounded to the nearest integer gives the projected congressional delegation by state.

A comparison of the number of congressional seats forecasted versus actual number of congressional seats for each state is reported in Table 8.8. Another nonparametric test, the Spearman rank correlation coefficient, can be used to measure the correlation between the actual and the fitted value of population growth transformed to yield the number of representatives by states.[8] This can be interpreted as a measure of the model's explanatory power and is reported in Table 8.9. Whether one compares the number of changes in congressional seats, the projected reapportionment of congressional seats during the last two decades and the current, the Spearman rank correlation coefficients (of 0.996, 0.99, and 0.99, respectively) and the cor-

Table 8.8
Representatives by State: Actual Versus Forecast for Election Year
After Apportionment

	Actual 1972	Forecast for 1972	Actual 1982	Forecast for 1982	Estimated 1992*	Forecast for 1992
Alabama	7	8	7	7	7	8
Alaska	1	1	1	1	1	1
Arizona	4	3	5	4	7	6
Arkansas	4	4	4	4	4	5
California	43	40	45	46	51	46
Colorado	5	6	6	5	6	6
Connecticut	6	6	6	6	6	6
Delaware	1	1	1	1	1	1
Florida	15	13	19	17	22	21
Georgia	10	10	10	10	12	11
Hawaii	2	2	2	2	2	2
Idaho	2	2	2	2	2	2
Illinois	24	24	22	21	20	22
Indiana	11	11	10	11	10	10
Iowa	6	7	6	6	5	5
Kansas	5	5	5	5	4	4
Kentucky	7	7	7	6	6	7
Louisiana	8	8	8	9	8	8
Maine	2	2	2	2	2	2
Maryland	8	8	8	9	8	8
Massachusetts	12	12	11	12	10	10
Michigan	19	19	18	19	17	17
Minnesota	8	8	8	8	6	8
Mississippi	5	5	5	5	5	5
Missouri	10	10	9	9	9	9
Montana	2	2	2	1	2	2
Nebraska	3	3	3	3	3	3
Nevada	1	1	2	1	2	2
New Hampshire	2	1	2	2	2	2
New Jersey	15	15	14	15	14	14
New Mexico	2	2	3	2	3	3
New York	39	40	34	36	31	31
North Carolina	11	11	11	11	12	11
North Dakota	1	1	1	1	1	1
Ohio	23	24	21	23	19	20
Oklahoma	6	5	6	6	6	6
Oregon	4	4	5	5	5	5
Pennsylvania	25	27	23	23	21	22
Rhode Island	2	2	2	2	2	2
South Carolina	6	6	6	6	6	6
South Dakota	2	2	1	1	1	1
Tennessee	8	9	9	9	9	9
Texas	24	24	27	25	31	29
Utah	2	2	3	2	3	3
Vermont	1	1	1	1	1	1
Virginia	10	10	10	10	11	10
Washington	7	7	8	8	8	8
West Virginia	4	4	4	3	3	4
Wisconsin	9	9	9	9	8	9
Wyoming	1	1	1	1	1	1

* 1989 "Statistical Abstract of the United States," U.S. Department of Commerce.

Table 8.9
Spearman Rank Correlation Coefficient and T-Statistics

Decade	1970s	1980s	1990s
Spearman Rank Correlation	.996	.99	.99
T-Statistic	8.96	8.94	8.94

responding *t*-statistics (of 8.96, 8.94, and 8.94, respectively) indicate that the forecast series conforms quite well to the actual reapportionment. The results clearly suggest that changes in the relative tax burden and past population growth may be used to project reapportionment.

POTENTIAL IMPACT ON THE HOUSE OF REPRESENTATIVES

One issue of particular interest to economists is the impact of changing population patterns on the House of Representatives. However, the political composition of Congress will depend on the degree of gerrymandering of congressional districts.

State legislators are the real power brokers because they generally draw the borders for new districts.

Incumbency and sweetheart deals often compensate for partisanship, but gaining seats in a body dominated by one party can reconfigure the prospects for redistricting. Democrats control both houses of the state legislature in 33 states, which includes 6 of the 7 states likely to gain congressional seats and 7 of the 13 states expected to lose seats.

Having the governorship in most states is another key element because a redistricting bill is like any other piece of legislation: It must make its way through the state legislature and be signed by the governor. The big winners in reapportionment—California, Texas, and Florida—currently have Republican (R) governors, but each was up for reelection in 1990. California's Senator Pete Wilson (R), reelected to the Senate in 1988, nevertheless announced in 1989 that he would run for governor, citing reapportionment as one reason for his move. Georgia, Arizona, and the "big three" were gaining states with gubernatorial races in 1990. Of the losing states, New York, Pennsylvania, Illinois, Ohio, Michigan, Massachusetts, Wisconsin, Iowa, Kansas, and Minnesota also had gubernatorial races in 1990.

In theory, having a Republican governor will help, but state political dynamics may override partisanship. In states where they do not control the state legislature, governors are forced to compromise. Having more Republicans in the House may not make it any easier for a Republican governor to lead back home. There is also no guarantee that state legislators or governors are the only players.

The expansion of the Voting Rights Act during the 1980s will make plans subject to a new test of fairness and nondiscrimination toward minorities and communities of interest. The old guidelines forced suits to prove intent to discriminate; new provisions merely require that the effect be to discriminate. The Justice Department and the courts will have a greater role in determining what plans were rejected.[9]

To illustrate the pervasiveness of gerrymandering, in 180 races for Congress in California since 1982, only one seat has changed parties. The late representative Phil Burton drew a map that, in 1984, allowed Democrats to win 60 percent of California's House seats even while Republicans won a majority of votes statewide. Californians are making attempts to curb gerrymandering. It would take the power to redistrict away from the state legislature and place it with a 12-member commission selected by three retired judges.[10] Gerrymandering protects incumbents from political challenges. Nationwide, 98 percent of incumbents were returned to office, and in 1988, only 38 out of 435 members won with less than 55 percent of the vote.[11]

The reapportionment of congressional seats based on population growth will have an impact on the distribution of congressional seats between the Democratic and Republican parties. Two questions immediately come to mind: Which party will benefit from the migration patterns? and How will gerrymandering affect the parties' gains or losses due to the shifting population?

CONCLUSIONS

Relative population shifts among states appear to be strongly negatively related to changes in the relative tax burden among states during the 1950-90 period. Further, these population shifts have often resulted in changes in the size of the state congressional delegation. Although a number of factors may explain these population shifts and the resultant changes in the size of state congressional delegations after reapportionment, the evidence suggests that state economic policy, by influencing state economic growth and factor migration decisions, plays an important role.

NOTES

1. Under the Apportionment Act of August 8, 1911, Congress effectively fixed the number of voting representatives to the House at 435. (The District of Columbia has a nonvoting delegate to the U.S. House of Representatives.) The number of voting representatives can exceed 435 if new states are admitted to the Union after the apportionment associated with the most recent census has occurred. Typically, the legislation enacting statehood also contains a provision requiring the return to 435

representatives after the next reapportionment. For instance, the admission of both Alaska and Hawaii in 1959 resulted in 437 representatives to the House until after the election following the apportionment resulting from the 1960 census (that is, until the next Congress convened in 1963).

2. In addition, Chapter 7 points out that state economic policies, by changing the stream of expected future after-tax profits, can influence the value of equity securities of companies principally located in the state undertaking the change.

3. Rather than moving from a political jurisdiction, government policies may lead to a dissolution of it. Recently, Buchanan and Faith (1987) have advanced a theory of "internal exit" to explain the phenomenon of secessions.

4. Of course, state and local governments raise tax revenues in order to provide goods and services desired by constituents. While it is possible that constituents may value the goods and services higher than or equal to their cost, it is assumed that they will be valued at less than their cost. Consequently, from a competitive point of view, changes in relative tax burdens among states are more important than the composition of government expenditures in influencing factor migration decisions. States lowering their relative tax burdens can be expected to experience accelerated economic growth and net factor immigration, whereas those increasing their relative tax burdens should exhibit a slower pace of economic expansion and net factor emigration.

5. It should be noted that the mobility characteristic of Americans is not constant over age groups. Younger workers are more likely to move across state lines than are older workers. The willingness of younger workers to move may exert some impact on birth and death rates across states.

6. Ideally, one would want to examine the relationship between *expected* changes in the relative tax burden of individual states and net migration. Owing to data limitations, the actual tax burden is used instead. This is tantamount to assuming perfect foresight among individuals.

7. For example, Sjaastad (1962) considers the costs of factor migration.

8. As used in our approach, the actual values of a series and the fitted values from the regression are each ranked by size. The correspondence between the rankings is then computed. The use of ranks rather than the actual values means that unusually high or low values do not distort the relationship. The significance level associated with a Spearman rank correlation coefficient is denoted by the t-statistic.

9. Elizabeth McCaughey, "Perverting the Voting Rights Act," *Wall Street Journal*, October 29, 1989, p. A18.

10. "Assault on the Gerrymander," *Wall Street Journal*, editorial, December 12, 1989, p. A14.

11. "High-Tech Vote Grabbing," *Wall Street Journal*, editorial, May 12, 1989, p. A14; and Paul A. Gigot, "Incumbent for Life: I Came, I Saw, I Gerrymandered," *Wall Street Journal*, November 4, 1989, p. A14.

REFERENCES

Becker, G. "A Theory of the Allocation of Time." *Economic Journal* 75, no. 299 September 1965): 493-517.

Buchanan, J., and R. Faith. "Secession and the Limits of Taxation: Toward a Theory of Internal Exit." *American Economic Review* (December 1987): 1023-31.

Canto, V., D. Joines, and R. Webb. "The Revenue Effects of the Kennedy and Reagan Tax Cuts: Some Time Series Estimates." *Journal of Business and Economic Statistics* 4 (July 1986): 281-88.

Canto, V., and A. Laffer. "A Not-So-Odd Couple: Small Cap Stocks and the State Competitive Environment." *Financial Analysts Journal* 45 (March/April 1989): 75-78.

Canto, V., and R. Webb. "The Effect of State Fiscal Policy on State Relative Economic Performance." *Southern Economic Journal* (July 1987): 186-202.

Hollander, M., and D. Wolfe. *Nonparametric Statistical Methods.* New York: John Wiley & Sons, 1973.

Sjaastad, L. A. "The Costs and Returns of Human Migration." *Journal of Political Economy* 70, no. 5, pt. 2 (October 1962): 80-93.

Smith, S. K., and B. Ahmed. "A Demographic Analysis of the Population Growth of States, 1950-1980." *Journal of Regional Science*, 30, no. 2 (1990): 209-27.

Tiebout, C. M. "A Pure Theory of Local Expenditure." *Journal of Political Economy* 64 (October 1956): 416-24.

U.S. Congress, House of Representatives. "The Decennial Population Census and Congressional Apportionment." 91st Cong., 2d sess., Report #91-1314, 1970.

U.S. Government, Commerce Department. *Statistical Abstract of the United States,* selected years, 1952-1989. Washington, DC: GPO.

9

The Jarvis-Gann Tax Cut Proposal: An Application of the Laffer Curve

Charles W. Kadlec and Arthur B. Laffer

On June 6, 1978, Californians approved Proposition 13—popularly known as the Jarvis-Gann initiative. Property tax rates on homes, businesses, and farms will be cut more than 50 percent to a rate of 1 percent of a property's 1975/76 assessed market value. Moreover, future tax rate increases will be curtailed sharply. Increases in tax collections from the reassessment of property will be limited to 2 percent a year as long as the property is not sold. And the majority required in the state legislature to increase any other tax rate will be increased to two thirds from a simple majority today.

Without considering any other economic effects, the tax rate cut will reduce property tax revenues from an estimated $12.5 billion in 1978/79 to about $5.5 billion. As a result, many groups—California businessmen, who fear higher nonproperty business taxes to maintain current spending levels; banks, which are understandably concerned about the values of their municipal bond portfolios; and public employed labor unions, which fear layoffs—oppose the tax cut. Moody's Investors Services, Inc. has suspended its rating on the existing $1.6 billion outstanding tax allocation bonds from California.

In our view, their concerns are exaggerated for two reasons:

- Property tax revenues will fall by less than $7 billion because of an increase in the property tax base.
- Total tax revenues most likely will rise because the increase in general economic activity in California will produce significantly higher income, sales, and other tax revenues.

THE ECONOMIC IMPACT

An immediate effect of the approval of Proposition 13 will be a decrease in the after-tax cost of house ownership. As a result, demand for single family houses will increase, and the market value of housing will rise. Higher property values, in turn, will spur new housing construction. Thus, in short order, the higher value of houses and the lower after-tax cost of home ownership will increase both the supply and demand for single family houses.

Similarly, the cost of rental housing will fall, and the supply of multi-family units will rise. Current rents reflect, in part, the rent-versus-buy cost trade-off to the household and the alternative uses of capital for rental unit owners. Thus, the cost reduction of home ownership implied by passage of Jarvis-Gann will reduce rents until the cost trade-off is restored. Just as important, the property tax rate cut will increase the after-tax rate of return on rental units. Since capital employed in rental housing is a close substitute for capital employed elsewhere, this increase will attract more capital and lead to the construction of more apartment units until the profitability of rental units returns to its market-determined equilibrium level. The increased supply of rental units also will cause rents to fall. Again, both the supply and demand for rental units will rise to a new equilibrium level.

Businesses also will be affected by the property tax cut. The after-tax cost of locating offices or plants in California will fall, thereby increasing demand for California real estate. And the after-tax returns to owners of commercial property will jump, leading to increased construction of commercial and industrial facilities.

Combined, the expected increase in supply and demand for residential and commercial construction will expand the property tax base in California significantly. Such a building boom will be but the leading edge in a surge of economic activity that will, in turn, produce more income, sales, and other tax revenues to state and local governments. For example, higher levels of employment among construction workers and among workers in other businesses supporting the building industry will directly boost total income and sales levels in the California economy. In addition, the California economy will benefit by luring economic activity away from other states. With property taxes lower, other businesses will expand existing activities or locate new activities within the state, creating still more jobs, more investment, higher real wages, and a new, high equilibrium level of economic activity.

Finally, Proposition 13 is expected to reduce significantly the level of government expenditure for social welfare programs. The improved economic performance of the state implies directly higher levels of employment and lower levels of state expenditures for unemployment, rent subsidies, aid to families with dependent children, and medical and other social welfare programs.

THE NET REVENUE EFFECT: AN ESTIMATE

In order to estimate the impact of a property tax cut in California, a cross section of 20 states was analyzed for the impact of changes in property taxes and, separately, all other taxes on the relative growth in personal income between 1965 and 1975. The 20 states with the largest property tax revenues according to state and local governments were used in the sample (Table 9.1).

Theoretically, any increase in a marginal tax rate in one state relative to other states would slow economic activity and result in a lower aggregate personal income. Thus, the states with the largest increase in marginal tax rates would be expected to have the smallest growth in personal income over the 10-year period. Consistent data on marginal tax rates were not available, so changes in the level of tax revenues as a percent of total personal income, the "tax burden," were used as a proxy for changes in tax rates. This analysis suggests that, on average,

• For each one percentage point increase in the property tax burden, personal income drops about 16 percent below its no-tax-increase level.

Table 9.1
Tax Revenues and Personal Income (in millions of dollars)

	1975			1965		
	Property Taxes	Other Taxes	Personal Income	Property Taxes	Other Taxes	Personal Income
California	7,909	10,493	138,719	3,325	3,398	59,817
New York	6,681	11,894	118,248	2,872	3,854	58,568
Illinois	3,131	5,007	75,798	1,429	1,406	34,837
New Jersey	3,019	2,289	49,591	1,170	651	22,395
Michigan	2,671	3,572	54,463	1,059	1,322	25,389
Massachusetts	2,509	2,233	35,156	930	685	16,408
Texas	2,343	3,961	68,327	979	1,206	24,531
Ohio	2,176	3,568	61,981	1,195	1,113	29,126
Pennsylvania	1,931	5.596	69,642	956	1,867	31,788
Florida	1,359	2,998	46,320	507	846	14,319
Wisconsin	1,249	2,064	25,640	582	701	11,368
Indiana	1,229	1,851	29,602	616	640	13,713
Connecticut	1,088	1,069	21,086	431	394	9,864
Minnesota	908	2,054	22,597	563	501	9,494
Missouri	876	1,615	26,023	401	600	11,871
Maryland	871	2,111	26,117	377	542	10,561
Washington	815	1,580	22,341	285	594	8,729
Georgia	800	1,702	24,734	255	577	9,432
Virginia	782	2,014	28,774	300	538	10,890
Iowa	754	1,075	16,783	429	333	7,441

Sources: Bureau of Census and Bureau of Economic Analysis.

- For each one percentage point increase in the other tax burden, personal income drops about 17.5 percent below its no-tax-increase level.

The actual and predicted levels of personal income in 1975, based on 1965 personal income levels for each of the states, are summarized in Figure 9.1. If the predicted and actual 1975 levels of personal income are the same, the point will fall on the solid line. If the predicted level was less than actual, the point is below the line, and vice versa.

The closeness of the fit is striking, given the many variables not quantified in the analysis—such as the differences in climates; average age of plant and equipment; skill of labor force; changes in tax burdens of neighboring states; and wide variations in the distribution of state and local expenditures among such competing budget items as schools, police and fire departments, welfare and social services, unemployment compensation, and highways. Nearly 40 percent of the difference between states in the growth of aggregate personal income over this period can be explained by the change in the burden of property and other taxes on personal income.

Based on this 10-year statistical relationship, passage of the Jarvis-Gann initiative could mean:

- A $110 billion increase in personal income above where it otherwise would be.
- A $4 billion loss in property tax revenue instead of the forecasted $7 billion loss.

Figure 9.1
1975 Total Personal Income by State: Actual Versus Expected

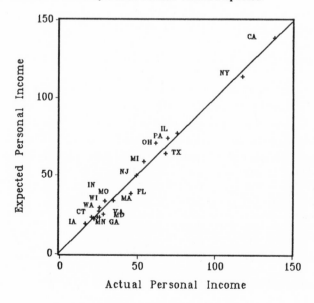

- An \$8 billion increase in other state and local tax revenues.
- A \$4 billion net increase in total state and local tax revenues.

The increases in the property tax base, personal income, and other tax revenues would flow, in part, from improved allocations of existing capital and labor within California made possible by the reduction in the property tax wedge and increased incentives to work and invest. In addition, increased amounts of both capital and labor can be expected to flow to California from other states and abroad.

Therefore, we believe that passage of Proposition 13 could boost aggregate personal income in California \$20 billion or more above what it otherwise would be during the next 12 months; that nearly half of the income and tax revenue impact will occur within the next 2 years; and that the full estimated \$110 billion increment to aggregate personal income in California will be realized within 10 years.

As a direct consequence of this growth in economic activity, social welfare spending should decline. The combined effect implies that California governments would, in short order, be back in surplus and that there is little cause for sharp reduction in spending, especially for such constitutionally mandated programs as schools and essential services such as fire and police protection.

INVESTMENT IMPLICATIONS

With the passage of Proposition 13:

1. Immigration of capital and labor into California from the rest of the nation and abroad will accelerate.

2. State or municipal bonds funded only by specific property tax revenues most likely will be impaired.

3. The quality of state and municipal bonds collateralized by general revenues most likely will be enhanced.

4. Sales and profits of corporations dependent on the California market or with large operations in the state (e.g., construction companies; banks; retail, wholesale, and industrial goods suppliers) will improve, on average, relative to all other companies.

5. A real-world test of the idea that cutting tax rates can lead to higher tax revenues is now forthcoming. Once this concept embodied in the Laffer curve is better understood and accepted, the probability of tax rate cuts at both the national and local levels will increase. The improved outlook for lower tax rates alone will affect stock and bond prices positively.

10

Is the California Tax Revolt Over? An Analysis of California's Proposition 111

Arthur B. Laffer
assisted by Christopher S. Hammond

The proponents of Propositions 111 and 108 are not rigorously trained to understand the impact these two propositions will have on the life-style of California. Nor are they broadly experienced to comprehend the magnitude of the disservice they do their fellow citizens. Undoubtedly, they believe deeply in what they preach, but they are just as wrong as if their statements arose from conscious deceit and conspiracy. The innocence of their ignorance does not shield California from the very real consequences of their deeds. The heat of their rhetoric belies the depth of their knowledge. In the words of Bertrand Russell:

> Persecution is used in theology, not in arithmetic, because in arithmetic there is knowledge, but in theology there is only opinion. So whenever you find yourself getting angry about a difference of opinion, be on your guard; you will probably find, on examination, that your belief is getting beyond what the evidence warrants.[1]

To assert that additional highway funds could be used productively in California is scarcely convincing as an argument for Propositions 111 and 108. To wag a finger at rush-hour congestion with that all-knowing conceit is disingenuous at the least and most likely dissembling. The case for passage of Propositions 111 and 108 does not measure up to the mark. Much more would have to be argued than can be argued to make the case for passage of Propositions 111 and 108.

The first condition that would have to be established is the actual extent

of California's highway needs. The urgency of California's needs is far
from obvious, especially when compared with other states. One's experience
with the byways and highways of New York, Cleveland, Boston, Detroit,
Chicago, or Dallas instills a great deal of appreciation for California.

But even if more highways were needed, there would still be no need to
raise taxes as is proposed by Propositions 111 and 108. And even if it were
necessary to raise taxes, the Gann spending limit does not need to be gutted,
as it would be if Propositions 111 and 108 were to pass.

The benefits that could reasonably be expected to result from the passage
of these propositions fall far short of the costs. California will be hurt for
years to come.

Propositions 111 and 108 would materially raise California's tax burden:
(1) an additional $0.09 per gallon gas tax, (2) an additional sales tax on top
of the gas tax itself, and (3) a weight tax on trucks. They would also weaken
the Gann spending limit beyond the point of recognition: (1) The new taxes
would not be subject to the limitation; (2) capital expenditure would be
excluded from the limitations; and (3) the formula for calculating the spending limits would be loosened. California would also be authorized to issue an
additional $3 billion worth of debt and commit California's taxpayers to both
interest payments and principal repayments for years to come.

What Propositions 111 and 108 promise in return is far greater state
spending on highways and light rail as well as greater spending on a whole
host of other state projects. There is something in these propositions for
almost every special interest group.

If passed, Propositions 111 and 108 would have a major impact on the
future path of California's economy. This impact is not as the proponents
would have us believe. Instead, California's growth would be lowered, and
within a few short years, California's unemployment rate would rise by
about 1.5 percent above where it would otherwise have been—all as a direct
consequence of Propositions 111 and 108.

Good theory is nothing if not the rigorous application of common sense
predicated on comprehensive experience. And goodness knows California
has experienced just about everything. To anyone open-minded enough to
learn from California's lessons of the past, the message is unambiguous:
The power to tax is the power to destroy.

Figure 10.1 plots state and local general revenues per $1,000 of state
personal income for California and the average for all states. Figure 10.2 is
a plot of California's unemployment rate and the unemployment rate for
the nation as a whole. And Figure 10.3 is derived from Figures 10.1 and
10.2. It is a plot of the difference between California's and the nation's tax
burden and the difference between California's unemployment rate and the
nation's. No one could possibly doubt the power of this statistical relationship. In California, higher taxes mean higher unemployment.

For the United States as a whole, there have been a number of studies
documenting rigorously the negative relationship between state taxes and

Figure 10.1
State and Local (Own-Source) General Revenue*

$ per $1,000
personal income

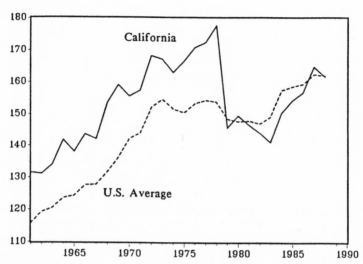

* Excludes federal grants-in-aid, insurance trust revenue, liquor store revenue, and public utility revenue.

Source: U.S. Bureau of the Census, *Government Finances in* (fiscal year).

Figure 10.2
Unemployment Rates for California and the United States

Percent

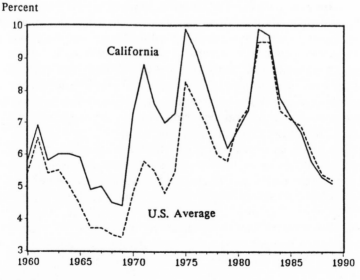

Source: U.S. Department of Labor.

Figure 10.3
Tax Burden Versus Unemployment

Difference Between
    CA and U.S.
(Percentage Points)

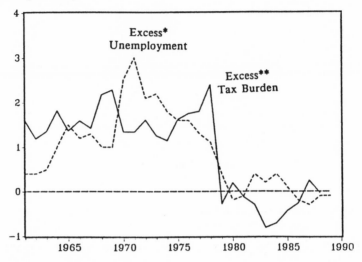

*   California rate minus U.S. rate.

**   California own source general revenues as a percentage of
personal income minus U.S. average.

a state's economic well-being. These findings reconfirm exactly what happens in California. Academic study after academic study has painstakingly documented the empirical association between a state's tax policy and its economic performance. Raising the tax burden raises unemployment rates.

But as convincing as the evidence is, legislators are quick to turn a blind eye and persist in their praise of higher taxation and spending. The numbers, however, tell the true story clearly. If California undoes the tax and spending controls put in place over the past 12 years, the economic prosperity of the last 12 years will stop as well. California will once again become a high unemployment state.

The conceptual case is equally as convincing as the evidence. Imagine two companies that sell the same products and are separated by 40 miles and the California-Oregon state line. Because both companies compete in a national market, that competition forces them to price their product at roughly equivalent prices. Because both companies operate in the same labor market, they have to pay their employees essentially the same after-tax wages. The two companies also face similar interest charges on their borrowings and have to pay similar costs for raw materials.

Now imagine that California increases its taxes and Oregon does not. What can the California company do? The California company cannot pass the new tax forward in higher prices or pass the new tax backward in lower wages. It will have to swallow the increased tax. In general, the increased tax in California will lead to reduced profitability for the California company, reduced asset values, and slower expansion.

With the passage of Propositions 111 and 108, California's personal income growth, too, will fall below its potential, leaving in its wake more poverty and more problems that go hand in hand with poverty. Immigration from other states would decline, as would tourism (Figure 10.4). It is a short step in logic to see how serious the consequences would be for most of California's real estate and construction industries.

As a result of lower growth, reduced profitability, and higher unemployment, the assumptions underlying California's projected budget for the rest of this century will not be met. State and local tax reciepts will fall short of the estimates, and expenditures—especially those to help those in need—will exceed expectations. While these supply-side effects will take time to materialize, they will, in due course, wreak havoc on the state's budget. Chronic fiscal crises mired in a sluggish economy will be the order of the day for California in the mid-1990s.

Figure 10.4
Population Growth

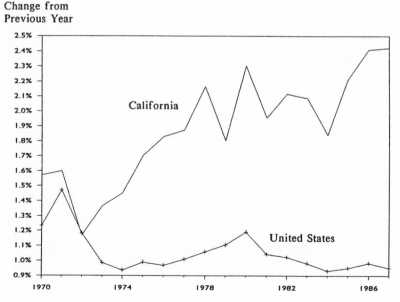

Source: U.S. Bureau of the Census.

If this argument on the ultimate budgeting impact of Propositions 111 and 108 seems farfetched, it is only because people are not used to thinking in terms of economic dynamics. One look at Massachuetts from "Taxachusetts" to the "Massachusetts miracle" back to "Taxachusetts" should be proof enough as to what can happen. Each state has its own unique history of taxation and economic growth, but the theme underlying each and every one of them is the same. Large tax increases are at best a short-run palliative for state budgets but are invariably a long-run disaster.

California's own fiscal history tells the same story. Over a decade ago, Charles Kadlec and I wrote an analysis of what we thought would be the consequences of Proposition 13:

> Therefore, we believe that passage of Proposition 13 could boost aggregate personal income in California $20 billion or more above what it otherwise would be during the next twelve months; that nearly half of the income and tax revenue impact will occur within the next two years; and that the full estimated $110 billion increment to aggregate personal income in California will be realized within ten years.
>
> As a direct consequence of this growth in economic activity, social welfare spending should decline. The combined effect implies that California governments would, in short order, be back in surplus, and that there is little cause for sharp reduction in spending, especially for such constitutionally mandated programs as schools and essential services such as fire and police protection.[2]

The analytic framework used then is just as true today. The passage of Propositions 111 and 108 and other tax increases that are bound to follow will severely damage the California economy and will not satiate the incredible appetite of our government.

A point illustrated by the California-Oregon example is that the origins of a tax—whether income, sales, gas, or property—are not material in determining the overall impact on the state's economy. Quite simply, the incidence of a tax is totally different from the burden of that tax. Mobile products and factors that can move quickly and cheaply will not suffer. Immobile factors, however, that cannot move easily will bear the lion's share of the tax hike. The longer the economy has to adjust to the increased tax, the greater will be the adjustment. It is hard to imagine anything less mobile than property and poor people.

As a result of the passage of these propositions, property values will fall, and California will take on the aura of its sister states Massachusetts, Connecticut, New York, New Jersey, and Arizona, to name a few (Table 10.1). Property values are always the first to suffer from escalating state taxation and are among the hardest hit areas as well. Those properties associated with

Table 10.1
Percentage Change in Residential Unit Prices from Third Quarter 1988 to Third Quarter 1989

Metropolitan Area*	Percentage Change	Metropolitan Area*	Percentage Change
San Francisco Bay	23.1%	Providence	0.1%
Seattle/Tacoma	22.5	Boston	-0.3
Honolulu	21.7	New Haven/Meridan	-2.9
Los Angeles	18.7	NYC/N. NJ/Long Island	-4.9
San Bernadino/Riverside	17.4	Phoenix	-6.1
San Diego	17.3	Worcester	-7.2

* All areas are metropolitan statistical areas as defined by the U.S. Office of Management and Budget. They include the named central city and surrounding areas.

Source: National Association of Realtors, *Home Sales Yearbook*, 3, no. 10 (October 1989): 56-58.

the longest commutes will suffer the most. The truth is precisely the opposite of what the proponents of Propositions 111 and 108 would have us believe.

While the proposed tax increases will initially cause property values to fall, ultimately these tax increases will slow California's growth and cause higher unemployment as well. The greatest brunt will fall on those people least capable of defending themselves. Illustrations of these effects are everywhere, and academic research journals are replete with the documentation of these principles. The concepts are sufficiently simple that even a politician should be able to understand them.

One aspect of the tax increase envisioned by Proposition 111 is the gratuitous dismemberment of the Gann spending limit passed in 1979. If one agreed with the central theme of Propositions 111 and 108, then it would be reasonable to exclude the spending mandated by those propositions. But there is only one reason why far greater and deeper cuts in the Gann limit are proposed. Proposition 111 is the necessary first step for an agenda of ever greater taxes in California.

The threefold changes in the Gann limit—exclusion of the new highway spending; reindexing the limits to the growth in personal income, instead of population growth plus the lesser of (1) U.S. CPI inflation or (2) California personal income per capita growth; and excluding capital spending from the limit—will virtually destroy the restraining power of the Gann limits.

Had the new limits been in effect, California would have experienced a $10 billion cumulative gas tax increase over the 1980-88 period. In addition, changing the formula used to calculate the spending limit would have resulted in a cumulative increase in the limit of $19.2 billion to 1990. Divided by the average population of 26 million people, it would have meant an average additional gas tax of $385 per person and $738 in additional spending for the state—a total of $1,123 per person. This number does not give any consideration to the exclusion of capital expenditures from the Gann limit.

Prospectively, the impact of the propositions on the relaxation of the spending limit could result in a cumulative increase of $53.3 billion over the next 10 years. Its passage would trigger a $15.3 billion tax increase. That amounts to a $547 additional tax per person and a $1,882 increase in spending limitations, for a total of $2,429 per person or $9,716 per family of four based on the 1988 population. These figures underestimate the true revenue and expenditure impact, for they do not account for the effect of removal of capital spending from the Gann spending limitations.

For 1988 alone, if the propositions had been part of Gann, the spending limit would have been $3.6 billion higher. Combined with the extra gas tax of $1.46 billion, they would add $179 per person to the California tax burden. These increases would place California even higher in the U.S. tax burden rankings, going from eleventh to eighth highest based on total taxes, and from tenth to sixth highest taxed state based on all-own-source general revenue.

The impact of Propositions 111 and 108 will be exceptionally onerous on the poor, minorities, and the young. Gasoline taxes are highly regressive and have their most biting impact on the poor and other disadvantaged segments of our society. While surely not done intentionally, these propositions, put on the ballot by our politicians, will be devastating to those least able to defend themselves. The conceptual underpinnings of these two propositions are just not logical. Economies cannot tax themselves into prosperity.

One of the least cogent arguments put forth by the proponents of Propositions 111 and 108 is that California's gas tax should be raised because it is low by national standards. The people who argue this way simply don't understand or don't want to understand that all taxes are paid by people and that it is the overall tax burden that affects behavior. How the government takes your money is irrelevant. What matters is whether the government takes your money.

It is nonsensical to argue that because one type of tax is below the national norm, it therefore should be raised, unless, of course, one also argues in favor of lowering taxes that are above the national norm. The argument can't go both ways. The advocates of the gas tax increase do point to California's lower-than-average gas tax but shun any mention of tax categories where California is abnormally high. They never once suggest lowering any tax at any time or anywhere. They've never met a tax they didn't like.

Table 10.2 lists revenue sources for the state of California and the national average for all states for selected years. This table should provide the reader with a perspective on how California ranks among the states today.

Table 10.2

Comparative State and Local Revenues for Selected Revenues in Selected Years

		Total Revenues($MM)			Per Capita-$	National
		1967	1978	1988	1988	Rank
Total Revenues	CA	$ 14211	$ 50079	$ 120365	$ 4251	6th
	US	107279	371607	884500	3598	highest
Own Source General Revenues	CA	9699	33248	79353	2803	10th
	US	76121	246368	609543	2480	highest
Total Taxes	CA	7940	27365	55169	1948	11th
	US	61241	193642	435675	1772	highest
Property Taxes	CA	4130	11011	15381	543	23rd
	US	26279	66422	132240	538	highest
General Sales & Gross Receipts Taxes	CA	1395	6021	14172	501	12th
	US	10143	41473	105168	428	highest
Income (Personal & Corporate) Taxes	CA	952	6709	17646	623	9th
	US	8062	43915	112090	456	highest

Source: U.S. Bureau of the Census, *Government Finances in* (fiscal year).

There are a number of other deleterious consequences that will result from the passage of Propositions 111 and 108. In the grand scheme of things, these additional consequences are sometimes viewed by economists as less weighty. Nonetheless, more of what little remains of California's open space will be cloaked in petroleum-drenched asphalt. Access to what had heretofore been relatively inaccessible wild areas will be dramatically increased.

What is most surprising is that the real concerns of traffic congestion are not dealt with by Propositions 111 and 108. And it is not as though we don't have the knowledge or experience to deal effectively with traffic congestion. We do. When faced with the potential crisis of the Olympics and all the associated traffic, careful planning and imaginative execution led to a very successful control of traffic. In fact, the traffic congestion during the Olympics was probably less than during normal times. Surely California's elected representatives can do as well as they did during the Olympics and thereby avoid all the unsavory consequences of massive tax and spending increases.

Congestion is driving's equivalent of having to wait in long lines to buy a product. Save for a few industries such as chic restaurants where long lines are the sine qua non of acceptance, long lines are a sure sign of poor management. The only reason long lines develop is because the product being offered is underpriced monetarily, and therefore the cost of waiting in line balances supply and demand.

California's government has a history of poor management. Today the crises of California's poor management encompass a whole range of governmentally controlled products such as water, pollution, congestion, and education. For some reason, our state government prefers rationing products at low or no cost to the user rather than pricing the product where supply equals demand. Congestion, quite simply, is the price a commuter pays for using the freeways during rush hour. Unfortunately, that is a price paid by the user but never received by the state to make things better. Everyone is worse off.

The correct solution is quite straightforward: Usage of the freeways during rush hour should have a monetary price. There should be a license fee to drive in a car with no other passengers or a highway use toll to ration valuable highway space during rush hour. The concept is clear—charge vehicles extra for using the roads where and when demand is great. A gas tax doesn't do that.

Propositions 111 and 108 totally ignore one of the most powerful movements in America and especially in California today: the slow growth movement. Even to the vizier extraordinaire, forecasting is a risky venture. And yet, if these two propositions pass and the slow growth movement gains momentum, we could experience firsthand just what happens when the irresistible force meets the immovable object. The outcome of having to build freeways to the tune of the new taxes and not being permitted to build highways where people now live could be 57-lane highways stretching from one border of Yolo County to the next. The picture is not very pretty, but it does illustrate some of the critical shortcomings of these propositions.

California's per capita state spending on highways is literally the lowest in the nation. Even federal per capita spending on highways in California is way below the national average. But then again, this is not a new phenomenon. The share of California's budget spent on highways has always been lower than the national average. In 1972, California spent 7.8 percent of its budget on highways, whereas the average for all states in that year was 11.4 percent. By 1982, California's budget share dedicated to highways had dropped to 4.4 percent, whereas the U.S. average was 8.07 percent. The most recent data for the year 1988 has California at 4.5 percent and the average for all states at 7.9 percent.

Our population growth has always been higher than the national average. There is nothing new about that either. Why these conditions would now be used to justify such radical measures as Propositions 111 and 108 doesn't make any sense except as rhetoric.

It makes no sense to raise taxes to increase highway spending when the proportion of our budget spent on highways is so low. If our spending needs were all that desperate, a simple redress of the abnormally small percentage of our state's budget spent on highways is readily available. It makes no sense to cut down the cherry tree to pick the last cherry.

The federal highway trust fund, as of the end of fiscal year 1989, has an accumulated surplus of $10,551 million. The federal mass transit fund had another $6,057 million surplus. Surely some attempt to use these idle federal funds makes more sense than raising state taxes.

Yet in spite of California's traditional willingness to shortchange highways, the consensus is that California's highways still rank among the nation's best. The problem, to the extent that California has a unique problem, stems from California's incredible success in attracting people from other states. These new residents don't need to be subsidized to come to California. They cause the congestion, and they should pay for its removal.

It is neither fair nor efficient for current residents of California to pay more in taxes to build roads and highways to new housing developments. New residents should pay the full cost for coming to California. Developers surely make enough money to pay for the full costs of their developments and then pass those costs on.

Whenever ballot measures are placed on the ballot by politicians, the arduous task of gathering signatures is circumvented. While clearly legal, this method of placing measures on the ballot imposes a serious political risk to the electorate at large. Invariably, compromise among competing political factions turns out to be conspiracy against the party not included in the compromise—the people. Propositions 111 and 108 have been loaded with special interest provisions to ensure as little formal opposition as possible. There is something for every organization and political lobbying group. Propositions 111 and 108 are a veritable Christmas tree bedecked with goodies and paid for by taxpayers. These compromises and giveaways have all been at the expense of the state's economic future and the opportunities afforded our young.

NOTES

1. Bertrand Russell, *Unpopular Essays* (New York: Touchstone, 1969).

2. Charles W. Kadlec and Arthur B. Laffer, "The Jarvis-Gann Tax Cut Proposal: An Application of the Laffer Curve," in *The Economics of the Tax Revolt*, ed. by Arthur B. Laffer and Jan P. Seymour (New York: Harcourt Brace Jovanovich, 1979), pp. 118-22.

11

A Proposal for a California Complete Flat Tax

Victor A. Canto and Arthur B. Laffer

California is on the brink of a serious slowdown. The consequences will be falling real estate prices, rising unemployment, a round of failures of financial institutions, and a serious budget crisis for state and local governments. The time is now to rethink the entire structure of state and local taxes. The long-term prosperity of California hangs in the balance.

The concept *business climate* is intrinsically elusive. The term is something of an enigma, suggesting implicitly, as it does, that business and labor are in conflict over formulation of an environment conducive to economic growth. Just the reverse is true. Business (or capital) and labor are complements in the economic process. Abusive taxation and regulation of business are detrimental to both labor and business.

Nonetheless, the notion of business climate is useful. The competitiveness of a state or region is determined by a myriad of factors—from weather patterns, proximity to major markets, and the quality of life to infrastructure, regulatory requirements, and fiscal policies. Most of these factors are all but impossible to quantify in a systematic way across states or even within a single state over time. Hence, they elude statistical analysis and, as often as not, are included intuitively under the rubric of "business climate."

In addition, the expected path of policies can be as important as existing policies in determining a state's competitiveness. This dynamic element of competition, too, is captured by the notion of business climate. In this sense, business climate is simply a catch phrase for the businessman's judgment as to the likely course of tax, regulatory, or expenditure policies. It includes such intangibles as the cost of defeating legislation that may detract from a company's profitability.

In short, business climate is a subjective estimation of the effect of state policies and economic environment on the profitability of a business over its expected life span. It captures not only the direct effect of the tax and regulatory codes but, just as important, the manner in which tax codes and regulations are implemented and enforced.

It follows, then, that concern over rising taxes, unpredictable regulatory requirements, or other governmentally imposed strictures will affect a state's competitiveness. The connection with the tax burden is more than a coincidence. There are sound theoretical reasons for focusing on the tax burden as the key tax variable likely to influence relative economic performance. Taxes levied on mobile factors will be passed on to immobile factors located within the state. The burden of state taxes will be borne by immobile factors.

Consider two identical mills—one mill located in Arizona, the other in California. Since both mills sell virtually identical products in the U.S. market, competition will force them to sell their products at approximately the same price. Given this situation, consider what would happen if Arizona increases its tax burden, whereas California's tax burden is unchanged. Because the market is highly competitive, the Arizona company would not be able to pass the tax hike on to its customers in the form of higher prices. The only option the Arizona company has is to pass the tax hike backward to its suppliers or employees.

Initially, at least, the Arizona mill would have to swallow the tax hike through lower after-tax profits and would have to lower wages, making the location of businesses and immigration to Arizona less attractive. In contrast, the relative reduction in taxes will make California more attractive.

In a dynamic context, the problem is more complicated. A plant with a 30-year life expectancy will not be located in a state where tax rates are expected to increase relative to the national average or where regulatory policies are expected to be capricious or unduly burdensome. Once a plant is built, management can do little in the short run to avoid such economic reversals. If such potential losses are to be avoided, the decision must be made at the time the location of a plant or facility is determined. The analysis may also be applied to individuals' location decisions. People tend to move to where they can improve their standard of living. This tenet has long been ingrained when it comes to Eastern European migration to the West or Mexican migration to the United States. But when this concept combines with the "one man [sic] one vote" principle, the affects are explosive.

States where taxes are high and/or increasing relative to the national norm tend to experience relative income and population declines. Likewise, in states where taxes are low and/or falling, income and population growth are often above average. During the 1978-87 period, California's tax burden went from the fourth highest taxed state in the U.S. in 1978 to the sixteenth highest in 1987. California's personal income, adjusted for inflation, increased 46 percent compared with 28.9 percent for the United States. The above-average economic performance occurred at a time when its overall tax burden was declining relative to the nation's.

Congressional seats are allocated to states according to population as measured by decadal census data. It therefore follows that state economic policies, in due course, help to determine political power. Population changes over the past decade projected onto the 1990 census suggest that California may pick up as many as six congressional seats.

States with high and/or increasing tax burdens during the 1978-87 period—New York, Ohio, Michigan and Illinois—are likely to lose congressional districts. In contrast, states with low tax burdens—Texas, Florida, Georgia, and Virginia—are gaining congressional seats. In California, taxes have fallen with a vengeance since 1978.

When taxes combine with democracy, Adam Smith merges with Charles Darwin. Not only do the anachronistic high-tax states wither away in political influence, but progressive low-tax states flourish. It boils down to only a matter of time.

In spite of the myriad of qualifications inherent in this type of research, the evidence is clearly consistent with the analysis. The burden of state taxation ultimately falls on the immobile factors located within the state. The relevant variable affecting economic behavior is the burden, not the form in which the taxes are collected. Therefore, if California is to improve its economic climate and competitiveness with other states, the impact of the tax burden must be taken into consideration. A reduction in the overall tax burden is a necessary precondition for the state's recovery.

The incidence of a tax can be different from the burden of that tax. The person upon whom a tax is levied may well experience no loss in net income if he passes the tax forward to consumers or backward to suppliers. Likewise, a person upon whom no tax has been levied may well suffer large net income losses as a consequence of taxes levied on others. In the words of Nobel laureate Paul Samuelson:

> Even if the electorate has made up its mind about how the tax burden shall be borne by individuals, the following difficult problems remain:
>
> Who ultimately pays a particular tax? Does its burden stay on the person on whom it is first levied? One cannot assume that the person Congress says a tax is levied on will end up paying that tax. He may be able to shift the tax; shift it "forward" on his customers by raising his price as much as the tax; or shift it "backward" on his suppliers (wage earners, rent, and interest receivers) who end up being able to charge him less than they would have done had there been no tax. Economists therefore say: We must study the final inci-

dence of the tax totality of its effects on commodity prices, factor prices, resource allocations, efforts, and composition of production and consumption. Tax incidence, thus, is no easy problem and requires all the advanced tools of economics to help toward its solution.[1]

Higher tax rates will slow California's growth. Personal income growth, too, will fall below its potential, leaving in its wake more poverty and more problems that go hand in hand with poverty. Immigration from other states would decline, as would tourism. It is a short step in logic to see how serious the consequences would be for most of California's real estate and construction industries.

STATE AND TAXES AND ECONOMIC PERFORMANCE: THE EVIDENCE

As a result of lower growth, reduced profitability, and higher unemployment, the assumptions underlying California's projected budget for the rest of this century will not be met. State and local tax receipts will fall short of the estimates, and expenditures—especially those to help those in need—will exceed expectations. While these supply-side effects will take time to materialize, they will, in due course, wreak havoc on the state's budget. Chronic fiscal crises mired in a sluggish economy will be the order of the day for California in the mid-1990s.

One look at Massachusetts from "Taxachusetts" to the "Massachusetts miracle" back to "Taxachusetts" should be proof enough as to what can happen. Each state has its own unique history of taxation and economic growth, but the theme underlying each and every one of them is the same: Large tax increases are at best a short-run palliative for state budgets but are invariably a long-run disaster.

California's own fiscal history tells the same story. Over a decade ago we wrote an analysis of what we thought would be the consequences of Proposition 13:

> Therefore, we believe that passage of Proposition 13 could boost aggregate personal income in California $20 billion or more above what it otherwise would be during the next twelve months; that nearly half of the income and tax revenue impact will occur within the next two years; and that the full estimated $110 billion increment to aggregate personal income in California will be realized within ten years.
>
> As a direct consequence of this growth in economic activity, social welfare spending should decline. The combined effect

implies that California governments would, in short order, be back in surplus, and that there is little cause for sharp reduction in spending especially for such constitutionally mandated programs as schools and essential services such as fire and police protection.[2]

The analytic framework we used before the passage of Proposition 13 was true then, and it's true now. The incidence of a tax is totally different from the burden of that tax. Mobile products and factors that can move quickly and cheaply will not suffer. Immobile factors, however, that cannot move easily will bear the lion's share of the tax hike. The longer the economy has to adjust to the increased tax, the greater will be the adjustment. It is hard to imagine anything less mobile than property and poor people.

As a result of the passage of Propositions 111, 108, and 116 in June 1990, property values will fall, and California will take on the aura of its sister states Massachusetts, Connecticut, New York, New Jersey, and Arizona, to name a few. Property values are always the first to suffer from escalating state taxation and are among the hardest hit areas as well. Those properties associated with the longest commutes will suffer the most. The truth is precisely the opposite of what the proponents of these propositions would have us believe.

While these tax increases will initially cause property values to fall, ultimately they will slow California's growth and cause higher unemployment as well. The greatest brunt will fall on those people least capable of defending themselves. Illustrations of these effects are everywhere, and academic research journals are replete with the documentation of these principles. The concepts are sufficiently simple so that even a politician should be able to understand them.

It is nonsensical to argue that because one type of tax is below the national norm, it therefore should be raised, unless, of course, one also argues in favor of lowering taxes that are above the national norm. The argument can't go both ways. The advocates of the gas tax increase do point to California's lower-than-average gas tax but shun any mention of tax categories where California is abnormally high. They never once suggest lowering any tax at any time or anywhere.

Table 11.1 lists revenue sources for the state of California and the national average for all states for fiscal year 1988. This table should provide the reader with a perspective on how California ranks among the states today.

Prior to the passage of Proposition 13, California's tax burden was higher than the national average; so was its unemployment rate. Population growth was slightly above the national average. The passage of Proposition 13 and the Gann spending limitations brought about a reduction in California's tax burden relative to the rest of the nation. California's unemployment rate declined relative to the nation even though the population growth more than doubled relative to the national average.

Table 11.1
Fiscal Year 1988 State and Local Government Taxes by Major Type

	($MM)	(% of Total)	($MM)	(% of Total)
	Total: All States		California	
Income taxes				
(Personal & Corporate)	$ 112,090	25.7 %	$17,646	32.0%
Property taxes	132,240	30.4	15,381	27.9
Sales taxes	105,168	24.1	14,172	25.7
Motor Fuels &				
Vehicle License taxes	27,299	6.3	2,355	4.3
Other Taxes	58,878	13.5	5,615	10.2
Total Taxes	435,675	100.0%	55,169	100.0%

Source: U.S. Bureau of the Census, *Government Finances in 1987-88.*

The tax rate reduction and spending restraint left California well positioned to take advantage of the fiscal policies enacted by the Reagan administration. In addition, a strong argument can be made that the spending limitation prevented the state authorities from making many of the mistakes made by Northeast governors during the implementation of the second round of Reagan tax rate cuts.

Flat tax proposals such as the Hall-Rabushka and Laffer flat tax greatly influenced the design of the Tax Reform Act of 1986.[3] Although some differences from a flat tax are apparent (i.e., the so-called bubble), the changes in tax rates have moved the United States closer to a flat tax.

The mix of tax rates may matter as much or more than the absolute amount of revenues collected. In the words of Henry George, the nineteenth-century American economist:

> The mode of taxation is, in fact, quite as important as the amount. As a small burden badly placed may distress a horse that could carry with ease a much larger one properly adjusted, so a people may be impoverished and their power of producing wealth destroyed by taxation, which, if levied in any other way, could be borne with ease.[4]

The important feature of the tax system is the conceptual framework upon which it is based. Henry George, in his chapter entitled "The Proposition Tried by the Canons of Taxation," enumerated as well as anyone the criteria by which tax policy may be analyzed:

> The best tax by which public revenues can be raised is evidently that which will closest conform to the following conditions:
>
> 1. That it bear as lightly as possible upon production—so as least to check the increase of the general fund from which taxes must be paid and the community maintained.
> 2. That it be easily and cheaply collected, and fall as directly as may be

upon the ultimate payers—so as to take from the people as little as possible in addition to what it yields the government.

3. That it be certain—so as to give the least opportunity for tyranny or corruption on the part of officials, and the least temptation to lawbreaking and evasion on the part of the taxpayers.

4. That it bear equally—so as to give no citizen an advantage or put any at a disadvantage, as compared with others.[5]

ALTERNATIVES TO THE CURRENT PROPERTY TAX STRUCTURE

Looked at in isolation, the current property tax system in California appears to have many of the attributes enunciated by Henry George. It bears lightly on production, it is easily and cheaply collected, and it is certain. The only attribute that the current property tax does not meet, which represents the likely constitutional challenge, is fairness.

The argument is that individuals in similar homes could pay vastly different property taxes owing to the feature that the tax base is determined by the initial purchase price. Thus, similar homes purchased at different times are likely to have different sale prices, thereby resulting in different tax payments by home owners.

There are alternative ways to deal with such a problem. The nature of the solution depends on the constraint that one may be willing to impose in arriving at the solution. Two alternatives are considered here. One focuses exclusively on replacing the property tax with another property tax. The second eliminates such a constraint and focuses on designing an optimal tax system.

The property tax solution is fairly straightforward, given that the current system approximates the attributes described by Henry George. The proposed alternative should retain the three basic attributes the current system meets and hopefully add additional features to meet the fourth and lacking attribute.

Theoretically, the solution is straightforward: It only requires finding a way of determining the market value of the property. However, past experiences in California and elsewhere with "assessed values" determined by state and local authorities could lead to disparities between market value and assessed values depending on the effectiveness (i.e., frequency with which property tax rolls are revised) as well as the accuracy of the measurement. A better solution would be to have the property owner declare the market value of the property and pay the property tax on the self-declared market value. To reduce the home owner's incentive to underestimate the value of the property, the state should have the specified right to purchase the property within a specified amount of time (say, two months) at a multiple of the assessed value, say, three times. If the state chooses to do so, then it should put the house on the market within a specified amount of time. Such a mechanism would ensure that the home owner would not, on average, declare the property value for less than one third of the market value. It also protects the home owner in case the state valuation differs from the home owner's valuation and the state mistakenly feels the home owner is undervaluing the property. When it puts the property up for sale, the bid price will not be as high as the state's assessed price and thus would fetch a lower price. There is nothing to prevent the home owner from repurchasing the property.

This option, although theoretically appealing, could have some difficulties. First, it would force the state to create a monitoring and acquiring department. The new bureaucracy would reduce the yield of the tax revenues. Second, it would create economic transaction costs to home owners from the state's mistakenly overvaluing the property. Conceptually, this could be resolved by developing a restitution mechanism—again creating additional bureaucracy and collection costs.

The third and most important objection relates to one of the original motives that led to the Proposition 13 revolution: The continuous revaluation of property assuming an upward trend, over and above inflation, implies that property taxes will be an increasing share of income for retired individuals and others on fixed incomes.

In addition to the three objections to the alternative property tax previously discussed, it is a mistake to consider individual taxes in isolation. To illustrate: While the tax burden by itself is well within the nation's average, suggesting that the state tax structure is in line with other states, the focus on individual taxes ignores the fact that different states rely on different taxes for their revenues. A state that has no income tax will rely more heavily on other taxes. The danger is that being average for each tax category may result in an overall tax burden higher than the average. Thus, focusing on individual states may lead some to recommend tax increases in categories that are below the national average. However, in doing so, the overall tax burden will increase. This will damage the state's competitive position.

Higher tax rates imply more of both tax evasion and avoidance. The more evasion and avoidance that exist, the more government spending will be required to monitor and enforce the tax codes. The existence of tax evasion and avoidance, therefore, at higher tax rates, further enhances the beneficial fiscal effects of tax rate reductions accompanied by a broad tax base.

In actual practice, the overall path of the economy is determined not only by how much revenue is collected through taxation but also by how it is collected and how it is spent.

One implication emerging for this analysis is that specific taxes designed to raise revenue for specific expenditures may inadvertently result in unnecessary distortion that reduces the efficiency of the economy, thereby lowering the level of economic activity, property values, and overall business climate.

The argument in favor of specific taxes for specific purposes merely represents a user fee and does not cause a distortion. Theoretically, the statement is correct; however, in practice, it is much more difficult to approximate the theoretical construct. Consider the case of a gasoline tax used to pay for highway construction. Proponents of such measures argue that it is a user fee. However, upon close examination, it is evident that this is not the case. To illustrate: Gasoline and other fuels are used in lawnmowers, tractors, and the like. None of those machines use the highways. If tax abatement and exemptions are granted for these uses (i.e., agriculture), then the differential taxation will lead to substitution effects. One only needs to be reminded of the experiences in the Northeast during the energy crisis. Home owners with oil heating and diesel automobiles siphoned the fuel from their boilers to use in their cars.

A gasoline tax also fails as an efficient user fee price. From an economic viewpoint, a flexible pricing schedule is desirable. During rush hour, the pricing should be such that it covers the fixed and variable costs of operating and maintaining the road. During traffic nonrush hours, only the marginal cost of operating the road should be charged. Thus, the peak load pricing is used to deter congestion but does not penalize non–peak load use. The differential price will induce substitution effects away from the peak price—thereby spreading the traffic flow more evenly over the different hours. The gasoline tax does not accomplish this. Finally, the gasoline tax is higher for less-fuel-efficient vehicles. While this may be desirable for other reasons, identical size cars with different engines cause the same amount of freeway congestion yet pay different taxes.

The detailed analysis points to the different distortions and substitution effects caused by a specific tax (i.e., gasoline tax) tied to a specific expenditure (i.e., road construction and maintenance). Additionally associated are the collection costs and expenses associated with the necessary bureaucracy to maintain and monitor each of the taxes.

All these arguments lead one to consider an alternative scheme: Tax collection is separated from the specific expenditure. In so doing, a tax system can be designed that raises the requisite revenues to finance the expenditure in the most efficient manner. The constitutional challenge to Proposition 13 presents a unique opportunity for California to reconsider the issue of what is the best way to raise the revenue to finance expenditures desired by the electorate.

A complete overhaul of the tax system following the canons of taxation outlined by Henry George points to a modified flat tax to replace a variety of state taxes. A flat tax will reduce the collection cost per dollar of tax revenues by minimizing duplication and the bureaucracy necessary to monitor and enforce the numerous taxes in the state. In addition, the efficiency gains resulting from a flat tax will increase the state's competitiveness. The complete flat tax is, first and foremost, an economic proposal. It eliminates much of the inefficiency in the current tax system by broadening the tax base and sharply reducing marginal tax rates. Its adoption would lead to a surge in growth and would create a more competitive economy.

The level of expenditures should be determined by the electorate and may very well be addressed through spending limitations. However, those issues are outside the purview of the present study.

The proposal, however, recognizes that state government should share in the rewards of this gain in efficiency. Hence, the tax rate is set so as to allow average tax rates to rise as existing depreciation and other grandfathered provisions under the existing tax law dissipate with the passage of time. This proposal, then, is a quintessential political document as well. It combines good economics with good politics, making it a forerunner of good public policy. Specifically:

1. *Fairness.* Tax rates on modest-income earners will be reduced considerably.
2. *Simplicity.* The straightforward calculation of the tax base and the application of a single tax rate simplify the entire tax system.
3. *Efficiency.* The reduction of marginal tax rates coupled with the broadening of the tax base will minimize many of the distortions that make the current tax system counterproductive. As a result, even while allowing for a rise in the average tax rate, the economy would undergo substantial expansion. The result would be a higher standard of living for the average Californian and an increase in revenues for the state and local governments.

Introduction of the flat tax to the political arena and to public discourse is likely to bring about some modifications in this basic proposal. Provisions also may be necessary to allow for tax loss carryforwards. Such changes, although technically important, would be of little consequence once the concept of the flat tax is accepted.

WHY A FLAT TAX

The theory of incentives provides the basis for the concept of a flat rate tax, which is so-called because a single tax rate applies equally to all sources of income and does not change as a result of the taxpayer's volume of income. Any exemptions, deductions, differential rates, or progressivity would, as a matter of linguistics, preclude the name *flat rate*. They also represent a deviation from the principles of efficient taxation. Such exceptions to the even application of a single tax narrow the tax base, lead to a higher tax rate, make for greater complexity, and increase tax avoidance.

Incentives can be either positive or negative. They are alternatively described as carrots and sticks or pleasure and pain. Whatever their form, people seek positive and avoid negative incentives. If a dog is beaten, for example, the animal's whereabouts will not be known, but the dog is certain not to be where the beating took place. If, however, a dog is fed, we know exactly where the dog will be. The principle is simple enough: If an activity should be shunned, a negative incentive is appropriate, and vice versa.

In the case of taxable income, people try to shift income from higher-taxed categories to lower-taxed categories. They purchase tax shelters, and in the extreme, they may even earn less income or literally evade the strictures of the Internal Revenue Service (IRS) and Franchise Tax Board at considerable personal risk. Because taxation in some form is necessary to sustain government spending, one canon of taxation has always been to have the largest possible tax base coupled with the lowest possible tax rate. By so doing, people are provided the least opportunity to avoid paying taxes and the lowest incentive to do so. In the words of Henry George: A good tax should "bear as lightly as possible upon production—so as least to check the increase of the general fund from which taxes must be paid and the community maintained." He also went on to say that a tax should "be easily and cheaply collected . . . so as to take from the people as little as possible in addition to what it yields the government."

A number of tax proposals over the years have attempted to reform one specific tax or another. Such reform attempts, however, are doomed at the outset. There can be no presumption even that the overall tax code will benefit from the most earnest of efforts to rectify one specific tax in a sea of flawed taxes. The interactive effects of all taxes taken in concert are barely imaginable when only one tax is viewed in isolation. True tax reform must take into account the entire tax code. Sincere efforts directed toward remedies of one specific tax are inherently tragically flawed by their lack of completeness.

Recently, in politics at the federal level, most attention has been paid to the current state of disarray of personal and corporate income taxes. It is widely recognized that in spite of the statutory progressivity of the tax codes, deductions, exemptions, and exclusions of all sorts rendered the income tax neither fair nor efficient. The legislative process made available tax shelters, deferrals, and various other tax avoidance schemes to those with access to fancy accountants and high-priced lawyers. People struggling to become economically comfortable who can neither afford nor have access to such inequitable devices pay taxes after taxes, rarely getting the rewards they so rightfully deserve.

In the realm of California state taxation, three groups of taxes account for the bulk of revenues: personal and corporate income taxes, property taxes, and sales and gross receipt taxes. They alone account for over 85 percent of total state and local taxes, as can be seen in Table 11.1. Therefore, any flat rate tax proposal should incorporate all three forms of taxation.

State and local property taxes have introduced economic distortions in local economies. The source of the distortion may be attributed to uneven application of property tax rates resulting from unevenness of the property tax base. Prior to Proposition 13, the high tax rate on property values and the disparity of assessed value gave rise to almost random variations in property taxes across communities. With the advent of Proposition 13, the intercommunity dispersion may have been reduced as rates were reduced and changes were made in valuation where the determination of the property tax base became determined by the purchase price of property. Proposition 13 introduced a different dispersion parameter. Other than the escalation clauses, a property could not be revalued unless the property was sold. This gave rise to identical houses with sales transacted at different times having different tax bases.

Attempting to redress the equity issue by levying differential rates or permitting extensive deductions, exemptions, and exclusions misses the whole point of a flat rate tax. Refusing to fold the property tax into a flat rate tax will also fail to provide the poor with actual relief. Comfortable images will once again have supplanted careful logic.

The practical difficulties inherent in any proposed flat rate tax scheme mandate far more consideration than would, at first glance, appear necessary from the uncomplicated nature of the theory.

CONFLICTING NOTIONS

In reality, issues of equity, solvency, and efficiency can conflict with the notion of a flat rate tax. Should, for example, the poor pay the same proportion of their income in taxes as do the rich? How about drinking, smoking, and gambling as activities versus charities, clean living, and conservation? Should all be taxed at the same rate? Even beneficial activities may, if necessary, succumb to a tax to provide the state with the requisite revenues. Clearly, considerations other than economic efficiency are of great importance. To reiterate the essential point, a piecemeal approach to tax reform will not work. Thus, a flat rate income tax is of little consequence unless considered in conjunction with other taxes.

TAX CATEGORIES

Today, even a summary of California's budget receipts requires page after page of entries in ever-smaller type to catalog a myriad of specific taxes. In total, many of these taxes raise little revenue. Their cost to the economy in terms of record keeping and collection represents an unnecessary burden. In general, all of these taxes should be eliminated forthwith.

Excise taxes on alcoholic beverages, tobacco products, firearms and munitions, along with traffic fines, parking tickets, fees at state parks, and the like, should be retained. It must be presumed that the state legislature.

when it passed those specific taxes, did so with the intent of discouraging their use rather than raising revenue. These are the so-called sin taxes. In total, these categories defined as being outside the purview of a flat rate tax base contributed approximately 8.5 percent of California revenues during fiscal year 1988.[6]

As part of an overall tax simplification tax reform, all other taxes and sources of budgetary revenues should be repealed. In their stead would be two flat taxes of equal rates: a flat rate personal income tax and a flat rate business value-added tax.

DEDUCTIONS

The tax base for both individuals and businesses has been eroded over the last 20 years by the enactment of numerous exemptions and deductions. In addition, a profusion of tax credits serves to reduce the effective tax rate paid by some taxpayers in this already-reduced tax base while doing nothing to reduce the tax burden on individuals or businesses that are otherwise in identical economic circumstances. Such credits reduce the government's tax receipts and the average tax rate while leaving marginal rates unchanged. In short, tax credits in virtually all forms are counterproductive.

Thus, to make the tax base as broad as possible, virtually all deductions and tax credits for individuals and tax credits for businesses should be repealed. In addition, the business tax base should be broadened to include the value added of labor as well as the value added of capital and land. Great care, however, should be taken to make certain that value added as it wends its way through numerous businesses is taxed once and only once. Double, triple, and even higher multiples of taxation in our current business tax code, no matter how well concealed, have cost our society unconscionable quantities of lost output and lost employment opportunities.

CALCULATION OF THE TAX BASE

Specifically, the tax base for individuals, businesses, and independent contractors would be calculated as follows:

Personal Income Tax

Taxable income for all individuals, save independent contractors.
   1. Take income from all sources—wages, salaries, interest income, dividends, net capital gains (short-term and long-term), royalties, fees, and the like.

2. Subtract charitable contributions.

3. Subtract mortgage interest payments on principal residence.

4. Subtract receipts of Social Security, unemployment benefits, and other transfer payments specifically designated as tax exempt.

5. The resultant figure is the taxable income base. Estimates of California's tax base are presented in Table 11.2. For comparison purposes, the U.S. tax base is also calculated.

Taxable income for independent contractors. To receive a business taxpaying identifying number for an individual requires explicit state permission that should be based on the recipient's demonstrated special employment circumstances that would warrant such treatment.

1. For the independent contractor possessing a taxpaying identifying number, the tax base for personal income tax purposes is the dollar value of total sales, including, but not restricted to, personal services less:

   • Purchases from other businesses and independent contractors bearing taxpaying identifying numbers of items used exclusively to generate sales and revenues.

   • Purchases of imported goods or services, with the requisite import

Table 11.2
Estimated Personal Income Tax Base, California and U.S. Total, 1987
(in billions of dollars)

	United States	California
Personal income	$ 3,766.1	$ 491.4
Plus capital gains	133.5	34.7
Less charitable contributions	(49.3)	(8.4)
Less mortgage interest payments*	(174.4)	(29.4)
Less transfer payments (tax exempt)	(548.8)	(71.6)**
Less imputed rent	(86.0)	(11.2)**
Equals Tax base for personal income	$ 3,041.1	$ 405.5

* Number includes "interest paid" as in sources.

** Estimate based on ratio (CA/US) personal income times U.S. aggregate.

Sources: U.S. Department of Commerce, *National Income and Product Accounts*; California Franchise Tax Board, *Annual Report*; Internal Revenue Service, *Statistics of Income Bulletin*, Spring 1989.

taxpaying identifying number, used exclusively to generate sales and revenues.

- Depreciation of pre–flat rate tax depreciable assets at their regular depreciation schedules.

2. Subtract one half of charitable contributions.

3. Subtract one half of mortgage interest payments.

4. Subtract one half of the receipts of Social Security, unemployment benefits, and other transfer payments specifically designed as tax exempt.

5. The resultant figure is the independent contractor taxable personal income base.

Business Value-Added Tax

Taxable value added for businesses.

1. For all entities possessing a business taxpaying identifying number, including independent contractors, the tax base is the total dollar value of all sales during the tax period less expenses:

- All purchases from entities that possess a taxpaying identifying number (including independent contractors).

- All purchases of imported goods with the requisite import taxpaying identifying number.

- Depreciation of pre–flat rate tax depreciable assets at their regular depreciation schedules.

- Bad debts incurred.

2. Subtract charitable contributions.

3. No other deductions are permitted.

4. The resultant figure is the value-added tax base.

An estimate of the business value-added tax base for fiscal year 1987 is reported in Table 11.3. The U.S. base is also provided for purposes of comparison.

THE TAX RATE

The tax rate is derived by dividing targeted revenues by the total tax base. On a statical basis, with no increase in average tax rates and using fiscal year 1988 as a guide, requisite flat tax revenue would be $50.4 billion on a combined tax base of $831.2 billion (Table 11.4). On this basis, the flat tax

Table 11.3
Estimated Business Value-Added Tax Base, California and United States, 1987
(in billions of dollars)

	United States	California
Gross Product ('87 est.)	$4,191.7	$533.8
Less business investment		
Fixed non-residential	(446.8)	(56.9)*
Business-fixed residential	(51.5)**	(6.6)*
Depreciation	(507.6)	(64.6)*
Less Business transfers	(28.1)	(23.8)*
Equals tax base for business value added	$3,157.7	$381.9

* Estimate based on ratio (CA/US) of Gross Product times U.S. total.

** Estimate based on all farm structures and 20 percent of non-farm structures.

Sources: U.S. Department of Commerce, *Survey of Current Business,* May 1988; *National Income and Product Accounts*; California Franchise Tax Board, *Annual Report.*

Table 11.4
California Flat Tax Calculations, 1984-88 (in billions of dollars)

Tax base previous CY	1984	1985	1986	1987	1988
Personal Income	$ 280.3	$ 313.2	$ 342.0	$ 373.2	$ 408.1
Business Value Added	302.6	326.8	358.5	381.9	423.1
Total tax base	582.9	640.0	700.5	755.1	831.2
Target state & local tax revenue	38.5	43.4	46.6	53.3	55.2
Tax maintained	3.2	3.4	3.7	4.3	4.7
Requisite flat tax revenue	35.3	40.0	42.9	49.0	50.4
Flat tax rate	6.06 %	6.23 %	6.12 %	6.49 %	6.06 %

Source: U.S. Department of Commerce, *Survey of Current Business, State Government Finance in* (fiscal year).

rate would be 6.06 percent applied to both taxable personal income and business value added. During the 1984-87 period, the revenue-neutral requisite tax rate would have fluctuated between 6.06 percent and 6.49 percent. The appropriate tax rate for independent contractors would be 12.98 percent (or double the business value-added or personal rate) applied to their tax base. Every percentage point increase in the tax rate on a statical basis would yield an additional $8.31 billion.

Although the business value-added tax (VAT) appears to be double taxation, our position is that it is not. The VAT tax base is approximately the same as that of the flat income tax. Therefore, as a first-order approximation, our proposal is a flat tax on all income of approximately twice the stated rate. The reason for using the two-tax structure is that there are minor differences in the way the bases are calculated, and a priori, we don't know which of the two bases is more fungible and hence results in greater tax avoidance.

The argument in favor of the flat tax is twofold: It increases the efficiency of the overall economy, and it reduces the collection costs.

Economists, in general, acknowledge that reduced tax rates will have long-run beneficial effects. However, they tend to underestimate how quickly the economy responds to the economic incentives. Ignoring the substitution effects may be perilous and lead to incorrect forecasts.

EFFICIENCY IN COLLECTION COSTS

A mechanism must be developed to efficiently collect revenues and efficiently provide public services. A broad-based, low-rate flat tax is a very efficient revenue collection mechanism. Local taxes should be collected through this mechanism, thereby minimizing the economic distortion and collection costs. Our belief is that services are more efficiently provided at the local level.

One issue to be addressed is the development of a mechanism to allocate the revenues generated by the proposed flat tax between the state and local communities. The starting point of the analysis is one of aggregate revenue neutrality. Therefore, initially it is assumed that the revenues will be allocated among state and local governments based on current proportions. Rules for allocating the aggregate amounts among the various communities are then discussed. Later, possible rules for changing the allocation are discussed.

Since local taxes average 34.6 percent (FY1988) of total state and local taxes, each community will be entitled to the same percent of the state value-added tax and personal income tax collected in that community.

This allocation formula takes into consideration the accumulated body of literature that indicates that location decisions are, in part, determined by the relative tax burden faced by economic agents. This proposal suggests that the tax-induced cost of doing business in one locality in the state relative to another will remain identical. Similarly, from the individual's point of view, the before- and after-tax income will also remain unchanged. Therefore, incentives to relocate to arbitrage differences in prices are eliminated from the formula.

The added cost of monitoring the location of the taxpayer need not create any additional bureaucracy. The structure in place provides enough information on an individual taxpayer's residency to allow the redistribution of the fractions of the taxes collected to the community where the taxpayer resides. Similarly, current institutional features for the sales tax also may generate sufficient information to allocate the position of the value-added tax to the individual communities.

The design of the two taxes—a business value-added tax and the personal income tax—also takes into account the nature of the community. For example, in a bedroom community, a small amount of tax revenues will be generated by the value-added tax; the bulk of the taxes will be generated by the income tax. Conversely, in the business district the bulk of the revenues will be generated by the value-added tax. Since the tax rate is the same for the two taxes, in both cases the amount of tax returned to the community will be dependent on the level of economic activity within the locality.

The income and/or population as a percent of the state income and population figures provides a first-order approximation as to how to allocate the revenues collected by the flat tax structure. Table 11.5 illustrates the close correspondence between the county share of the income taxes in 1988 and the personal income and population shares during 1987. A regression analysis between the revenue share and each of the two alternative allocation variables is reported in Table 11.6. Upon inspection, it is evident that the fit is quite close. Furthermore, one cannot reject the hypothesis that, on average, the share of taxes in each county matches the share of personal income and/or population. The coefficient for each of the explanatory variables is not statistically significantly different from one, whereas that of the constant term is not statistically significantly different from zero.

The regression-fitted values may be compared with actual values in order to identify the outliers. For example, Contra Costa's share of the state population appears to be significantly lower than its share of the state personal income and state tax revenues. Clearly, the population formula would reduce the revenues allocated to Contra Costa County.

In the case of Los Angeles and San Bernardino counties, the share of taxes is lower than the counties' share of personal income and population. In contrast, for Orange, San Mateo, and Santa Clara counties, the share of taxes is higher than the counties' share of the state's population and personal income. Therefore, a simple reallocation formula based either on population or personal income or both will have a significant revenue impact on those counties.

Table 11.5
County Shares of State Taxes, Personal Income, and Population

County	Income 1987	Population 1987	Taxes* FY '87-88
Alameda	4.63%	4.42%	4.65%
Alpine	0.00%	0.00%	0.01%
Amador	0.07%	0.09%	0.08%
Butte	0.44%	0.61%	0.41%
Calaveras	0.07%	0.11%	0.08%
Colusa	0.05%	0.05%	0.06%
Contra Costa	3.27%	2.69%	3.38%
Del Norte	0.04%	0.07%	0.03%
El Dorado	0.36%	0.41%	0.34%
Fresno	1.75%	2.16%	1.64%
Glenn	0.07%	0.08%	0.06%
Humboldt	0.32%	0.41%	0.29%
Imperial	0.25%	0.40%	0.25%
Inyo	0.05%	0.06%	0.07%
Kern	1.41%	1.83%	1.78%
Kings	0.22%	0.32%	0.18%
Lake	0.13%	0.18%	0.13%
Lassen	0.06%	0.10%	0.05%
Los Angeles	30.65%	30.67%	29.81%
Madera	0.20%	0.29%	0.19%
Marin	1.40%	0.82%	1.25%
Mariposa	0.04%	0.05%	0.04%
Mendocino	0.21%	0.27%	0.20%
Merced	0.41%	0.60%	0.33%
Modoc	0.02%	0.03%	0.02%
Mono	0.03%	0.03%	0.06%
Monterey	1.14%	1.24%	0.99%
Napa	0.39%	0.38%	0.38%
Nevada	0.22%	0.27%	0.22%
Orange	9.69%	8.01%	10.49%
Placer	0.52%	0.54%	0.58%
Plumas	0.05%	0.07%	0.06%
Riverside	2.97%	3.33%	2.94%
Sacramento	3.12%	3.43%	2.96%
San Benito	0.10%	0.12%	0.09%
San Bernardino	3.59%	4.38%	3.33%
San Diego	7.75%	8.27%	7.74%
San Francisco	3.45%	2.67%	3.45%
San Joaquin	1.22%	1.61%	1.16%
San Luis Obispo	0.60%	0.73%	0.71%
San Mateo	3.05%	2.25%	3.27%
Santa Barbara	1.30%	1.23%	1.27%
Santa Clara	6.22%	5.11%	6.93%
Santa Cruz	0.80%	0.80%	0.73%
Shasta	0.38%	0.49%	0.39%
Sierra	0.01%	0.01%	0.01%
Siskiyou	0.11%	0.15%	0.10%
Solano	0.91%	1.09%	0.81%
Sonoma	1.34%	1.28%	1.29%
Stanislaus	0.90%	1.18%	0.90%
Sutter	0.17%	0.22%	0.16%
Tehama	0.11%	0.16%	0.10%
Trinity	0.03%	0.05%	0.03%
Tulare	0.74%	1.05%	0.59%
Tuolumne	0.12%	0.16%	0.13%
Ventura	2.33%	2.27%	2.31%
Yolo	0.43%	0.46%	0.40%
Yuba	0.12%	0.20%	0.10%
TOTAL	100%	100%	100%

* Tax share includes state personal income taxes (calendar year 1987), state sales taxes and state and local property taxes.

Sources: California State Board of Equalization; California Franchise Tax Board.

Table 11.6
Regression on Tax Share by County (*t*-statistics in parentheses)

	'87 Population	'87 Personal Income
Constant	0.000093	0.00023
	(0.1243)	(0.8589)
Population share	0.9946	--
	(61.0145)	--
Personal income share	--	0.9864
	--	(166.9536)
R Squared	0.9852	0.9980
S.E.	0.0052	0.0019
F-Statistic	3722.774	27873.49

Using income as the sole criterion may present what one may term *scale* or *size problems*. To illustrate: Consider the case of two communities of equal population yet with different income levels. In general one may expect that both will require the same size schools, and so on. Therefore, the fixed-cost expenditures of maintaining the schools are likely to be the same. There may be other examples where the disparities in size and/or fixed costs may force local communities to undertake the same expenditures even though community sizes are different.

These two considerations suggest that in addition to income other variables may be incorporated in the decision criteria. One that immediately comes to mind is taking into account relevant population levels. However, in order to ensure that no systematic biases exist in favor of bedroom communities versus business communities, consideration may be given to the relevant population figures used to allocate funds because the needs of these communities, although different in the nature of the services required (i.e., schools versus police protection, parking, etc.), are directly related to their respective populations. In the bedroom community, the relevant population is the number of people residing in the community, and in the business district, the relevant population is the number of people working within the community. Those two variables represent an adequate scale variable of the needs for specific services to be provided by the different communities. The only remaining issue to be determined is whether the amount to be allocated per person in each community should be the same whether for residents or for workers.

Up to this point, we have identified two different variables that may be used to determine the local revenue to the individual communities. In order to approximate the current revenue, we have related the share of revenue to the individual community to develop an empirical formula that will be as close as possible to revenue neutrality for each individual community.

The allocation formula attempts to minimize differences in taxation of different revenue sources that may alter the location to different communities because of differences in tax burden. However, that is not to say that differences are completely eliminated. Communities may make different choices as to how to spend their monies. The difference in the mix of public services offered by the different communities will alter the location decisions of economic agents. Individuals who value education will tend to move to communities with good public schools. That is the essence of the Tiebout hypothesis. What our proposal does is to eliminate the revenue-raising mechanism and its corresponding distorting element from the location decision. However, insofar as different mixes of services are funded, then the location decision will be affected by the public service, and that will shape the nature and character of the individual community, which in turn will reinforce the selection of public services. Therefore, the process will create diverse communities based on what people want to consider alone and not on the joint determination of what and how to raise the revenue to pay for it.

The calculation of the tax rate, the formula for distribution between state and local taxes, and the formula for allocating taxes among the various communities are meant to be illustrative only. The final formula should be determined by the interested parties: state governments, local governments, and taxpayers. Although this may appear to be a difficult and complicated task, there is already an infrastructure in place that may allow all parties involved to determine the outcome: the initiative process.

For example, if the state and league of local governments decide that the rate and formula for allocating funds ought to be changed, they could, without collecting the required signatures, include such formulas as one of the initiatives, and the voters could decide. If the initiative doesn't pass, then the status quo remains. Similarly, if the state and league of local governments do not reach a consensus, then two initiatives may be put in place, and the voters may choose either one or none of them. It may be worthwhile to limit the state and the league of local governments to one alternative each. If no consensus is reached within the league of local governments, it is their option to go out and collect signatures for however many variants may be selected.

Similar restrictions should be placed on the formula distributing the local revenues among the different communities.

The flat tax specifically addresses how the tax is collected. The structure is designed to minimize the disincentives induced by tax rates, given the amounts of revenues to be collected. A revenue-neutral tax, by definition, will, on a static revenue basis, raise the same amount as the current structure. However, since the broad-based, low-rate tax minimizes the distortions, efficiency gains will be realized, and the state's competitive environment, California-based asset values, and California's economic activity will increase.

The value-added and personal income tax base are roughly equivalent to the state gross income. Therefore, the revenue-neutral tax rate for the two taxes will be around one half of the tax burden (Table 11.7).

Earlier in this chapter an argument was presented that linking specific taxes with specific expenditure patterns would unambiguously distort the state's economy and thereby reduce the level of economic activity relative to a flat tax structure. However, given that the state government must ultimately finance its expenditures through taxes, a link between aggregate spending and aggregate tax revenue must be established. In order to achieve a balanced budget, the tax revenues must, on average, equal state and local expenditures. Therefore, on average, the tax burden must equal the state and local expenditures per dollar of gross income. This implies that, on average, the tax rate for each of the two taxes must be approximately half the state and local expenditures as a percent of gross income.

If overall tax rates are not directly linked to expenditure patterns, special interest group politics will result in a process where expenditures may be excessive and will drive tax rates, thereby reducing the state's competitive environment. This argument suggests that an explicit linkage between tax rates and expenditures be established.

The design of such a mechanism is outside the scope of this study. Nevertheless, it is worthwhile to mention three alternatives that have been widely used with various measures of success at the state level. They are a balanced budget amendment, line-item veto, and spending restraints. Although recently California relaxed its spending limitations, it is worthwhile to note that in spite of the well-known shortcomings of Proposition 13 and the Gann spending limitation, these policies did help restrain the level of spending and improved California's competitive position.

Table 11.7
State and Local Tax Burden and Flat Tax Rates, California and U.S. Total,
Fiscal Years 1987 and 1988 (in millions of dollars)

	1987	1988
California:		
State and local taxes (FY)	$ 53,272	$ 55,169
Personal income		
(previous Calendar Year)	452,973	491,393
CA Tax burden: taxes/PI	11.76 %	11.23 %
Estimated CA flat tax rates	6.49	6.06
Total: All States		
State and local taxes (FY)	405,149	435,675
Personal income		
(Previous Calendar Year)	3,522,203	3,768,696
Tax burden	11.50 %	11.56 %
Estimated flat tax rate	5.31	5.26

Source: U.S. Bureau of the Census, *Government Finances in* (fiscal year).

In California, higher taxes mean higher unemployment. No one could possibly doubt the power of this statistical relationship.

For the United States as a whole there have been a number of studies documenting rigorously the negative relationship between state taxes and a state's economic well-being. These findings reconfirm exactly what happens in California. Academic study after academic study has painstakingly documented the empirical association between a state's tax policy and its economic performance. Raising the tax burden raises unemployment rates.

But as convincing as the evidence is, legislators are quick to turn a blind eye and persist in their praise of higher taxation and spending. The numbers, however, tell the true story clearly. If California undoes the tax and spending controls put in place over the past 12 years, the economic prosperity of the last 12 years will stop as well. California will once again become a high unemployment state.

NOTES

1. Paul Samuelson, *Economics* (New York: McGraw-Hill, 1973), pp. 164-65.

2. Charles W. Kadlec and Arthur B. Laffer, "The Jarvis-Gann Tax Cut Proposal: An Application of the Laffer Curve," in *The Economics of the Tax Revolt*, ed. Arthur B. Laffer and Jan P. Seymour (New York: Harcourt Brace Jovanovich, 1979), pp. 118-22.

3. R. Hall and A. Rabushka, "A Simple Income Tax with Low Marginal Rates," Hoover Institution, Stanford University, July 1982; Arthur B. Laffer, "The Complete Flat Tax," A. B. Laffer Associates, February 22, 1984.

4. Henry George, *Progress and Poverty* (New York: Robert Schalkenbach Foundation, 1960), pp. 408-21.

5. Ibid., pp. 408-21.

6. U.S. Bureau of the Census, *State Government Finances in 1987*. Includes selective sales receipts and license taxes. Washington, DC, September 1988.

Index

About the Contributors

VICTOR A. CANTO is president of A. B. Laffer, V. A. Canto & Associates. A former professor at both the University of California at Los Angeles and the University of Southern California, he has written numerous articles in the areas of international economics, public finance, and macroeconomics. His articles have appeared in many of the leading economic journals, and he has authored, edited, or coedited a number of books including *Monetary Policy, Taxation, and International Investment Strategy* (Quorum Books) and *Supply-Side Portfolio Strategies* (Quorum Books), both coedited with Arthur B. Laffer.

ARTHUR B. LAFFER is Chairman of A. B. Laffer, V. A. Canto & Associates, an economic consulting firm in La Jolla, California, and is well known for formulating the "Laffer Curve"—the relationship between tax rates and total revenues. Dr. Laffer served as a member of President Reagan's Economic Policy Advisory Board, was a consultant to the Secretaries of Treasury and Defense during the Nixon and Ford administrations, and served as Chief Economist at the Executive Office of the President, Office of Management and Budget during the Nixon administration. In addition, he has held professorships at Pepperdine University and the University of Southern California and has taught at the University of Chicago.

ROBERT I. WEBB is an Associate Professor of Commerce at the McIntire School of Commerce of the University of Virginia. He has published articles in journals such as the *Journal of Econometrics*, the *Journal of*

Business and Economic Statistics, the *Southern Economic Journal*, and the *Journal of Futures Markets*. A former trader for the World Bank and member of the Chicago Mercantile Exchange, he has also served as senior financial economist at the Chicago Mercantile Exchange, the Executive Office of the President, Office of Management and Budget, and the Commodity Futures Trading Commission.

CHRISTOPHER CHARLES is Director of Research with Wulff Capital Management in San Francisco.

CHRISTOPHER S. HAMMOND is a Research Associate with A. B. Laffer, V. A. Canto & Associates.

CHARLES W. KADLEC is Vice President and Industry Strategist with J. & W. Seligman & Co., Inc. in New York.

JOHN E. SILVIA is First Vice President and Economist at Kemper Financial Services.